ART and DESIGN
in CHILDREN'S PICTURE BOOKS

ART and DESIGN
in CHILDREN'S PICTURE BOOKS

An Analysis of
Caldecott Award-Winning Illustrations

LYN ELLEN LACY

American Library Association   Chicago and London   1986

Designed by Charles Bozett

Composed by Impressions, Inc.
in Palatino on a Penta-
driven Autologic APSµ5
Phototypesetting system

Printed on 50-pound Glatfelter,
a pH-neutral stock, by
Malloy Lithographing, Inc.
Bound in B-grade Holliston
linen cloth by John H. Dekker
& Sons.

Library of Congress Cataloging-in-Publication Data

Lacy, Lyn Ellen.
 Art and design in children's picture books.

 Includes indexes.
 1. Caldecott medal books. 2. Illustrated books,
Children's—Awards. 3. Picture-books, Children's—
Awards. 4. Book design—Awards. 5. Children's
literature, American—Awards. 6. Illustration of
books—Awards. 7. Children—Books and reading.
I. Title.
Z1037.A2L33 1986   028.5   86-1163
ISBN 0-8389-0446-7

With love to my mother
and in memory of my father

Contents

Pictorial Resources

The reader is strongly encouraged to acquire a hardbound copy of each Caldecott Medalist title from 1938 through 1986 to study while reading ART AND DESIGN IN CHILDREN'S PICTURE BOOKS. These titles are listed below by their author, coauthor, author/illustrator, translator, or adapter entries to facilitate acquisition from library, media resource center, or bookstore. Full bibliographical entries are found following chapters in which the titles are discussed.

Art appreciation of picture-book illustrations must take into account the whole book as a work of graphic art. In ART AND DESIGN IN CHILDREN'S PICTURE BOOKS, attention will often be directed to a picture book's format. For fullest appreciation of total picture-book effects created by these distinguished American illustrators, please have their books nearby.

Award Winners Discussed

(An asterisk [*] indicates one of thirteen major titles used to illustrate artistic concepts.)

*Aardema, Verna. *Why Mosquitoes Buzz in People's Ears.* Illus. Leo and Diane Dillon.
Bemelmans, Ludwig. *Madeline's Rescue.*
Brown, Marcia. *Once a Mouse . . .*
Brown, Marcia. *Shadow.*
Brown, Margaret Wise (pseud. Golden MacDonald). *The Little Island.* Illus. Leonard Weisgard.
*Burton, Virginia Lee. *The Little House.*

Chaucer, Geoffrey. *Chanticleer and the Fox*. Illus. Barbara Cooney.

d'Aulaire, Ingri, and Edgar Parin d'Aulaire. *Abraham Lincoln*.

de Regniers, Beatrice Schenk. *May I Bring a Friend?* Illus. Beni Montresor.

*Emberley, Barbara. *Drummer Hoff*. Illus. Ed Emberley.

Ets, Marie Hall, and Aurora Labastida. *Nine Days to Christmas*.

Field, Rachel. *Prayer for a Child*. Illus. Elizabeth Orton Jones.

Goble, Paul. *The Girl Who Loved Wild Horses*.

*Hader, Berta, and Elmer Hader. *The Big Snow*.

Haley, Gail E. *A Story A Story*.

Hall, Donald. *Ox-Cart Man*. Illus. Barbara Cooney.

Handforth, Thomas. *Mei Li*.

Hodges, Margaret. *Saint George and the Dragon*. Illus. Trina Schart Hyman.

Hogrogrian, Nonny. *One Fine Day*.

*Keats, Ezra Jack. *The Snowy Day*.

Langstaff, John. *Frog Went A-Courtin'*. Illus. Feodor Rojankovsky.

Lathrop, Dorothy P. *Animals of the Bible*.

Lawson, Robert. *They Were Strong and Good*.

Lipkind, William, and Nicolas Mordvinoff. *Finders Keepers*.

Lobel, Arnold. *Fables*.

*McCloskey, Robert. *Make Way for Ducklings*.

*McCloskey, Robert. *Time of Wonder*.

McDermott, Gerald. *Arrow to the Sun*.

Milhous, Katherine. *The Egg Tree*.

*Mosel, Arlene. *The Funny Little Woman*. Illus. Blair Lent.

Musgrove, Margaret. *Ashanti to Zulu: African Traditions*. Illus. Leo and Diane Dillon.

Ness, Evaline. *Sam, Bangs and Moonshine*.

Nic Leodhas, Sorche. *Always Room for One More*. Illus. Nonny Hogrogrian.

Perrault, Charles. *Cinderella: Or the Little Glass Slipper*. Illus. Marcia Brown.

*Petersham, Maud, and Miska Petersham. *The Rooster Crows*.

Politi, Leo. *Song of the Swallows*.

Provensen, Alice, and Martin Provensen. *The Glorious Flight: Across the Channel with Louis Blériot, July 25, 1909*.

*Ransome, Arthur. *The Fool of the World and the Flying Ship*. Illus. Uri Shulevitz.

Robbins, Ruth. *Baboushka and the Three Kings*. Illus. Nicolas Sidjakov.

*Sendak, Maurice. *Where the Wild Things Are*.

Spier, Peter. *Noah's Ark.*
Steig, William. *Sylvester and the Magic Pebble.*
Thurber, James. *Many Moons.* Illus. Louis Slobodkin.
*Tresselt, Alvin. *White Snow Bright Snow.* Illus. Roger Duvoisin.
Udry, Janice May. *A Tree Is Nice.* Illus. Marc Simont.
*Van Allsburg, Chris. *Jumanji.*
Van Allsburg, Chris. *The Polar Express.*
Ward, Lynd. *The Biggest Bear.*
Zemach, Harve. *Duffy and the Devil.* Illus. Margot Zemach.

Introduction

Since 1938 titles selected as the most distinguished American picture books for children have annually been awarded the Caldecott Medal by the American Library Association. Too often these books receive the kiss of death from adults who present them to children as "best" books, or as isolated titles with little relevance to other books the children are reading. Even worse, Caldecott books have in the past been offered as important landmarks in children's literature, to be studied in chronological order! The disheartening result of these approaches is that many children steer clear of any book with a gold Caldecott sticker on it.

Thus, a grave disservice has been done to a truly *fun* collection of books chosen by Caldecott committees of ALA's Association for Library Service to Children for the quality of their illustrations in relation to their stories. The recipients of the Caldecott Medal are illustrators—a total of over four dozen artists—many of whom have devoted entire careers to creating pictures for children. The diversity in the collection by Caldecott winners is illustrative of different societal attitudes over the decades, and a review of these books, some of which are decidedly dated, provides an instructive perspective on changing tastes.

ART AND DESIGN IN CHILDREN'S PICTURE BOOKS has been written out of a deep respect for this collection of American picture books as a whole, for their creators individually, and for their audience of children throughout the years.

The Caldecott Award and I have always been friends. As a child in the 1940s I was given the Medal-winning title each year by my parents. A very special memory is that when *Make Way for Ducklings* was five years old and I was seven, I rode on the swan boat in

Boston's Public Garden that McCloskey pictured. My father stood with his camera on one of the bridges, and today a small snapshot of me on that boat, years ago, sits framed on my desk.

In the late 1950s I studied the Caldecott winners in a college course on children's literature. I remember most how the violence in *Finders Keepers* stunned me with its sharp contrast to the sweet titles I had loved in my childhood. Years later I grew to understand that the book was indeed intended to disturb. In the 1960s I shared new Caldecott titles with my own three little children Ruth, Peter, and John. During this period nearly every year a Medal-winning title set a new standard for art and subject matter in children's picture books. *The Snowy Day* introduced us to collage and to a black child as primary character during tense years of desegregation. *Where the Wild Things Are* included monsters and antisocial behavior reminiscent of Dr. Benjamin Spock's book on child rearing. In *Drummer Hoff* we were presented with what we thought of as abstracted art as well as an abstracted antiwar statement about Viet Nam.

In the 1970s I became an elementary-school librarian and media specialist in the Minneapolis Public School District. That decade's Award-winning folklore titles perfectly complemented the multicultural educational goals in the schools. An additional attraction for each of these books was that illustrations reflected each story's cultural or historical background. *The Funny Little Woman* showed statues of the Jizo, Japanese guardian gods of children and other small, weak creatures. *Why Mosquitoes Buzz in People's Ears* was illustrated with resplendent African batik designs, and *The Girl Who Loved Wild Horses* faithfully reproduced motifs from the art of early Indian artists. The Caldecott Award in the 1970s recognized artistic innovation as well as cultural diversity, thereby expanding children's access to other worlds of art and literature. I began to devote more time to teaching about the illustrations and the texts of the Caldecott Medalists.

Excitement over the Caldecotts of the seventies was the impetus behind the first of my many "Caldecott years": nine months at school spent with children of various age levels looking closely for and listening carefully to the nuances in art and language as found in the entire Award-winning collection. I soon found that as many artistic and literary topics existed for students' further investigation as there were titles, and careful planning was required to reach closure by the end of a year. In order to weave together discussions from one week to another, a thematic or genre approach was easily developed, with titles grouped as fables, folk songs, origin tales, history, rhymes, holidays, and so on. Although this approach soon took a back seat to more in-depth studies devoted to art appreciation, such simple thematic approaches are quite valid in structuring an introduction to children's appreciation of literature. Vestiges of the original plan are often evident in ART AND DESIGN IN CHILDREN'S PICTURE BOOKS, since the book reflects the order in which I still prefer to discuss certain titles with children. Many of my students also enjoyed hearing how the illustrators applied personal experience, research, or pure imagination to their pictures; such anecdotes can also be found in ART AND DESIGN IN CHILDREN'S PICTURE BOOKS.

I gathered such information from many sources, but none were more rewarding than some of the illustrators' Caldecott Award acceptance speeches. These were published by Horn Book in three volumes for 1938 through 1975. Speeches for subsequent years may be found in the ALA journal *Top of the News* or as recordings by Weston Woods Studio. Especially inspirational for me was Robert McCloskey's acceptance of the 1958 award, for *Time of Wonder*. He challenged teachers with the following words:

> I think it is most important for everyone really to see and evaluate pictures and really to see and evaluate his surroundings . . . to develop a visual sense . . . to "read" pictures . . . to know when someone is fooling us with pictures.

On a printed page if the relationship between art, text, and the area around them

> is not well thought out, we shall have a page that is not pleasing to the eye. . . . Every child ought to study design and drawing along with reading, and writing, and arithmetic. . . . I get mad when I see this important part of life shoved way over to one side in our curriculum and labeled "Art". . . . Let us teach design, and let us get it out of the museums, let us get it off the pages and drawing boards and let us put it to work.

McCloskey had called for *visual literacy* almost a decade before that phrase was coined by John L. Debes of Eastman Kodak, and I was encouraged by his remarks to dig deeper into my teaching of the Caldecotts to develop a more significant foundation for critical viewing through picture-book art. Strategies to increase student awareness of book design were obviously important; so was a basic introduction to artistic elements used by illustrators for intended effects on the audience. The children and I both needed to know more about how an artist uses elements of line, color, light and dark, shape, and space in a two-dimensional graphic design such as a picture book. Over the next several years, I enrolled in art classes, attended workshops, toured galleries, read all kinds of art books, experimented with drawing and painting myself, interviewed local artists and art educators and art students, and gleaned from my research what I consider to be most applicable to a study by young children of picture-book art. One of the most valuable resources was the Minneapolis Public Schools Fine Arts Department's K–6 art curriculum guide. It contains astute analysis of student readiness for art concepts at certain ages and practical guidelines for appropriate instruction, which became second nature to me as I explored art and picture books over the years. ART AND DESIGN IN CHILDREN'S PICTURE BOOKS presents my own understandings of what I have found to be generally accepted views about artistic elements, the graphic arts in general, and picture-book design in particular. It is only one of many possible approaches.

All my ideas were presented to children. I called attention to compositional design and to artistic details in illustrations; slowly, they built a basic art vocabulary. During a whole series of "Caldecott years," the children and I acquired visual tools for critical discrimination of pictures, not only in books but elsewhere in our environment.

Kindergarteners were as adept at grasping fundamental concepts of art as were older children. One of my five-year-old students, an active Ojibwe child named Laura, was disruptive in story hour and stubbornly checked out the same book, *Drummer Hoff*, every single week. During a class discussion about illustrations in *Baboushka and the Three Kings*, Laura was uncharacteristically quiet. Finally, she thoughtfully remarked that *Baboushka*'s pictures looked to her like those in *Drummer Hoff*. The other children and I were excited by Laura's observation, and we began to look through all the Medalists for more examples of figures represented in the same manner; then we looked through other picture books on the shelves; then we began to draw with triangles, circles, and squares and created bottle-shaped or stick-figured characters for storytelling pictures of our own.

Tuning in and following through on children's own enthusiasms over pictures or story are crucial ingredients in the success of any "Caldecott year." Our investigation into similarities of art in *Drummer Hoff* and *Baboushka* became a springboard from which my students flew off into new directions—especially Laura, who began checking out books of all kinds and continued to come to me with her discoveries. When she remarked in class on another day that the illustrations in *Jumanji* were like "pictures of clay people," I could have kissed her on the cheek, and of course the children and I began a search for photographs of sculpture to study.

After such experiences over a lifetime with the Caldecotts, it is appropriate that in the eighties I began to write about them. My efforts include a proposed series of filmstrip scripts for producer Paul Gagne of Weston Woods. One resulting audiovisual presents a biography of Randolph Caldecott himself as well as appreciation of his illustrations, and the others in progress present an appreciation of Caldecott winners, including many of the individual titles Mort Schindel and his studio have for over twenty-five years transformed to film. The present manuscript, overseen by senior editor Herbert Bloom and Bettina MacAyeal of ALA Publishing Services, provides material on the Caldecott illustrations and stories; these resources may prove useful to adults who wish to present this material to the children themselves. To the people of Weston Woods and ALA I owe everlasting gratitude—both for five years' worth of deadlines and for encouragement that kept me at the keyboard, even though I continued teaching full-time and raised my teenagers alone.

A little help from my friends in Minnesota turned out to be much more than a little from much more than just friends, and to them also I extend my gratitude. Long-time teaching colleague and friend Beth Berggren, who became national art consultant and lecturer for Dixon Ticonderoga Company (formerly American Crayon/Prang), stepped forward to critique ART AND DESIGN IN CHILDREN'S PICTURE BOOKS. Her expertise covered not only elementary art education but also professional art techniques. Family friend Lyndel King completed her doctoral degree in art history and was named curator and then director of the University of Minnesota Art Museum; she generously offered her superb credentials as critic regarding art history and fine arts concepts. Former English teacher, now sister-in-media, Rosemary Carlson encouraged my attempts to provide personal and literary as well as artistic background for the illustrators and their books. Fellow teacher and friend Dave Gatewood read countless revisions with sensitivity for what kids might most need to know. Engineer and artist Gay Austin conjured up a home computer to speed up my work and knew more about many things than other people do about a few.

My children grew up with these people around them and like chameleons took on many of the same qualities: Ruth became Lyndel's protégée and my critic, going on to graduate school in art history at New York University. Peter has been an astute sounding board, always ready to listen and suggest ideas with more merit for children. John began to write short stories and turned his own mental images into verbal ones.

I have nothing but admiration for what my Minneapolis Public School colleagues do each day for children. I offer my heartfelt thanks for support in this project over the years to principals Morris Vogel, Margaret Lincoln, and Elmer Koch, director of Educational Media Services Gladys Sheehan, superintendent Richard Green, and fellow staff members at Wilder, Seward, and Cooper elementary schools.

Along the way I corresponded with the eight living illustrators among the fifteen who are given major attention in this book. They were offered an opportunity to participate in analyses of their art, and I was gratified that they all responded favorably, with few corrections or suggestions, and sometimes even found time to chat. From such informality in an Ed Emberley letter I learned just how astute five-year-old Laura had been. Emberley was pleased by the anecdote because he had indeed been impressed by Nicolas Sidjakov's pictures in *Baboushka and the Three Kings* and was sure the book had had a direct influence on the way he chose to illustrate *Drummer Hoff*. If I should find Laura now and tell her that, I'm sure she wouldn't remember a thing about our class so long ago. But I do, and a great deal of the joy in my writing is inspired by memories of all the children. I can never thank them enough.

1

Visual Literacy, Children, and Picture Books

The world can be a visual delight—and so can the works of art that mirror it. The visual arts can be a lifelong wonderment and source of pleasure, and one's ability to enjoy them is enhanced by an understanding of the artistic elements, including line, color, light and dark, shape, space, and texture and their effects on the audience. Even very young children—prereaders—can begin to recognize these elements so as to expand their understanding of pictures and refine their response to them.

Teachers, librarians, parents, and others who read aloud to children are well placed to introduce these elements through art appreciation of picture books. This book is intended as a resource for those who wish to provide such an experience for children.

Historical criticism of picture books as well as art history and criticism are all subjects for recommended reading; they have been treated elsewhere most eloquently by eminent scholars, practitioners, reviewers, and critics in the fields. The intent here will not be to repeat all that has been said before but to review some historical and critical aspects that lead toward a better understanding of high-quality picture-book art's place in fostering visual literacy in children today. ART AND DESIGN IN CHILDREN'S PICTURE BOOKS will also be limited to the past exciting half-century in high-quality award-winning picture books from the United States. Criticism of other contemporary titles, of mass-market books (those generally less expensive and considered of lesser artistic and literary quality), or of titles from other times and cultures will be left to writers with expertise in the fields.

Generally speaking, the basic skills that need to be taught for evaluation of visual material are: to distinguish between reality and unreality, to appreciate use of details that contribute to the whole, to identify unique properties of the medium used, and to understand the main idea intended by the visual message. In visual material reality or unreality is usually implied by the creator's use of appropriate symbols. Such details as colors and shapes are used to create an intended effect; properties of natural or machine-made media also contribute to the effect by their unique abilities and limitations. Intent of a message is conveyed by the creator's choice of a viewpoint that often reflects also an emotional or intellectual stance the artist wishes the audience to take toward the subject matter.

Most children today can learn these concepts quickly for they are much more visually oriented than past generations due to the amount of time spent watching television. Our children riding the crest of high technology toward the twenty-first century must be taught more than ever not only how to read, write, compute, and contribute to the world around them but also to see, feel, and think creatively in order to contribute in a complex world ahead. A uniquely appropriate medium exists with which to begin such visual appreciation: pictures intended, developed, rendered, and produced for children, the pictures in their picture books.

Art in Picture Books

Picture books provide enjoyable opportunities for visual exploration, interpretation, and reflection. Unlike transitory electronic images, books are permanent, and children may reflect on them as long as they like and return to them as often as they like, questioning, accepting, or discarding what they see.

Artistic style is a matter of aesthetics and taste, and controversy over eternal values of beauty and truth has waged heatedly in criticism of children's books just as it has in the fine arts. Style in art reflects a society's standards or rebels against them, for art is a language that is constantly changed by and adapted to its speakers and its listeners. Artists have said they physically see things differently from others—pain and joy, loveliness and wretchedness, the tragic and the absurd. These opposing forces lie at the heart of their work and are sometimes thought of by them as curse as well as blessing. This different way of looking at things means artists move beyond facts into creation of personal perceptions that may become variously a celebration of people, a mood piece, a dance, an extension of oral tradition, an invitation to participation, or a spiritual awakening. As expression of perceptions, artistic style can be anything an artist chooses to make of it. The audience's role should not be as much an expression of personal liking or of social judgment as an evaluation of whether a particular work successfully communicates the artist's perception within the limits of its style and its conceptual intent.

BACKGROUND FROM FINE ART

Works of art are generally broken down into *representational* presentations of recognizable subject matter and *nonrepresentational* works having no reference to anything outside themselves. Nonrepresentational art, typified by Piet Mondrian compositions in shapes or lines and colors appreciated for their innate qualities alone, is so rarely found in children's picture books that discussion here is focused on representational art and its stylistic modifiers of *realism, stylization,* or *abstraction.* Realism attempts to convey an exact appearance of subject matter with no distortion for expressive purposes. Stylization alters or modifies the appearance to emphasize preconceived universal physical characteristics, ideal types not as they truly are but as they should be. Abstraction demonstrates more interest in manipulation of subject matter into its parts than concern for naturalistic appearance.

Next in importance are further general modifiers that define styles of two-dimensional artistic rendering itself: *linear, painterly, lines with paint added,* and *mixed-media imagery.* Linear style emphasizes the drawn line or, in painting, the draftsmanlike approach of outlines and contour lines for closed shapes and space. Painterly style emphasizes more sensuous rendering of open shapes and space by areas of color and tone rather than lines. A style in which paint is added within lines emphasizes color and tone applied within outlines for closed shapes and space. Mixed-media images such as collage emphasize use of such materials as cloth, wood, and paper for texture and closed shapes or space; additional drawing or painting may or may not be included.

Movements or periods in the fine arts result from attitudes and techniques held in common by artists; examples are Romanticism, Impressionism, and Expressionism. Each artist within a movement, however, has a unique personal viewpoint, so that it is usually unwise to characterize an artist's collected work by period alone. Like all other artists, illustrators respond to biographical, geographical, and social influences that can make period labeling in book illustrating as misleading as it has been in fine art in the past. Basic awareness of realistic, stylized, or abstract representation through linear or painterly work, lines with paint added, or mixed-media rendering provides enough categorization for a critical process that enhances artistic appreciation but still allows individual opinions to be reached.

ARTISTIC ELEMENTS

The critics' role is legitimized by their abilities not only to express liking or disliking for a work of art but also to express reasons why, in terms of artistic elements and their intended effects on their audience. These elements are *line, color, light and dark* (often called *value*), *shape, space,* and *texture*. Texture in picture books with very rare exception has an implied appearance rather than actual tactile quality, and so this important element will be grouped with visually implied contour and depth; all three are achieved in the majority of pictures by an artist's use of the five other elements. The combined uses to which artists put these fundamental elements results in an interrelationship for emphasis, a sense of balance or imbalance, and continuity or overall unity in picture books as well as in the fine arts.

Line as an element can include visible drawn lines of many kinds—thin or thick, straight or curved, horizontal or diagonal, continuous or broken—or serve invisibly in pictures as a compositional framework such as a theatrical horizontal base extending left to right, a framed circular pattern that leads the eye around, or a frenetic underlying diagonal that jerks attention from one point to another. Drawn *edge lines* outline and contour figures, but so also can undrawn *line effects* in painting, as color meets color for shading and implied contouring to create the illusion of three dimensions. An interplay of lines can be used for implied depth of foreground, middle ground, and background; contrast or repetition of lines can imply texture; and the kind of invisible linear framework employed gives either symmetrical or asymmetrical weight and balance to the composition. Line as a most basic element records what artists see and is used to express their impressions of fluidity, vigor, or subtlety.

Color refers to pigments' abilities to absorb, transmit, or reflect light to create a visual illusion of *primaries* red, yellow, and blue, theoretically mixed in a triadic coloration system to create *secondaries* green, orange, and violet, and *tertiaries* red-orange, red-violet, blue-violet, blue-green, yellow-green, and yellow-orange. The triadic system is one of several systems explaining the creation of colors and will be used in ART AND DESIGN IN CHILDREN'S PICTURE BOOKS because of its common usage in American education of children. *Hue* is the exact name for a color; *color forms* are tones (created by the addition to a hue of its opposite), shades and tints (created when black or white is added), and gray, white, or black themselves (considered lacking in hue). Varieties of color transitions and contrasts can be used to imply contour by modeling, texture by shading and highlighting, and depth by warmly advancing or coolly receding. Complex visual harmonies are considered to exist when colors are used in combinations and with regard for their *intensity* of dullness or brightness; response to color and color harmony is also recognized to reflect personal preferences more than any of the other elements.

Light and dark as an artistic element is concerned with an artist's demonstration of interest or disinterest in a natural or an artificial *source of illumination* and in the contrast or gradation of *value* in colors and color forms for implied contour, texture, and depth. An emotionally powerful but intellectually elusive element, value is intertwined with uses of lines both visible and invisible as well as with uses of colors. It relies for effect on an audience's preconceived attitudes about lightness and darkness.

Shape is two-dimensional in pictures, as opposed to three-dimensional *form* in sculpture, and is usually thought of as irregularly *organic*, as found in nature, or *geometric*, as found in the superficial or mathematically precise world of humanmade objects. Shape in art is delineated by the *figure* itself or the *ground*, the area around the figure, and is considered *closed* when continuously outlined or *open* when outlined in a broken manner that allows the ground to enter. Shape can be thought of as created by an artist's uses of lines, colors, and value. It contributes to stylistic differences perhaps more than any other single element by its organic or geometric tendencies and through systems of *proportion*—natural, idealized, hierarchical, or distorted.

Space as an element is "into" a picture, and the illusion may be *deep, shallow,* or *flat* (also called planar). Uses of line, color, light and dark, and shape are combined to create space as an artist's perspective that becomes the audience's viewpoint. The artist chooses whether or not to invite participation by the audience itself through *aerial* (atmospheric) or *linear* (geometric) perspective systems. Changes in color and value as well as shape sizes, placements, and overlapping all contribute to foreground, middle ground, and background in a two-dimensional work of art. Artistic space may be distorted to throw the viewer off-balance, and sometimes multiple viewpoints are incorporated in filmic techniques that create unusual dimensions for time and place in a picture.

Composition is the relationship of all these parts to each other and to the whole, and an artistic composition takes into account such principles for overall design as movement, rhythm, repetition, contrast, and variety the artist may want to demonstrate through use of the elements. A composition may be firmly anchored within its frame (*closed composition*) or suggest further activity beyond one's view outside the frame (*open composition*), may draw the audience into its depths or guide the eye across and out, may be on a grand scale or an intimate one. Classic compositions reveal something new every time one sees them—a shadow, a nuance of skin tone, a line of an eyebrow, or a shape of the head missed before. Classic illustrators as well as classic fine artists use the tools of their trade to best effect, and these tools are the artistic elements common to both but uniquely employed by each: line, color, light and dark, shape, and space.

WHOLE BOOK DESIGN

High-quality book illustrating is closely related to fine-art picture making, but the language of the illustrator is not exactly the same as that of the fine artist. From the world of mass production in the graphic arts must be applied an understanding of technical and compositional demands that give picture books unique properties also to be considered in art appreciation. If two-dimensional one-of-a-kind fine art can be considered the grandfather of picture books, then perhaps reproducible graphic art should be called the grandmother of children's picture books today. Tracing lineage from such auspicious ancestry may provide criteria for appreciation of the best in contemporary illustrating that will satisfy both sides in the family of art and legitimize a working definition of the quality picture book as other than stepchild until now claimed wholeheartedly by neither.

Intelligently looking at pictures in picture books requires consideration of the whole book design, the exterior and interior formats chosen by the illustrator and the publisher to meet different literary and artistic objectives for different kinds of audiences. Size and shape of the book itself offer perimeters for the illustrator's *field of action*. In fine art the field of action is the canvas or paper upon which the artist paints or draws; in picture-book illustrating it is the size of the page, single or double spread, on which artwork will ultimately be reproduced, often after enlarging or reducing. Just as fine artists may or may not prefer to work with different sizes and shapes of canvas, some illustrators lend their talents to different physical book formats while others work in only one so that each book sits with their others as a collection on the shelf. Lap books are primarily intended for individual enjoyment or for only a few children at a time, while large-scale books allow everyone in a larger audience to see the pictures. Good illustrators take into account the appropriate size of a projected book for illustrative purposes just as a painter considers whether the proposed work is to be viewed from near or far away.

Whereas mixed-media artists may express themselves in irregularly shaped or free-form works of art, the fields of action for book illustrating are shaped like those for painting and drawing: square, horizontal rectangular, or vertical rectangular.

The dust jacket and cover provide the illustrator an initial opportunity to design a single illustration on the front, a pair of illustrations in which one is on the front and another is on the back, or a wraparound in which the front illustration continues across the spine onto the back. The cover or jacket is like a poster that reflects mood, text, and artistic style to be found within. Whereas the fine artist traditionally limits placement of a title and signature to the area along the bottom of a work of art, the illustrator must balance within a composition itself the book's title and creators' names and has even been known to consider within the design future placement of a promotional sticker should the book be given an award such as the Caldecott Medal.

When the book is opened, a series of pages offer many more possibilities for an illustrator's field of action than the fine artist has with one canvas stretched upon a frame. From the very beginning, single or double pages in the front matter provide fields of action often employed as dramatic prelude for the full visual text yet to come. Endpapers, half title, title, copyright, and dedication pages may each or all demonstrate artistic design as an extension of the cover, or beneath the print information may be bits of visual information that constitute background or the beginning of the story itself. Like little silent movies, initial sequences of pictures in the front matter are used by many picture-book illustrators to provide a build-up and thus become an integral part of the continuity in overall book design.

Once the text begins, single pages may be used in part, as with spot illustrations or vignettes that balance areas of type within the same field of action. Other scenes take up full pages, either framed by marginal space or bleeding off the pages' edges. Horizontal expanse of double pages, called landscape format, may be used as wordless narration, in which text precedes the visual or interpretation is left to the audience's imagination, or with text superimposed or printed elsewhere on the page. Combinations of double- and single-page spreads are considered transitionally interesting, but consistency and symmetry in quality book design usually dictate that one double spread demands another. Successful artists are aware of the necessity for designing artwork around the gutter where pages are bound at the book's hinge.

Another crucial consideration concerns size and shape of type in relation to artwork on the field of action. Typeface must be in harmony, not only with artistic style demonstrated in the pictures, but also with the formal or informal literary style itself. Layouts most consistently used are (1) text placed *opposite* illustrations on adjacent pages, considered here the most formal arrangement; (2) text positioned *beneath or above* illustrations, often alternating in high or low position within the same book, considered formal; (3) text *shaped* with irregular boundaries to fit inside, around, between, or to the side of illustrations, considered informal; (4) text *combined* with two or more arrangements in the same book, very informal; (5) text totally *absent* as in a wordless book, the most informal. Choices of text placement affect design and sequencing necessary for words to proceed in a consistent pattern from page to page, and the good illustrator has considered placement of the words as formally or informally part of illustrative layout in harmony with the intent of the text.

To these components of book design the illustrator brings an artistic style and choice of medium. Style may be photographically realistic or cartoonlike; paintings, drawings, woodcuts, etchings, or collages may be accomplished by watercolor (or its opaque form, gouache), oils, acrylic glazes, pastels, ink, charcoal, airbrushing, or mixed media. Improvements in technology have made feasible reproductions of any style using almost any medium, but picture books are a sum of their parts, and inaccurate illustrative conceptions or careless bookmaking in high-quality works can result in inferior products for children that are just as banal but four times more expensive than mass-market books found in the drugstore.

The Picture Book Audience

As increased expressiveness on the part of illustrators is found in illustrations, picture books have become artistically intriguing to older children and adults. Many picture-book illustrators have left behind concerns of the nursery to venture forth into the living room where other family members find merit in their contributions. As high-quality works have become more and more expensive to publish, they are increasingly made attractive to adults whose enthusiasm in bookstores, libraries, and professional periodicals has been observed and who are after all the ones to actually buy books.

DEFINITION OF THE AUDIENCE

The picture book viewed as an object of art, literature, and literacy to be found on coffee tables as well as in cribs has created debate in some circles over the way the medium itself is now to be defined. Controversy surrounding the definition of a picture book seems to stem from the conflicting views regarding a most appropriate audience—those for whom the art, text, and literacy set are intended to play a role.

A most appropriate picture-book audience is one for whom the books are read aloud by someone else, resulting in a pictorial and aural experience rather than a reading experience. The best picture-book audience, whether young or old, should be one who watches and listens. Older children can benefit greatly from experiences with picture books but should still be read aloud to or encouraged to tell themselves the story. To a definition for picture book as a two-dimensional graphic art form in which the whole book is designed around illustrations that extend the text and contribute to an intended effect on an audience can be added the picture book's role as providing a primarily pictorial and aural experience.

PREREADERS

Although all children can benefit from art in picture books, a vacuum will be created however if and when high-quality picture books are removed from hands of the very young and given over entirely to be enjoyed by an older audience. Prereading youngsters have general characteristics that make them the most receptive to a picture-book format, and the medium can play a vital role in this particular audience's development. Subject matter in picture books for prereaders may be as sophisticated or as simplistic as it is for an older audience, artistic styles of all kinds are welcomed, and whole book design may be on a grand scale or small. However, appeal to minds and hearts of the very young requires that a series of pictures be properly paced so as to reflect spoken text (or implied text as in wordless books) and include a portrayal of more rather than less of the action, scenery, or characterizations described.

A definition of picture book for the prereader thus does not generally include types such as an illustrated storybook, in which a long text has more verbal images than are pictured, or an easy-to-read title in which the audience's concentration on decoding words detracts from the pictorial and aural experience. A collection of poster or easel art would also usually stand outside the definition of picture book for the prereader, because a series of picturesque tableaux most often serves to mount art for its own sake rather than as paced reflection of a text.

In general, prereaders rather than older children are thought more successful as a picture-book audience for several reasons. By and large they still believe in fantasy, hold images in awe even when they do not move, are curious about visual images as symbols since their verbal language is more limited, and are intuitive rather than literal, empathetic rather than self-conscious, innocent rather than experienced.

VISUAL LITERACY FOR PREREADERS

Most prereaders possess other attributes that older children may have outgrown and that make a picture book a unique tool for critical evaluation in the four basic areas of visual education.

For instance *reality versus unreality* is a concept still being refined by most prereaders; their ego-centeredness is often combined with an active fantasizing that allows them to define reality as whatever they may choose to believe it is. In books they generally like both make-believe stories and subjects that center around themselves or their own interests. They are just beginning to differentiate independently between the unreality of one and reality of the other, and they are best introduced to foreign subjects through pictures that visually represent other peoples, times, places, or ideas being described by words.

A characteristic of the very young, however, is that in visuals they often accept only realistic pictorial *style* as properly portraying real *subjects* and will summarily discard as unreal any subject depicted in artistic abstraction or schematic expressiveness. For children to be visually literate their definitions of images must not be confused with subject matter itself. Images must be recognized as real *regardless of artistic expressiveness* if they symbolize what is understood by research or observation to exist in the world as we know it and as unreal only if they represent otherworld creations from the artist's imagination or dreams. Subjects themselves must be recognized as real if they are based solely on nonfictional accounts of the world around us and unreal when based either on fictional accounts of the world or on fantasy itself. Exploring this crucial difference in a picture book is excellent technique for prereaders in particular, because a brief text and series of illustrations offer opportunities for slowly paced analysis of images compared with subject matter. Such analysis lays a vital foundation for their interpretation of other visuals, such as television programs, in which reality of images belies fictional subject matter and confuses young minds with a real-looking world in which unreal subjects centered around constant chaos or feverish hilarity reign supreme.

Use of *detail* to contribute to a whole is a second aspect of visual literacy applicable especially to prereaders as an audience for picture books. Very young children enjoy noticing things that are alike or different and are eager to point out or name things around them, but they also believe that everyone sees these things as they do and indeed feels about them in ways similar to their own. These youngsters are quick to offer opinions about what is a pretty picture or an ugly one and perhaps who draws "good" or "bad," confusing personal taste with compositional excellence and subjective appreciation with objective criticism. Through exploration of artistic details used for effects by illustrators in picture-book compositions, these children develop a vocabulary for visual language that not only enables them to discuss with others their likes and dislikes but also encourages more critical examination of other visuals in the environment.

Children in this age group are known themselves to use the artistic elements in the following ways for their own compositions. *Line* is an outline for their figures. It is held in high esteem for its ability to create likenesses, and it sometimes serves as a horizontal base along which to arrange figures in a semblance of space. *Space* otherwise is as flat as the working surface, and figures are arranged weightlessly and freely within the field of action according to the child's instinctive feelings for design. *Shapes* are crude images, logical and meaningful to the child as symbols. *Scale* or *proportion* is distorted or hierarchical in relation to the importance attached to the figures (but young children are known to trace, copy, or color in coloring books because proportions most admired for replication are naturalistic or idealized). *Color* is at first enjoyed for its own sake, later personalized by expressions of favoritism, and finally applied to objects through learned association with them. *Light and dark* is the least understood of the elements, and children hardly ever demonstrate an interest in this in their own work except in a formal or stylized way. *Texture* as actual tactile experience is enjoyed in crafts of all kinds but is seldom found implied in two-dimensional works by children. Examination of more detailed uses for artistic elements by illustrators enables children to more objectively evaluate success or failure of intended effect in composition. Such a study may even plant the seed of life-long tolerance for diverse artistic styles and other aesthetic points of view.

Picture books as a medium have *unique properties* that are also most useful when promoting visual literacy of prereaders as compared with more experienced older audiences. Younger children have not yet seen a preponderance of books and do not realize from firsthand reading the variety of information contained in them. They are becoming more conscious of designs in the environment but have not often been exposed to art in an original form as it was meant to be encountered. They may not frequently be asked for their opinions about art or text and have few preconceived notions about such subjects. Prereaders are also just beginning to grasp the idea of sequencing and connotative as well as denotative expression in words as well as pictures; they have just discovered that pictures can have more than one meaning and that personal predictions can be made about a text's outcome before a last page is turned. Use of picture books with these children often competes well against electronic visuals because the book's format can be enjoyed at leisure; it is an object that can be used effectively at a slow pace to teach as well as entertain. Its slighter text appeals to shorter attention spans but may encourage thoughtfulness of response; it can be picked up again and again to divulge new and different delights. Finally, it provides through shared read-aloud experience a strong feeling of kinship with others as well as a private and protective attitude of ownership as a thing unto itself.

The last area of visual literacy is the need for understanding a picture's *main idea*, and again prereaders are an audience in need most of education in the necessary conceptualization of concrete versus generalized experience. Very young children are more interested in process or concrete activity than in results or statements about such activity seen as a type, and their only value judgments are likely to be whether or not they found the activity itself interesting and whether or not they felt talked down to by descriptions of it. However, the illustrator may provide a depiction of activity that provides children with opportunities to form value judgments they can apply in their own lives. Family, community interdependence, use of tools, nature, wild creatures, celebrations, play, and fantasy are favorite concrete experiences depicted in picture books that help the prereading audience gather facts from the specific in order to understand the general. If illustrators and readers do not underestimate the abilities of very young children to generalize about role modeling, group behavior, and problem-solving, the prereader's concept of self can expand. Even a very young child can begin to adopt a world-view that values other environments aesthetically, emotionally, and intellectually.

Picture-Book History and Production

The picture book for children arises from a tradition of illustrative art that dates to prehistory. Advances in technology and changes in culture fostered the appearance—and evolution—of the picture book.

HISTORY OF ILLUSTRATION

The first illustrators were cave painters who commemorated the hunt or shamans who invoked images of the supernatural for religious and medicinal purposes. Words and images have always gone together, and written language such as ancient Chinese has often relied on visual symbolic sequences to represent ideas rather than words. In medieval times illustrators were the scribes who not only penned individual manuscripts but also decorated their margins, illuminated initials, and embellished the bound volumes' outer edges. These artisans were replaced by the first printers who reproduced illustrations, initially in woodcut and then by lithography, in order to please a new reading public that demanded visual enhancement for comprehension of printed matter.

Because illustration was considered ornamentation for text and a method of making information more appealing to the masses, early illustrators were regarded first as craftsmen and then as folk artists but never as serious or fine artists. The title "fine art" came to be reserved for creations that provided self-expression rather than illustrative communication that took into account its viewing audience. Folk art, on the other hand, was utilitarian, faithful to traditional cultural motifs, and intended as decoration, instruction, or documentation for a specified audience; it was therefore thought more suitable as a definition for early book illustrating. Illustration was considered decorative when used to adorn gray expanses of print matter, instructional when visually elucidating concepts under discussion, and documentary when visually recording character or event described by words. Illustrators like N. C. Wyeth and Howard Pyle who spent their adult lives beautifying books were consequently never taken as seriously as fine artists like Honoré Daumier, Edgar Degas, and Georges Rouault, even though all of the latter at one time also made illustrations for public consumption.

Visual narration or storytelling by an illustrator serves also a decorative, instructional, documentary, or even combined function, but to be truly narrative in books a sequence of pictures must additionally indicate a close relationship between cause and effect from one visual to another and may result in a visual account in its own right. The great nineteenth-century English artists for children, Kate Greenaway, Walter Crane, Randolph Caldecott, and Beatrix Potter, created fine examples of early visual narration by bringing comedy and social satire to their illustrations for picture books, but since children were their audience they were considered lords and ladies of the nursery and were never received at the court of fine art. Only the abiding love and admiration of subsequent generations of artists, children, and professionals in the field of children's literature have promoted some of their works from the ranks of folk art to that of classical graphic art design.

In the twentieth century more attention began to be paid to the creative as well as technical talents of graphic designers who produce two-dimensional work intended for reproduction, compared with fine artists who create one-of-a-kind works. Picture-book making as a modern-day graphic art form seems to have coincided in some respects with artists' revitalization of the medium of printmaking. So-called art prints had popularized works of the old masters by making inexpensive copies easily accessible to the public for years, but mid-nineteenth-century printmakers began to create their own designs and to make such skillful reproductions themselves or in close collaboration with a printer that the copies came to be called *multiple originals*, each considered a work of art and deserving of attention in its own right. Such printmaking involved reproduction techniques that defined the graphic artist's work as either a relief print (use of a raised surface as in woodcut), intaglio (use of dampened paper pressed into inked lines as in etching or engraving), serigraphy (use of stencils to treat areas separately as in silk screening), or planography (use of a chemically sensitized surface as in lithography). Printmaking through the years became a unique artistic medium practiced readily by contemporary fine artists. Prints and proofs were exhibited around the world in galleries and museums, and courses in the medium began to be taught in art departments on college and university campuses.

Meanwhile the picture-book illustrators who had often popularized texts by others were recognized as graphic artists who also created original designs. In addition they took into account sequencing of words as well as visuals throughout a series of designs. Sensitive collaboration with editors and art directors at publishing houses resulted in high-quality book illustrations that became contemporary works of art. Advances in planographic reproduction produced better books, enticing many renowned artists like Leo and Diane Dillon, cartoonists Edward Gorey and William Steig, theatrical designer Beni Montresor, and sculptor Chris Van Allsburg from their work for adults into the increasingly sophisticated realm of illustrating for children.

In general the graphic arts grew to perform many of the same diverse functions as the fine arts, from spiritual commemoration to political satirization. Graphic arts storytelling fell mainly to the photographers, printmakers, and picture-book illustrators. Since many of the latter had been attracted into the field from fine art, artistic considerations began to compete in some circles with the attention paid to design and reproduction techniques.

Fine artists in a graphic-arts medium could not be labeled folk artists since the first thing many of them discarded was the old notion of illustration as purely decorative, instructional, or documentary. Illustration took on new meaning as revolutionaries arrived on the scene to introduce in children's books personal expressiveness achieved by surrealistic viewpoints, cubistic simplification of figures, or schematized distortion that reduced visual imagery to its elements. To the straightforward, cause-and-effect, theatrically visual narrative in which the book is a stage and a reader is the audience, these new artists added the complicated filmic narrative implying motion and the choreographed narrative, to be imagined as accompanied by music. They brought multiple levels of understanding to wordless narration and the dream sequence. In short, the new picture-book illustrators were spawned by the electronic age itself, nurtured by its technological advances, and sent on their way to compete in a visually oriented society accustomed to abundant and often simultaneous imagery.

Artistic styles and moods in picture books varied as new and differing emphases were evolved by these artists. But reliance on basic types of subject matter appealing to children generally remained, and the medium continued to be looked down upon outside the field as a minor graphic art in spite of the growing evidence of major expressive influence from the world of fine art. Then high-quality picture-book illustrations without texts began to be reproduced as prints and posters that appeared in galleries and exhibits where many adults could look at them closely for the first time. These adults may have read picture books to children, but they had concentrated on the words and left pictures for the youngsters to enjoy. Now they were not only seeing contemporary picture-book art through new eyes but were buying it to hang on their walls. Some children's illustrators began to be discussed seriously and their techniques were seen to be remarkably similar to those of other art: rhythm, repetition, and spatial relationship conveyed energy, motion, and life itself in their pictures. These principles of design seemed to be accomplished by similar uses as well for the artistic elements of line, color, light and dark, shape, space, and implied texture. The picture book for children entered the adult world of art appreciation.

THE PICTURE-BOOK ARTIST

The picture-book artist must still consider basic illustrative functions of decoration, instruction, and documentation. Illustrators of fact, fiction, folklore, or poetry must comprehend fully both the content and spirit of the text and be led by them to build a visual world supplementary to the words. The illustrator's creations are vitally integral to a picture book because young children have such a limited range of experiences that they need visuals to bolster their understanding of words. In a set of illustrations that truly illuminate a text, the whole book design is correct, medium and artistic style are appropriate, details are credible, and a proper mood of seriousness or frivolity is communicated.

The illustrator exercises power independent of the words, however, by choice of textual subject matter to illustrate and by the way artistic elements are used to expressively portray those subjects. Emphasis on certain subjects and omission of others create a series of illustrations that may stand as a visual text with message of its own, adding dimension to the written words and serving as a differing but harmonious point of view. Just as the storyteller's point of view gave form and direction in ancient oral tradition so too can the illustrator's viewpoint give form and direction to story, poem, or information by visually interpreting the subject or by meandering enticingly away into highlights personally considered amusing, intriguing, or enlightening. Use of the artistic elements for portrayal of any subject matter in an *expressive* manner gave rise to high-quality picture books as a graphic art form worthy of serious attention and resulted in some children's illustrations themselves viewed variously as visual poetry, visual protest, or visual humor just as may be found in the fine arts.

The illustrator as visual narrator of a story is additionally involved in portraying consistent characters throughout one continuous plot that has a beginning, a middle, and an end. Characters must have personalities that visually contribute to cause-and-effect relationships. Some authors have personified animals or inanimate objects as primary characters in their texts, offering the illustrator unusual challenges in visual storytelling.

Not all picture-book illustrations of high quality can be evaluated alike with regard to their expressive abilities since texts differ from the strictly factual to the wildly imaginary, and illustrators understandably view their functions as demanding different approaches. Documentary or instructional illustrations that are successfully expressive, for instance, go beyond clarification of information but generally remain connected to texts. Treasured expressions of decorative illustrating, on the other hand, create separate but equal lives for art and text as the audience is invited to dwell on the pictures while listening to the words, to imagine what if while interpreting what is. Fair evaluation of success must take into account the illustrator's chosen function, the appropriateness of individual improvisation, and an appreciation for the restricted medium of the picture book itself.

A critic of picture books must also take into account when the title was published. Before World War II the number of quality American picture books published each year was comparatively small; since then a remarkable growth in children's books has occurred due to our society's changing attitudes toward child raising, increased interest on the part of publishers and artists, and the establishment of children's literature courses, special library collections, and award committees of all kinds. Comparisons of the different ways in which texts with common themes have been illustrated by different artists and during different eras enhance children's appreciation of divergent uses of the artistic elements and of methods employed in picture-book illustrating over the years.

ILLUSTRATION AND PRINTING TECHNOLOGY

Nineteenth-century illustrators such as Greenaway and Caldecott had their illustrations carved out of wood blocks by such sensitive printers as Edmund Evans, who reproduced the wood engravings and added illusions of coloration often within a limited span of hues.

Next in the technological parade came letterpress or rotary gravure which used raised relief for printing. This was eventually discontinued for several reasons. To be economical, artwork had to be confined in an area blocked out separately from text. In addition, use of the raised surface forced ink onto paper in a way that diminished quality except when paper had an expensive high gloss.

The next step was lithography, which duplicates continuous-tone illustrations and photographs on uncoated paper by use of a plane, or flat, surface. In the early days of picture-book illustrating, this surface was a finely polished, porous, and smooth stone or *lithograph* (such as a flat slab of Bavarian limestone) upon which a drawing was made in reverse with a greasy crayon. This pattern was etched with an acid solution that also made it water-resistant. The stone was dried, washed, soaked in water, and then rolled with greasy printer's ink. The ink was repelled by areas of water on the stone and attracted to areas of oil. With the aid of a press, copies could be made from the inked image.

Early lithography or planographic printing, however, was cumbersome because the paper had to be dampened, stones were heavy and awkward, and slow flatbed presses were unable to simultaneously print text and pictures. For faster reproduction, lithographic stones have been replaced by zinc or aluminum plates that are cheaper, easily obtained, and more versatile; in addition, illustrations can be transferred to them photographically. The flatbed has been replaced by larger, hydraulically operated offset printing presses on which the flexible metal plate can be wrapped around a cylinder. The plate itself is dampened by rollers, then inked, and the inked image is offset onto a rubber blanket cylinder; the paper is printed as it comes between the blanket and impression cylinders to produce the final image. To print text simultaneously with picture, text is first phototypeset and a proof is made which is then photographed onto the plate with the art before printing.

In offset printing, however, colors have to be painstakingly pre-separated, often by the illustrator personally. Many of today's picture-book illustrators still prefer to preseparate their artwork by hand, although some publishers offer the choice of color preseparation or working in full color at a reduced royalty income for the artist. In full-color photolithography, a camera is used to photograph the original art, usually through four separate filters (in very high-quality full-color work other filters may be added). Each color appears on its own negative film as a series of large dots where color is saturated and smaller dots where it is weak. These images are transferred to printing plates that have a coating of light-sensitive emulsion that repels ink except at those places where dots from the film appear (120 or more per square inch). An offset press may consist of one, two, four, or five one-color printing presses joined together; most multiple printing is accomplished with one pass of the paper through the press. In four-color printing, for instance, the presses could be inked with any four colors, but generally the best results are achieved by use of magenta, cyan, yellow, and black inks in combinations of overprinting. Advances in technology have also produced electronic or laser scanning for color separation and correction, and systems using microcomputers have been developed for making printing plates directly from originals without the intermediate step of photography.

ROLE OF THE PUBLISHER

Careful printing, quality paper, and handsome binding all contribute to overall design in quality picture books, and success or failure in these regards can be attributed to the publisher and printer, although some artists involve themselves in the publishing process all the way through to the final product. Juvenile-book sections in American publishing houses have an editor, art director, consultant, or designer whose task is to oversee production of the book itself. If a manuscript is accepted, the right illustrator for expansion of text must be found, taking into account the potential audience, illustrative perceptions of an artist, and original intent of the author who is sometimes not involved further with decisions about artwork or book design. Illustrators of their own works as well as of others' works must be reassured or gently criticized, they must be made aware of color and space limitations, and their artwork must be accurate, clear, and reproducible.

Illustrators present ideas in dummies for artistic layout and for choice of typeface but designers must look at the unified arrangement of the whole book before art and text finally go to press. Theirs is a creative contribution in itself. An uncertain market and effects of the economy place pressures on them; spiraling costs for manuscripts, artwork, printing, and distribution of books often give rise to editorial as well as fiscal conservatism just when the most liberal advances in technology offer unparalleled opportunities for quality picture reproduction. As competition from other media for children escalates, book production must be dynamic rather than cloying, innovative rather than trendy, respectful of children's sensibilities as well as of adult critics, and most of all fun to look at.

The Caldecott Collection

An award honoring a quality picture book's success in artistic expressiveness is a relatively recent phenomenon on both sides of the Atlantic. As more and more writers and artists entered the field, children's books began to compete for the attention of youngsters and the money of adults and, as in all competitive activities, rules for contests of different kinds were soon established. The races were on, and winning or losing became a significant concern in the lives of leading artists, their families, their publishers, and their audiences. Of tens of thousands of children's books in print in the United States, only a relative few can be winners or even also-rans; and as increases in reprinting costs force even recent books out of print, one of the most successful assurances for comparative permanence is that a title be mentioned as a winner of an award or listed on someone's selection of "best" books for children.

Of the many awards and selected lists of children's books, the Caldecott Medal roster is one of the oldest in this country. It ranks among the most respected, by outsiders as well as insiders in children's literature, and its recognition of illustrating and illustrators is unique. The collection of over four dozen Caldecott Award winners represents a chronological spectrum of American artists from pre–World War II to the present, a wide variety of artistic expressiveness and intent, and most of all the unabashed joy and personal integrity with which many adults of talent have presented the picture book as a work of art to be quietly appreciated in the noisy, active lives of children.

At the beginning of each new year, a committee of adults, now called the Caldecott Committee from the Association for Library Service to Children of the American Library Association, has looked over the entire outpouring of U.S. picture books from the preceding twelve months. The committee accepts nominations and votes for one selection as each year's "Most Distinguished American Picture

Book for Children," an illustrator or illustrators to receive the Medal itself, and often other noteworthy titles to be designated Honor Books. "Distinguished" over the years has been variously defined by committees as "marked by eminence and distinction: noted for significant achievement," "marked by excellence in quality," and "individually distinct." "Picture book" is variously defined as one that "essentially provides the child with a visual experience," "has a collective unity of story-line, theme, or concept," and "displays respect for children's understandings, abilities, and appreciations." "Children" is defined as "persons of ages up to and including four-teen and picture books for this entire age range are to be considered."

Other awards and selected lists contain as many prestigious picture-book offerings and represent as many talented illustrators as does the Caldecott collection, but no other collected body of work in this country is as well known for providing early quality book experiences for young children. None includes more obtainable titles or has been more subjected to as much critical and bibliographical scrutiny. No other large group of titles has been more represented in audiovisual format, more sought after in manuscript form by institutional depositories dedicated to the preservation of children's literature, or offers a wider variety of subject matter and artistic treatment for appreciation by older as well as younger children. As a review of societal mores and artistic styles deemed suitable at different times in America's changing views of childhood, no other experience for young and old alike offers better insights into the complexities of making judgment statements in the field of children's literature. And finally, no other collection can enhance appreciation of all picture books as a graphic art form as can the Caldecott books in a hands-on evaluation with youngsters themselves.

As Robert Lawson said in his 1941 acceptance speech for *They Were Strong and Good*, perhaps no award at all should have been made during years when the books published were generally un-distinguished. Today a few titles whose art, text, or intent are of questionable quality stand on the shelf beside outstanding contri-butions that have enriched the lives of children for generations. In ART AND DESIGN IN CHILDREN'S PICTURE BOOKS, analysis of merit is attempted solely in light of the late–twentieth-century audience that these books now address. Any re-evaluation should apply ac-cepted tenets in art criticism to the whole book. Thematic, cultural or social, and classically didactic approaches to children's literature can then be joined by a formalistic aesthetic approach that takes into account the intended audience and the entire creative process that produces a picture-book experience.

ART AND DESIGN IN CHILDREN'S PICTURE BOOKS is structured to present an introduction for interested adults and children to the whole picture book as a graphic arts medium. The discussion will consider background influences on selected illustrators as reflected in their works. Also discussed are characteristics of prereaders that make them a receptive audience for a particular work, variations in book design, uses of the artistic elements, and their effects on the audience. Fifteen American illustrators have been chosen for primary focus, representing Caldecott Medal–winning artwork over five decades and demonstrating various biographical, political, social, imaginary, geographical, or cultural influences in addition to stylistic influences from the fine arts.

Personal backgrounds that set each illustrator's work into a picture-book context have been compiled from interviews, articles, Caldecott acceptance speeches, and biographies, some of which appear as selected recommended readings in the bibliography following this chapter. Possible influences from the fine arts can be demonstrated by adults who gather as many examples of like artwork as possible for children to study. If visits to art museums or galleries are impossible, then the reader should seek out art prints, slides, and/or books with color reproductions. A selected bibliography of sources for art, art appreciation, and art education is also included at the end of this chapter. It is, however, a limited list selected from numerous available works.

In-depth exploration of each of the artistic elements—line, color, light and dark, shape, and space—as used in picture-book art is offered by appreciations of thirteen Medal-winning titles by the above-mentioned illustrators. The first titles cited in each of five chapters are given most emphasis to introduce an element, and other titles are subsequently analyzed to provide support and expansion for exploration of the element. Such exploration is followed by analysis of audience response to the artistic element, except in the final chapter on artistic use of space. Here techniques and effects are so fundamentally intertwined that the two are discussed together.

The eight illustrators living during the writing of this book were all consulted regarding analyses of their artwork, and their clarifications, helpful explanations of technique, and elaborations on background were incorporated. The approaches to art appreciation through picture books described here have proven successful when incorporated into elementary-school classrooms as well as art and library/media classes when children are intellectually and perceptually ready for such extensive exploration. For interested adults and children, suggestions for further study are included in each chapter.

At the end of most chapters a section entitled "Looking Ahead" includes for titles under discussion a brief commentary on artistic elements to be explored more fully in chapters yet to come. For example, in the chapter on line, artistic elements of color, light and dark, shape, and space have not yet been discussed and perhaps will not be fully understood by the reader at that point. However, it would be a disservice to consider art appreciation of *Make Way for Ducklings* and *Time of Wonder* and make no mention of Robert McCloskey's use of all the artistic elements. Therefore, brief remarks are included in "Looking Ahead" and may be more meaningful to the reader after subsequent chapters have been digested. "Looking Back" provides appreciation of elements discussed previously and applied to the title in question, except in the final chapter, in which exploration of space necessarily relies on an artist's use of all the other artistic elements combined.

"Looking Around" suggests other Award winners in the collection that are recommended for further study of the artistic element being explored; these titles are in many cases as vitally pertinent to a point under discussion as are the major titles selected. Careful selection of major titles was made on the basis of proven success with children in the experience of this author, who is merely one of many parents, teachers, librarians, frustrated artists, and fans out of the scores who have spent enjoyable years appreciating the Caldecotts.

Recommended Sources

ART, ART APPRECIATION, AND ART EDUCATION

Arnheim, Rudolf. *Art and Visual Perception.* Berkeley: Univ. of California Pr., 1974.

"The Art of Seeing." Sound filmstrip. Jamaica, N.Y.: Eye Gate, 1972.

"The Art of Seeing." Six sound filmstrips. Chicago: Clearvue, 1979.

"The Artist Looks at Life." Seven sound filmstrips. Lewiston, N.Y.: McIntyre Visual Publications, n.d.

Barron, John N. *The Language of Painting: An Informal Dictionary.* Cleveland: World, 1967.

Batterbury, Ariane Ruskin. *The Pantheon Story of Art for Young People.* Rev. ed. New York: Pantheon, 1975.

Bell, Ione, Karen Matison Hess, and Jim R. Matison. *Art: As You See It.* New York: Wiley, 1979.

Birren, Faber. *Creative Color.* New York: Van Nostrand Reinhold, 1961.

———. *Principles of Color.* New York: Van Nostrand Reinhold, 1969.

Bolognese, Don, and Robert Thornton. *Drawing and Painting with the Computer.* New York: Watts, 1983.

The Britannica Encyclopedia of American Art. Chicago: Encyclopaedia Britannica, 1973.

Campbell, Ann. *Paintings: How to Look at Great Art.* New York: Watts, n.d.

Canady, John. *What Is Art?* New York: Knopf, 1981.

Chapman, Laura H. *Approaches to Art in Education.* New York: Harcourt, 1978.

Chase, Alice Elizabeth. *Famous Artists of the Past.* New York: Platt & Munk, 1964.

———. *Famous Paintings: An Introduction to Art for Young People.* New York: Platt & Munk, 1962.

———. *Looking at Art.* New York: Crowell, 1966.

Cumming, Robert. *Just Imagine: Ideas in Painting.* New York: Scribner, 1982.

———. *Just Look . . . a Book about Paintings.* New York: Scribner, 1979.

Edwards, Betty. *Drawing on the Right Side of the Brain: A Course in Enhancing Creativity and Artistic Confidence.* Los Angeles: Tarcher, 1979.

Eisner, Elliot W. *Educating Artistic Vision.* New York: Macmillan, 1972.

Feldman, Edmund B. *Art as Image and Idea.* Englewood Cliffs, N.J.: Prentice-Hall, 1967.

Gaitskell, Charles D., and Al Hurwitz. *Children and Their Art: Methods for the Elementary School.* New York: Harcourt, 1975.

Glubok, Shirley. *The Art of America in the Early Twentieth Century.* New York: Macmillan, 1974.

Grigson, Geoffrey. *Shapes and People: A Book about Pictures.* New York: Vanguard,1964.

——— and Jane Grigson. *More Shapes and Stories: A Book about Pictures.* New York: Vanguard, 1967.

———. *Shapes and Stories: A Book about Pictures.* New York: Vanguard, 1964.

Holme, Bryan. *Creatures of Paradise: Pictures to Grow Up With.* New York: Oxford Univ. Pr., 1980.

Janson, Horst Woldemar, with Samuel Cauman. *History of Art for Young People.* 2d ed. Rev. by Anthony F. Janson. New York: Abrams, 1982.

Lanier, Vincent. *The Arts We See: A Simplified Introduction to the Visual Arts.* New York: Teachers College Pr., 1982.

Lansing, Kenneth M., and Arlene Richards. *The Elementary Teacher's Art Handbook.* New York: Holt, 1981.

Lauer, David A. *Design Basics.* New York: Holt, 1979.

"Little Adventures in Art." Four sound filmstrips. Chicago: Clearvue, 1979.

Look Again. Childcraft—The How and Why Library, v. 13. Chicago: Field Enterprises, 1968.

Madeja, Stanley S. *The Arts, Cognition, and Basic Skills.* Based on a conference held at Aspen, Colorado, June 19–25, 1977. St. Louis: Cemrel, 1978.

Maillard, Robert, ed. *Masterpieces in the History of Painting.* New York: Holt, 1961.

Moore, Janet Gaylord. *The Many Ways of Seeing: An Introduction to the Pleasures of Art.* Cleveland: World, 1968.

The Phaidon Art Collection. 3v. Chicago: Encyclopaedia Britannica, 1976.

Praeger Encyclopedia of Art. 5v. Chicago: Encyclopaedia Britannica, 1971.

Preble, Duane. *Artforms.* New York: Harper, 1978.

Ruskin, Ariane. *Seventeenth and Eighteenth Century Art.* New York: McGraw-Hill, 1969.

"Unicef Art." Five sound filmstrips. Chicago: Clearvue, 1979.

Waterfield, Giles. *Faces.* New York: Atheneum, 1982.

Williams, Linda Verlee. *Teaching for the Two-Sided Mind: A Guide to Right Brain/Left Brain Education.* Englewood Cliffs, N.J.: Prentice-Hall, 1983.

"Wilton Art Appreciation Program." Six sound filmstrips. Wilton, Conn.: Reading & O'Reilly, 1980.

CHILDREN'S LITERATURE, PICTURE BOOKS, AND ILLUSTRATORS

Arbuthnot, May Hill. *Children and Books.* 3d ed. Chicago: Scott, Foresman, 1964.

Bader, Barbara. *American Picturebooks from Noah's Ark to the Beast Within.* New York: Macmillan, 1976.

Bator, Robert, ed. *Signposts to Criticism of Children's Literature.* Chicago: American Library Assn., 1983.

Bauer, Caroline Feller. *Handbook for Storytellers.* Chicago: American Library Assn., 1977.

Bettelheim, Bruno. *The Uses of Enchantment: The Meaning and Importance of Fairy Tales.* New York: Knopf, 1976.

Billington, Elizabeth T., ed. *Randolph Caldecott Treasury.* New York: Warne, 1978.

Caldecott, Randolph. *Randolph Caldecott's John Gilpin and Other Stories.* New York: Warne, 1978.

"Caldecott's Favorite Stories." Four sound filmstrips. New Rochelle, N.Y.: Spoken Arts, 1968.

Champlin, Connie, and Barbara Kennedy. *Books in Bloom: Creativity through Children's Literature.* Omaha: Special Literature Pr., 1982.

Cianciolo, Patricia. *Illustrations in Children's Books.* Dubuque, Iowa: W. C. Brown, 1976.

———. *Picture Books for Children.* 2d ed. Chicago: American Library Assn., 1981.

Commire, Anne, ed. *Something about the Author.* 28v. Detroit: Gale, 1962– .

———. *Yesterday's Authors of Books for Children.* 2v. Detroit: Gale, 1977–78.

de Montreville, Doris, and Elizabeth D. Crawford, eds. *Fourth Book of Junior Authors and Illustrators.* New York: Wilson, 1978.

—— and Donna Hill, eds. *Third Book of Junior Authors.* New York: Wilson, 1972.

Engen, Rodney K. *Randolph Caldecott: "Lord of the Nursery."* London: Oresko Books, 1977.

"Enjoying Illustrations." Sound filmstrip in series 3 of "Literature for Children." Los Angeles: Pied Piper, 1978.

"Ezra Jack Keats." Signature Collection motion picture. Weston, Conn.: Weston Woods, 1969.

Frost, Joan. "Art, Books and Children: Art Activities Based on Children's Literature." Omaha: Special Literature Pr., 1984.

Fuller, Muriel, ed. *More Junior Authors.* New York: Wilson, 1963.

"Gail E. Haley: Wood and Linoleum Illustration." Signature Collection sound filmstrip. Weston, Conn.: Weston Woods, 1978.

Hearne, Betsy, and Marilyn Kaye, eds. *Celebrating Children's Books: Essays on Children's Literature in Honor of Zena Sutherland.* New York: Lothrop, 1981.

Heck, Colette M. "A Bio-bibliography of Winners of the Caldecott Award, 1938–1955." Master's thesis, Catholic University of America, 1956.

Hoffman, Miriam, and Eva Samuels. *Authors and Illustrators of Children's Books: Writings on Their Lives and Works.* New York: Bowker, 1972.

Holtze, Sally Holmes, ed. *Fifth Book of Junior Authors and Illustrators.* New York: Wilson, 1983.

Hopkins, Lee Bennett. *Books Are by People.* New York: Citation, 1969.

"How a Picture Book Is Made." Signature Collection sound filmstrip. Weston, Conn.: Weston Woods, 1979.

Hoyle, Karen Nelson, and staff, comps. *The Kerlan Collection Manuscripts and Illustrations for Children's Books: A Checklist.* Minneapolis: Kerlan Collection, University of Minnesota Libraries, 1985.

Hyman, Trina Schart. *Self-Portrait: Trina Schart Hyman.* Reading, Mass.: Addison-Wesley, 1981.

Karl, Nancy. "Exploring the World of Peter Spier." O'Fallon, Mo.: Book Lures, 1983.

Kingman, Lee. *The Illustrator's Notebook.* Boston: Horn Book, 1978.

——, ed. *Newbery and Caldecott Medal Books: 1956–1965.* Boston: Horn Book, 1965.

——. *Newbery and Caldecott Medal Books: 1966–1975.* Boston: Horn Book, 1975.

——, Joanna Foster, and Ruth Giles Lontoft, comps. *Illustrators of Children's Books: 1957–1966.* Boston: Horn Book, 1968.

——, Grace Allen Hogarth, and Harriet Quimby. *Illustrators of Children's Books: 1967–1976.* Boston: Horn Book, 1978.

Klemin, Diana. *The Art of Art for Children's Books: A Contemporary Survey.* New York: Potter, 1966.

Kunitz, Stanley J., and Howard Haycraft, eds. *The Junior Book of Authors.* New York: Wilson, 1951.

Lacy, Lyn. "Randolph Caldecott: The Man behind the Medal." Signature Collection sound filmstrip. Weston, Conn.: Weston Woods, 1983.

Lanes, Selma G. *The Art of Maurice Sendak.* New York: Abrams, 1980.

———. *Down the Rabbit Hole.* New York: Atheneum, 1971.

"The Lively Art of Picture Books." Signature Collection motion picture. Weston, Conn.: Weston Woods, 1964.

"Maurice Sendak." Signature Collection motion picture. Weston, Conn.: Weston Woods, 1963.

McCann, Donnarae, and Olga Richard. *The Child's First Books: A Critical Study of Pictures and Texts.* New York: Wilson, 1973.

Mealy, Virginia. "Caldecott Capers." O'Fallon, Mo.: Book Lures, 1983.

"Meet the Newbery Author: Arnold Lobel." Sound filmstrip. Westminster, Mo.: Random, n.d.

Meigs, Cornelia, and others. *A Critical History of Children's Literature.* New York: Macmillan, 1969.

Meyer, Susan E. *A Treasury of the Great Children's Book Illustrators.* New York: Abrams, 1983.

Miller, Bertha Mahony, Louise Payson Latimer, and Beulah Folmsbee, comps. *Illustrators of Children's Books: 1744–1945.* Boston: Horn Book, 1947.

——— and Elinor Whitney Field, eds. *Caldecott Medal Books: 1938–1957.* Boston: Horn Book, 1957.

Muir, Percival H. *Victorian Illustrated Books.* New York: Praeger, 1971.

Paulin, Mary Ann. *Creative Uses of Children's Literature.* Hamden, Conn.: Shoe String, 1982.

Peterson, Linda Kauffman, and Marily Leathers Solt. *Newbery and Caldecott Medal and Honor Books: An Annotated Bibliography.* Boston: Hall, 1982.

Polette, Nancy. *E Is for Everybody: A Manual for Bringing Fine Picture Books into the Hands and Hearts of Children.* 2v. Metuchen, N.J.: Scarecrow, 1976, 1982.

———. *Picture Books for Gifted Programs.* Metuchen, N.J.: Scarecrow, 1981.

Preiss, Byron, ed. *The Art of Leo and Diane Dillon.* New York: Ballantine, 1981.

Richards, Bob. *The Making of a Book.* New York: Holt, 1980.

"Robert McCloskey." Signature Collection motion picture. Weston, Conn.: Weston Woods, 1962.

Roberts, Ellen E. M. *The Children's Picture Book: How to Write It, How to Sell It.* Cincinnati: Writer's Digest Books, 1981.

Roberts, Patricia L. "The Female Image in the Caldecott Medal Award Books." Ph.D. diss., University of the Pacific, Stockton, Calif., 1976.

Roginski, Jim, comp. *Newbery and Caldecott Medalists and Honor Book Winners: Bibliographies and Resource Material through 1977.* Littleton, Colo.: Libraries Unlimited, 1983.

Sadker, Myra Pollack, and David Miller Sadker. *Now Upon a Time: A Contemporary View of Children's Literature.* New York: Harper, 1977.

Schwarcz, Joseph. *Ways of the Illustrator: Visual Communication in Children's Literature.* Chicago: American Library Assn., 1982.

"Sendak." Signature Collection motion picture. Weston, Conn.: Weston Woods, 1986.

Shulevitz, Uri. *Writing with Pictures: How to Write and Illustrate Children's Books.* New York: Watson-Guptill, 1985.

Smith, Irene. *History of the Newbery and Caldecott Awards.* New York: Viking, 1957.

"Story of a Book." Sound filmstrip. Los Angeles: Pied Piper, 1970.

Sutherland, Zena, and others, eds. *Children and Books.* 6th ed. Glenview, Ill.: Scott Foresman, 1981.

Viguers, Ruth Hill, Marcia Dalphin, and Bertha Mahony Miller, comps. *Illustrators of Children's Books: 1946–1956.* Boston: Horn Book, 1958.

Ward, Martha E., and Dorothy A. Marquardt. *Illustrators of Books for Young People.* 2d ed. Metuchen, N.J.: Scarecrow, 1975.

Wintle, Justin, and Emma Fisher. *The Pied Piper: Interviews with the Influential Creators of Children's Literature.* New York: Paddington Pr., 1974.

Woolman, Bertha. *The Caldecott Award: The Winners and the Honor Books.* Minneapolis: Denison, 1981.

Zemach, Margot. *Self-Portrait: Margot Zemach.* Reading, Mass.: Addison-Wesley, 1978.

Send inquiries about the Caldecott Committee and the Medal to:

Association for Library Service to Children
American Library Association
50 East Huron Street
Chicago, Illinois 60611

2
Line: *Make Way for Ducklings* and *Time of Wonder*

Make Way for Ducklings by Robert McCloskey will be fifty years old in 1991; by now the story of the Mallard family has worked its charm on three generations of youngsters. *Ducklings* is the fifth Caldecott Award winner and the oldest Medalist to remain as popular today as after its initial publication. *Time of Wonder* won the Award sixteen years after *Ducklings*, making McCloskey the first artist to win the Medal a second time. *Wonder* is the first of two books illustrated in color by this author/illustrator and the third story in a group about the McCloskey family itself.

Robert McCloskey

"I never get to be the first to read them *Make Way for Ducklings*. The children have always heard it before," laments a primary-school librarian with many years' experience in reading aloud, "but they always want to hear it again!" She went on to say she'd "have to get up pretty early" to precede the nursery and preschool attendants, kindergarten teachers, family friends, parents—and now grandparents—who have all turned to *Ducklings* as a precious read-aloud for younger children. But even though the youngsters know the story from classroom, home, or babysitters, the librarian still opens it up year after year to another interested audience at story hour. "I enjoy it too," she adds as partial explanation for her second-reading successes, "because it's a nice little story with such very good pictures."

One reason, certainly, for *Ducklings'* longevity is its ability to give joy for many readings with preschool and primary-age children. Sitting through the "nice little story with such very good pictures" can be even more rewarding in these rereadings and is to be encouraged for the pure pleasure of meeting an old friend once again. Art appreciation should be approached enthusiastically but with sensitivity for the appropriate time when children may be receptive to learning new things about their old friend.

A congenial group sharing can be considered with this book in a library, classroom, or day-care setting, due to the generous size of the hardbound edition (it is one of the largest of the Caldecotts) and because of McCloskey's masterful use of space on the pages, which makes the action easy to follow. As an individualized experience the book is without equal, for *Ducklings* as a lap book has such details as feathers that beg to be touched and simplicity of language that cries out for private reading, like the name game for the ducklings: Jack, Kack, Lack, Mack, Nack, Ouack, Pack, Quack. A media specialist relates that she once projected the filmstrip version for the enjoyment of hearing-impaired students. Their teacher stood near the screen to sign the story for them as it was read aloud to her, and when she spelled out these names in sign language, the youngsters giggled over the silliness just as hearing youngsters do. As the ducklings were named they were also pointed out on the screen, but after the seventh the teacher had lost track of the last one and said under her breath, "Where is the little bugger?" One of the deaf children, obviously keeping count and sensing that the delay might mean Quack's tragic omission, scooted quickly to the screen, where he pointed at the eighth duckling staring out from behind the tuft of grass. The child smiled at his teacher with wisdom and contentment, and she knew that here was another *Ducklings* fan, back for one more reading.

A rereading that offers such delight in finding Quack again continues as pleasure enough through the years because McCloskey has presented an audience of four- to seven-year-olds a story and pictures they can relate to on emotional, cognitive, and creative levels. The family is of uppermost emotional importance to this age span, and *Ducklings* is first of all a family story. It makes good reading as enrichment in all the curricular areas that include studies of family relationships and group interdependencies. Second, the natural world is a subject of overriding curiosity to children of this age, and *Ducklings* is a nature story about ducks, giving textual information as well as lots of pictures. Last, younger children are very receptive to realistic drawings of shapes, landscapes, and townscapes, all found in the representational artistic style of McCloskey.

Without question *Ducklings* has become a classic picture book for children that is uniquely American in personality. Its first audience was the generation of children growing up in the forties, many of whom were quite puzzled over this storybook that set itself so firmly in the reality of Boston, Massachusetts. Authentic landmarks lent an air of specificity to the illustrations that many children were unfamiliar with in their picture books, which by and large had been set in nameless, timeless fairylands or anonymous landscapes. *Ducklings*, however, presented Boston, a real American city as it and its people had looked just a few years earlier when McCloskey had drawn them.

Perhaps the novelty of touring Boston was the reason children kept coming back for a second and third look. Images of a real place provided them with a glimpse of their world that was almost unheard of in their own literature at that time. McCloskey had previously given his 1940 children's book, *Lentil*, a real-world setting in his boyhood home of Hamilton, Ohio. Later, in *Homer Price* and *Centerburg Tales* he continued telling stories based on his own childhood. He also portrayed family and friends from the area around his summer home off the coast of Maine in *Blueberries for Sal, One Morning in Maine, Time of Wonder*, and *Burt Dow, Deepwater Man*, while continuing to add his illustrating talents to a half dozen works by such other writers as Clair Bishop and Keith Robertson. *Journey Cake, Ho!* illustrated by McCloskey and written by his mother-in-law Ruth Sawyer was a 1954 Honor Book selection. But in 1941 he pictured Boston's State House, Public Garden, Louisburg Square, and even a Corner Book Shop at Mount Vernon and Charles Streets, and *Ducklings* has remained uniquely charming over many years because of its specificity.

The simple plot in *Ducklings*—a new brood of ducklings must be transported safely from nesting place to permanent home—was also presented as a real-life situation and continues to ring true for children today. And indeed, newspapers around the country periodically print photographs showing a scene much like the one from *Ducklings* in which a policeman holds up traffic for ducks to cross a street. McCloskey himself has related that the story idea grew from a real incident he observed as a young man walking through the Public Gardens. He developed the idea by sketching buildings, streets, and the park, then thoroughly researched mallards through books in the library, specimens at museums, and experts in ornithology. The part of this story that children love best is that McCloskey also bought four little ducklings to study when he returned to his apartment in New York. It seems that the noise prompted complaints from neighbors, and the ducks' splashing in the bathtub caused the lady downstairs to object about leaks in her ceiling. But before the artist gave up his studies, he had filled many sketchbooks with "running, walking, standing, sitting, stretching, swimming, scratching, sleeping ducklings," all poses accounted for in *Ducklings.* "No effort is too great to find out as much as possible about the things you know you are drawing," he has said. He can in fact recall many occasions when he was called upon for advice— not as an artist but as a duck expert.

Besides providing young readers with an experience of real place and realistic ducklings, McCloskey may also prompt a more so- phisticated realization—perhaps for the first time—of an important theme in literature: the clash between nature and society. Many other authors before and since have incorporated this theme into seemingly simplistic works for younger children, the Curious George series by H. A. Rey being perhaps the most rambunctious, hilarious example, at least to the children. In this literary historical perspec- tive, *Ducklings* makes yet a fourth contribution of a realistic nature: it is not ageless. The age of the story itself is made clear. McCloskey makes this an easy aspect to share with the children because he has put "41" on the automobile license plates. Kids like cars and bikes and trikes and boats, so a discussion about obvious modern-day differences in these things leads without difficulty into an explo- ration of the ways in which McCloskey's world in *Ducklings* has been transformed into our world of today. Encouraging the children to imagine how freeways and television antennas would make even more precarious a duck family's trip across town heightens young- sters' sensitivity about our ever-changing environment.

Sensitivity toward the changes in people themselves can be fos- tered also through an approach on a high level to McCloskey's picture book, a title older students might otherwise bypass as an easy book for little kids. Needless to say, adults readily identify the role changes evident from 1941 to the present, but children need practice in order to develop this critical awareness for themselves— to have attention called, for instance, to the fact that few police walk a beat these days, and seldom can you find streets swept by men with long-handled brooms. Most important to point out is the figure of Michael himself as artistic cliche and the fact that, indeed, such stereotypes as this started out exactly from certain types of pop- ularized images long ago. McCloskey's Michael was assuredly not as stereotypical in 1941 as he appears today, the symbolic representation of hearty Boston Irish cop just like actor Pat O'Brien in some old movie. Because of the seeming timelessness in story line, *Ducklings'* age must be mentioned to children so they can better understand that this early portrayal of "cop" would not be as realistic in today's fast-paced world.

Michael as stereotype leads naturally to the final observation about the world the artist has portrayed in his book. From much research and personal study the illustrator has shown a real Boston, a real event, and real mallards—all of which might result in a work of nonfiction if the fact did not remain that McCloskey's ducks talk. Mr. and Mrs. Mallard speak English only a few times, and then to each other or their babies—with humans they revert to quacking— but these occasions have been created from the author's imagination, and thus *Ducklings* must be described for children as the type of literature that, however realistic it may appear, is still a form of fantasy. Few storytellers before or since can be said to have excelled in this difficult picture-book genre to the degree achieved by Mc-Closkey: fantasy fiction clothed in totally real surroundings.

The fantasy aspect of the book was influenced, perhaps, by animal fables and nineteenth-century fantasists who through long novels introduced the idea that common creatures in the hedgerows communicate intelligently to each other, form societies, act foolishly or courageously, love, and even dream. These forerunners in fantasy literature would have seen the humor in Mr. Mallard's taking a week's vacation to cruise along the river, leaving Mrs. Mallard behind to navigate the journey crosstown alone with her excitable little brood. They would have loved the stuffy swan on the swan boat and the boy on his horrid bicycle. Kenneth Grahame, the author of *Wind in the Willows*, would have adored Quack and his siblings. McCloskey's representational linear style for his illustrations in *Ducklings* is in keeping with the time-honored tradition of using drawn lines for implied texture and contour, as in the work of Albrecht Dürer and of Chinese artists through the centuries.

McCloskey's second Caldecott winner, *Time of Wonder*, is most successful when it is presented as a family story: as we have seen, the family is of utmost importance to youngsters aged four to seven. As the best introduction to the McCloskey family, first read *Blueberries for Sal*, a 1948 Honor Book that depicts wife Peggy and little daughter Sal, and *One Morning in Maine*, a 1953 Honor Book that adds two-year-old Jane, McCloskey himself, Penny the dog, and even Mozzarella the cat. Establishing the family as a real one—with events, like the loss of a tooth, that all five- and six-year-olds can relate too—helps immeasurably when *Wonder* is opened to pages 54–55[1] and the four family members plus Penny can be pointed out again, with Jane and Sal having grown bigger. *Wonder* presented as the last book about these characters becomes immediately more interesting to a young audience.

Also intriguing to many children is the mystery behind the fallen trees in this same illustration, and explaining that a hurricane has swept across the island suggests the idea that *Wonder*, like *Ducklings*, can additionally be enjoyed as a book about nature, a theme most appropriate for this age group. Telling the children that a fierce late-summer storm will be a highlight in this story guarantees their attention, and they will wait patiently for the "stormy part" once you finally turn to read at the beginning. Now the richness of the poetic text may be savored—the "ribbons of smoky spray" and the sound that "like a half whisper—is the sound of growing ferns." Lovely details can be searched out: the fiddleheads, raindrops, "yellow fog," gulls, porpoises and a hummingbird.

McCloskey devoted three years to the creation of paintings and prose poem for *Wonder*, set at his island home in Penobscot Bay, Maine, where he and his family spent long summers. He featured as main characters in the story Sally, aged twelve when the book was published, and Jane, then nine years old, and from the first paragraph of text we know the "you" is of course directed to them but certainly also to children everywhere who might care to join the girls in their adventures. McCloskey names for us all the little islands and all the neighbors in their lobster boats or seaplanes and all the cruise schooners in Bucks Harbor. In short, just as in *Ducklings*, the author/illustrator builds for us a firm foundation in real places, real people, real events, the real world. But here there are no talking ducks to create a fantasyland; rather, there are only gulls who giggle with a "seabird sense of humor" and porpoises that puff in play around the boat. And in *Wonder* we have escape from the city into a wilderness at its loveliest rather than *Ducklings'* clash of nature with society. TV antennas have certainly come to Penobscot Bay, and jets are surely known to spoil a starlit night, but one likes to think McCloskey's island world remains timeless with its sloops and yawls, ketches and motorboats.

Although the artist's paintings are as representational as his line drawings in *Ducklings* have been described to be, the watercolors are more impressionistic in their portrayal of the outdoors bathed

---

[1]*Time of Wonder* has its own pagination, which will be used here.

in color and light. These paintings are reminiscent of Camille Pissarro, Claude Monet, and Alfred Sisley, leaders in the nineteenth-century Impressionist movement. McCloskey's reputation as a painter was established in the 1930s when he studied art as a young man at the National Academy of Design; he won the President's Award as well as the Prix de Rome. He later exhibited his work at the academy and at the Society of Independent Artists in Boston.

Wonder was one of the first Award winners that seems intended for an older, more experienced and mature picture-book audience. Generally speaking, the more sophisticated children in a group today are still the most receptive to McCloskey's mood and setting. Much about his work can be enriched by a viewing of the live-action film *Robert McCloskey* in the Signature Collection by Weston Woods. After *Wonder* the artist made another watercolor contribution—*Burt Dow, Deepwater Man*—but for many years he has not lent his talents to the field of children's books. Children and adults are the poorer for it.

Book Design

Ducklings' endurance is due in part to the quality Viking hardbound edition. Its large, vertical-rectangular cover opens up into attractive, expansive horizontal-rectangular double-page spreads. Every double spread is testimony to McCloskey's mastery of picture-book design: left and right pages consistently exhibit his marvelous sense of balance. He makes optimum use of the large format for illustrations drawn from three eye-level viewpoints, each with rewarding details to linger over—whether feathery closeups, exciting street scenes, or wide-angled rooftops.

Even the gutter caused by the book's binding has been taken into account for each two-page composition and does not interrupt the action or disturb us by its presence. Instead it acts as a vertical center dividing line that actually enhances balancing elements found on each side. Only once does the binding cause serious grief: on pages 35–36[2] an entire duckling has literally fallen away into this gutter, leaving just seven babies to waddle along behind Mrs. Mallard. (The Weston Woods filmstrip version of *Ducklings* restores the eighth duckling to his place in line—as we can hope Viking Press

[2]Pagination begins on the first page with text.

might do some day in an edition that widens the inner margin for this one double spread.)

To better appreciate McCloskey's expert skill in the designs for these large compositions, simply try to shorten an illustration by masking with paper or rule along the top or bottom of a page, as if the book had a square shape. Much is lost as regards total harmony, energy, or grace, since background and even empty space have been utilized for each picture. Regrettably, the Viking and Puffin paperback editions of *Ducklings* are not only smaller than the hardbound but are also this rather square shape. The resulting loss of detail and harmony make them less appropriate for use in art appreciation. However, the Weston Woods filmstrip and iconographic film or videocassette version are recommended as supplementary enrichment due to their faithful adherence to the original as well as their creative highlighting on the screen of details in artwork and in dramatic development. Random House School Division offers the book with read-along cassette.

Ducklings is a classic example of earlier picture books in which content of text and illustration complement each other in absolutely parallel style, with a formal arrangement of text beneath or above illustrations. McCloskey has said that the book started with the pictures and the idea, followed by the brief story line. The result is that often we have more emphasis on artistic detail in the drawings— a congested street corner, fine old row houses, a crowded capitol complex—and less detail in text, where McCloskey simply lets us know that we are looking at Beacon Street, Louisburg Square, the State House. So on these pages a rather skeletal text is fleshed out by the illustrations, although both need each other, in the best tradition of picture-book structuring.

Just as often, though, text elucidates illustration; otherwise things might get dreadfully monotonous. For instance, on pages 27–28 the illustration alone might surely suggest that Mr. Mallard was abandoning his brood back on shore—where the family's wide-eyed, stiff-necked poses could easily be mistaken for downright alarm—but McCloskey explains that the father will "meet you in a week, in the Public Garden," a reunion we witness with relief at the end. Illustration alone would not have sufficed; elaboration in text parallels the picture but increases our understanding and extends the story beyond what the art can do.

On one occasion only, this pattern of text/illustration parallelism is broken, and for the exciting event McCloskey chose to let the illustration carry the weight of storytelling: on pages 11–12 we are not told why all of a sudden the Public Garden "is no place for babies," but we are shown the "horrid thing" that has gotten Mrs. Mallard "all of a dither." This visual elaboration on the Mallards' predicament presents better than words the alienation they feel, and structural timing was ideal for the author-illustrator to abruptly require us to interpret for ourselves the ducks' frustration over a bicycle.

From both artistic and literary standpoints, the design of this picture book shows an unerring sense of balance—or the need for abrupt imbalance. We will further explore McCloskey's control of double-page spreads and text/illustration placement when we later discuss three illustrations from *Ducklings* as an introduction for children to the artistic element of line.

Viking Press issued both hardbound and paperbound editions of *Time of Wonder* in identical sizes and shapes as *Ducklings*. When one opens *Wonder*, however, seldom is evident the marvelous planning to left and right that delighted us so in *Ducklings*. Here the majority of illustrations are found to occupy about two thirds of each double page, and the gutter slices through these pictures in a most disappointing way. White space to the top, bottom, and left of each illustration isolates the text in a very formal position to the left of the pictures. The four illustrations that engage the full double-page field of action with text superimposed are more harmonious in their balance on the pages.

The book design detracts from the loveliness of McCloskey's watercolors and poses difficulties in appreciation of the Medal-winning art. (The Weston Woods sound filmstrip version of *Wonder* presents all illustrations as full frame and makes a suitable substitute for the book when one is presenting artistic elements and structural design.) One might wish that McCloskey and Viking had chosen for *Wonder* the same format as for the author-illustrator's *Blueberries for Sal*, a horizontal-rectangular cover that when opened would have provided opportunity to place *full* compositions on the right-hand page and use the left-hand page for spotlighting of free-verse text.

The text for this series of seashore scenes is appropriately rhythmic in a strong cadence, with a straightforward beat like a sea chantey. Its colorful language and lulling repetition are lovely to the ears. The prose poem comprises thoughts, images, and impressions that often are related to the art quite informally or in a few cases are not found at all in the pictures. McCloskey's intention in *Wonder* was to create a feeling for the sea, for a place, for wonderment itself with words as well as with watercolor brush. Despite the obstacles of faulty book design, he nonetheless succeeds in many of his enchanting paintings.

Art Appreciation of *Make Way for Ducklings*

"It's a good feeling to be able to put down a line and know that it is right," McCloskey has said, and it is just this use of *line*—invisible as well as visible—that makes *Ducklings* a perfect choice as introduction for children to line as a first, most basic element in art. We will investigate thoroughly the kinds and effects of artistic line in this picture book, reinforced later with a consideration of *Time of Wonder*, McCloskey's second Caldecott Award winner. The aim is to provide children with a definitive study of *line* as a crucial design element in these and other books from the collection.

Any of the double-page spreads in *Ducklings* would make excellent material for study, but three have been selected as best examples of (1) McCloskey's three viewpoints (eye levels), (2) the different kinds of visible and invisible lines used for balance and order in composition, and (3) the three main effects for storytelling purposes produced by these compositions. The illustrations for study will be called here "Looking for a Place" (pages 1–2), "Swim and Dive" (pages 29–30), and "Michael Rushed Back" (pages 43–44), and you will surely want to have these pages before you as we discuss each of them. After pointing out later to the children what has been discussed about these three illustrations, you might enjoy reinforcing the concepts through examples found in every other picture in *Ducklings*—some of which make one point or another even more dramatically than the three chosen here.

KINDS OF VISIBLE LINES

Crayon or charcoal drawings such as McCloskey's can seem to be as fresh and richly toned in print as the day they were executed because of the lithographic printing process used for such picture books that affords great delicacy in halftones and lines crucial to artistic expression. However, variety offered by the use of colors is absent in *Ducklings*, and so the artist must define shapes, imply texture, and spatially orient the scene solely through kinds of *lines*. "Looking for a Place" is the first double-page spread in the book and presents a wealth of drawn or *visible* lines to identify in four categories: (1) thin, fat, or shading (a contrast of light and dark areas used to create the illusion of solid form); (2) straight, curved, or a combination of the two; (3) horizontal, vertical, diagonal, or circular; and (4) continuous or broken.

For instance, fat, curved, continuous lines form the bodies, heads, and feet of the mallards in flight. Wings are drawn with fat lines and shading, wing feathers are shown by continuous straight lines that turn into broken curved shading, and all four wings are either vertical or diagonal lines in relation to the horizontal bodies themselves. Trace around the figures of Mr. and Mrs. Mallard with your fingertip as you read again the description above, then imagine that a pencil was held in that hand for you to draw these ducks (as so many children have tried to do) as well as McCloskey has. What your imaginary pencil has drawn is called an *edge line*.

Edge lines are just as interesting down below in this illustration. Children can follow them with their fingertips and should be encouraged to say aloud the categorical differences as they recognize them: here is a thin, straight, vertical edge line for a telephone pole and also for a tree trunk. The edge line for the lake seems continuous, fat, and horizontal until it breaks, curves, turns, and disappears altogether to be replaced by a darker area representing the grass. This kind of grass area that has been used as a line brings us to the next concept about artistic line: the idea of a visual demarcation we can all recognize—where one thing stops and another begins—but a demarcation that is not a physical edge line drawn by pencil, pen, crayon, or charcoal. This is often called a *line effect* rather than a line per se and is especially useful to McCloskey for contour in his illustrations.

Line effect for McCloskey can give an edge line, but by contrast only, a gradual transition from one shade (seen as color in other books) to another shade, as opposed to a distinctly drawn line. Through shaded line effects in the shadows on the hillsides, the artist has given the illusion of contour in the landscape, and then, with the uppermost line effect, the distant hills meet the sky in sharpest contrast of all—the stopping point for the hills, the horizon. Look back at the mallards once again, and you can now see the shaded line effects that give contour to the points at which both right wings are attached to the ducks' bodies. More can be learned about line effect when we discuss *Time of Wonder* with its watercolor illustrations.

In conclusion, "Looking for a Place" can be seen as an illustration composed of marks (*lines*) and contrasts (*line effects*) of all kinds arranged in recognizable images—a house, a tree, the hills, two ducks—and McCloskey's artistic style can be called a representational or realistic one because his drawings are true to life and, although simplified, are without distortion in shape or perspective.

VERTICAL AND HORIZONTAL INVISIBLE LINES

Invisible lines used for compositional structure by McCloskey fall into the category of directional lines: horizontal, vertical, diagonal, and the closed circular. These lines form an underlying skeleton for a picture, much as our own bodies are shaped by our bone structure or the stud framework defines a house. In the previous discussion of *Ducklings'* hardbound book design, much attention was paid to the vertically oriented cover, opening up into horizontally oriented illustrations unavoidably sliced by the vertical line of the gutter. This gutter is the first invisible or undrawn line that contributes to the design of each double-page spread, as best demonstrated in "Looking for a Place."

Imagine the placement of Mr. Mallard in the picture one inch to the right, where his head would be severed by the gutter—a laughable example of poor planning, perhaps, but known to occur in far too many picture books. More subtly, mentally place the lake also one inch to the right so that the water would appear to run off into the gutter rather than culminate in its little bay on the facing page. Subtle or ridiculous, both examples by their absence show McCloskey to be a master designer of his pictures before the book ever went to press. Father's head is intact, and the lake has not run dry; the artist as picture-book designer is here faultless.

A mallard at top center of each page is rather a good example of obvious balance between two shapes, called in artistic terms symmetric or formal balance on either side of the invisible center vertical line—the gutter—that has divided the "field of action" (the outer boundaries for a work of art, in this case the double-page spread). Less obvious to children is the balance in the scene below. It is not found in solidly symmetrical objects as much as in points of interest, which form an invisible line the human eye is likely to follow. Theoretically we first look at the ducks in this picture, then we look down to the lake (the reader's eye has been proven to be attracted to lighter areas of pictures; additionally here, the lake is what the Mallards are looking at). Then the eye moves to the village crossroad, and then perhaps back up again to the ducks, cutting a rectangular path that delineates the field of action. Paths may differ with individual viewers—some say they start at the lake and go up to ducks—

but the point is that there are four points of interest in this solidly rectangular field: two ducks, a lake, and a village crossroad.

Once more trace with your fingertip along the entire shore of the lake to outline a shape that approximates indeed the space occupied by the village crossroad, including the two houses on the edge of town. Here we have asymmetrical balance in the relationship between the "weight" of a shape and a space. This concept is more difficult for children to grasp than that of symmetry but is equally vital in appreciating McCloskey's use of the invisible line of the gutter. Balance and weight in art are closely linked by numerous factors that make discussion here rather cumbersome and complicated when we are primarily interested in use of *line*. In the briefest and simplest of terms, asymmetry in "Looking for a Place" is achieved by one part of a large subject (shape of the lake) being equal in weight to ten parts of small subjects (houses in town) added to two parts (crossroad), added yet to two more parts (houses on the edge of town), all together in a space. ("Michael Rushed Back" offers a more dramatic study of asymmetry, which will be discussed later in the chapter.)

The lake's crossing over the gutter an inch or so to the other page breaks up what might otherwise be seen as a rather static, four-square, tightly boxed-in composition. Basically, however, this illustration is a four-square arrangement, since an invisible horizontal line also divides "Looking for a Place" into a top half and a bottom half. This horizontal center undrawn line can be discovered running through the hillside's darkest shadows an inch below the line effect at the horizon. (How convenient to have the word *horizon* to aid us with a definition of *horizontal line* for children.) Clearly now, the illustration is seen to have an important invisible inner structure of four sections, each with its point of interest, and our eyes can go back and forth—up, down, and across like a ball being bounced on a Ping-Pong table—because we are confident in an ordering force that underlines the field of action.

The horizontal invisible line is the main directional influence in this particular illustration. It may be likened to the baseline often used in drawings by primary-age children, with objects arranged along it. McCloskey's use of a horizontal framework is of course much more sophisticated as an organizational tool in that he creates objects along a foreground, middle ground, and background. Most adults—much less children—find it impossible to achieve such a sense of artistic space.

The most intricate interpretation of this picture reveals that the horizontal stabilizing influence indeed divides the entire double-page spread into *three* planes, with text itself as foreground, ducks as middle ground, and valley as background. The majority of pages in *Ducklings* are illustrated along such a horizontal frame, which slices from left to right and intentionally encourages us to turn to see the next page. Important to note is that this horizontal line is always broken by vertical visible lines that hold our attention long enough for us to absorb the meaning of each page. In "Looking for a Place," one dark and dramatic vertical line outlines Mr. Mallard's right wing; another delineates a downward gesture of Mrs. Mallard's wings as she "points" to the lake below.

VISIBLE LINES FOR IMPLIED TEXTURE

"Swim and Dive" (pages 29–30) ranks as one of the most adored pictures in children's literature. We can deepen our satisfaction with McCloskey's accomplishment here by continuing to expand our study of artistic line. Eight swimming, sitting, stretching ducklings are each drawn at a slightly different angle. The mother's position is reserved as the anchoring spot for all the activity around the perimeter.

The use of visible lines in this illustration is one of the best examples for the appreciation of implied texture: the impression of soft down on the babies we would love to touch, and the silkiness of mother's stiff wing feathers we might dare to stroke. Different printings of the Viking hardbound edition present a perplexing variance in quality of lithographic process, and searching for a copy of the book with deepest contrast between ink and paper is worthwhile for best appreciation here of texture.

Of course no real down or actual silk exists; rather, thin, straight, broken wisps of lines and flat strokes of controlled, contrasting shading imply such tactile qualities. The mother's head and all of the ducklings are shaped, except for beaks, feet, and waterline, by these wispy "feathered" lines that identify where each figure stops and the surrounding water, or another duckling, begins. In this picture more than in any other illustration in *Ducklings*, McCloskey has chosen to emphasize lines for implied texture, and he presents the most representational, realistic close-up one could ask for.

The only strong, continuous *edge line* is that around the mother's body. This line is interrupted a few times by the figures of the babies but always reappears forcefully to persist in its shaping of the heaviest figure in the composition. Other fat, unbroken edge lines form beaks, a webbed foot, and waterlines along the ducklings' lower bodies, whereas both continuous and broken *curved lines* and *line effects* compose the contours of ripples caused by these bodies in the water. A veritable maze of horizontal, vertical, and diagonal lines is formed as the ducklings twist and turn—left, right, up, and down—in playful chaos.

CIRCULAR INVISIBLE LINES

A visual reliance on the form of the mother as anchor in this composition, despite the fact that she has been bisected by the binding's gutter, gives proof once more to our contention that McCloskey excels in masterful picture-book design. Any one of the smaller figures thus severed would have been damaged by distortion, but the larger figure can survive intact because of her diagonal angle, her off-centeredness, and the placement of her head complete and at yet another diagonal angle. To have composed such a close-up on a large double-spread field of action without the gutter noticeably interfering is quite an accomplishment. To have additionally employed this same gutter as an invisible vertical line for structural purposes contributes to the meaning of the work.

A clue to the picture's composition is found in the placement of four intact ducklings to each side of the vertical center line. This symmetrical balance gives equal importance to each duckling, like some gathering for a family photo in which all the toddlers are equally fidgety. Because of the mother's placement off-center, more of her form lies on the left-hand page. As a result, the ducklings on this side are a bit more crowded than their siblings. Within the right-hand space, one duckling's gone underwater (to avoid falling into the gutter?), two are slightly overlapping but still full forms, and one is a short distance away yet still very much a part of the group: he seems secure enough in his family position to momentarily ignore everyone.

This illustration also exhibits some clues that indicate dependence on an invisible horizontal center line though not as dramatic as the orientation to a horizon in "Looking for a Place." Horizontal center begins at the top of the body and head of the feeding duckling on the far left and proceeds right across the mother's beak to the base of the distracted duckling on the right. We are still oriented in a horizontal environment but we are not being as encouraged to turn the page.

We must emphasize the invisible vertical and horizontal center lines here because of their ability to determine a *center point* in the work of art. Such a point is unerringly sought by the human eye and is undeniably strong in its capacity to draw the audience into a picture. In a field of action, the area where the invisible horizontal crosses the invisible vertical center line is called the center point. In "Swim and Dive," it is not coincidence that the two most prominent features of the mother (her beak and her sloped wing feathers), as well as the two darkest spots in the picture (both appearing as intense shading for Mrs. Mallard), all cluster in this area to the left and right of the gutter in the middle of the spread.

The center point is additionally important for this particular picture because it acts as a structural hub from which *invisible lines*, both diagonal and horizontal, radiate to the ducklings. Through their placement the ducklings then form a rim around the mother. The figures in their wheellike pattern lead from one to the next in a frame around the mother. As our eyes circle around, they reach the last duckling distracted by the insect and continue up to the perfectly placed line of text which completes the framing.

Thus the field of action for "Swim and Dive" is actually a sphere imposed onto a horizontal-rectangular double-page spread, and the center point is crucial to that discovery. Adding reinforcement to this structure is the posture of each duckling along the way, no matter which way the eyes proceed or in fact upon which duckling they begin the circle. Augmenting further this invisible scaffold are paths of look and gesture, invisible lines of communication between two figures within the work or between a figure and the audience. Mrs. Mallard might well be said to indicate where we should begin our circular pattern, for she looks most decidedly at one specific baby. He looks back at her, as does another of the ducklings. Three are more interested in us, and two are oblivious to everyone. The one that is looking at an insect directs our attention to McCloskey's text, an integral part of the overall balance.

And balance there most certainly is in this picture because, despite the flutter of activity (imagine the noise!) everyone is momentarily frozen in place for this most charming family portrait framed within an oval.

VISIBLE LINES FOR IMPLIED CONTOUR AND DEPTH

The decision was easy to include for study an illustration that featured Michael the policeman; the difficulty lay in choosing which one of five such grand pictures to study. Michael appears early in the book, feeding the Mallards, then reappears in a marvelously dramatic series of four illustrations in which he comes to the ducks' rescue. From this series, "Michael Rushed Back" (pages 43–44) has been selected as best for introduction to the remaining uses of line covered in our basic study. Later in the chapter, we will apply what has been discussed, not only to other pictures of Michael, but to illustrations throughout *Ducklings.*

The figure of Michael offers the best example for children of the use of *contour lines* to communicate the illusion of three-dimensional volume. Trace with your fingertip the outline of the policeman; Michael's shape is confined within a strong, fat, nearly continuous *edge line* that curves and turns vertically, horizontally, and diagonally. If it were not for the protrusions of his hands and nightstick, he would cut a fairly simple, bulky figure, with little distracting detail in clothes and with facial features easily seen to express alarm.

Wonderfully fat he is, and through use of *contour lines, contour line effects,* and *shading* his massiveness comes across from the printed page. For instance, the edge line for Michael's pants leg twice breaks to turn onto the leg as a contour line that describes the location where the pants fold or billow out. At his shoulders, back, and arm these contour lines can be seen as well; they give us a sense that Michael's body fills the clothes he wears. Allusion to his rotundity is also found in use of contour line effects, more subtle delineations achieved by contrast between dark and light areas going around his middle and also down his leg. Shaded areas provide an implied texture that adds to the substantial form, while the light areas of his coat confront us with the bulging girth. The big shoes and sturdy dark hat force confinement within a defined space, and Michael's whistle is the only thing to have broken free—but more about this whistle later.

Behind Michael is a thick horizontal line for the edge of the road, which is filled with McCloskey's automobiles that by this stage in the story quickly signal the central problem: Mrs. Mallard's trouble getting her brood across town. An image in art becomes a symbol when it comes to stand for something in addition to its mere presence in the work, and here McCloskey has intentionally put on display for the audience's interpretation a lineup of cars smack in Mrs. Mallard's path—just as he had earlier used the bicycle as a symbol for danger in the park.

The road is a visible horizontal baseline (as were the hills in "Looking for a Place"). This middle-ground line positions Michael in the foreground and cars, ducks, and town in the background. The town beyond the road attracts our attention after we have studied Michael, partly because this is one of our few glimpses of Boston from normal eye level and the pleasing vignette is an interesting maze indeed of buildings and streets. But attention is also paid to this little scene within the larger scene because of McCloskey's skillful arrangement of lines to imply depth. Visible lines are abundant—fat and thin ones, continuous and broken, vertical and horizontal and diagonal, every one straight in order to form very geometric shapes except where a few trees, cars, and people are concerned. The diagonal line of the street turns to go up a hill; otherwise the artist would have been committed to continuing this busy townscape all the way back to a horizon. This street line has created an illusion of depth, an illusion reinforced by the loss of detail as chimney lines become blurry, cars become smaller, and buildings overlap buildings. (More understanding of depth can be expected when we study the artistic element of space in chapter 6, but the important idea here is that McCloskey achieved depth almost entirely through lines. The fact that shadows cast on the buildings contribute to this illusion must be mentioned, but light and dark as an artistic element will be discussed fully in chapter 4.)

This townscape picture-within-a-picture is useful now to introduce the strength and ordering force found in visible vertical line, that perpendicular plumb line that roots upright shapes to the ground and can by its height aid an artist in creating the illusion of depth. Visible vertical lines are the strong supports for the buildings—figuratively holding up the shapes they make, balancing one wall against another. They do not lead our attention off the page to left or right as visible horizontal lines have been shown to do; instead, vertical lines join with the horizontal ones to make geometrical shapes, frames with straight edges, sharp corners, four sides tensed and poised. In combinations—like soldiers in formation that grow smaller as the formation stretches into the distance—they imply depth. McCloskey's little townscape is an architectural delight in its use of visible vertical lines that in art signify dignity, self-sufficiency, and resistance to gravity's pull; used in combination with a few horizontal lines, the scene beckons us to enter its depths.

In the midst of all this, the ducklings have been reduced to mere spots on the sidewalk, so small we might easily overlook them.

DIAGONAL INVISIBLE LINES

In contrast to the intimate close-up in "Swim and Dive," we now have the most distant long shot of Mrs. Mallard and her brood, who would be nearly lost to sight without some intentional compositional guidance from the artist. Since there exists no meaningful eye appeal in a bunch of spots on a sidewalk, we return to the figure of Michael for clues. When last we saw him, Michael was on his way somewhere—and he still is: rushing right past us, looking beyond our position in the audience, in such a hurry that his foot is barely on the page, the nightstick thrust tightly forward as balance for his big stride. He charges to the right off the page, and we might be impelled to quickly turn to the next picture to find out where he is going—except for the whistle.

Tethered to a top coat button, the whistle manages to fly behind Michael like a free pixie spirit. It points in the direction opposite Michael's intended hasty path. Literally, it points toward the townscape; figuratively, it points our way back into the picture in case we missed something. We do not then turn the page too soon, but instead we follow the whistle's path of gesture along an *invisible line*, back into the maze of buildings whose vertical lines have a downward thrust to the sidewalk. This underlying structure in the picture is a gentle reminder that there are minute spots on the sidewalk. McCloskey did not want us to miss them.

Just in case this remarkable ploy with the whistle is not successful in drawing our attention to the mallards, McCloskey additionally utilized the center point found where the invisible horizontal center line intersects the invisible vertical center line of the book's gutter. This center point occurs at the car window closest to the gutter behind Michael—and since the car headlights, a passerby, and the car across the street all appear to be "looking" toward the spots on the sidewalk, we also look. As if this second clue were not enough, McCloskey gives our vision one last nudge, patiently leading us in from the left edge of the double-page spread, along a footpath given shape only by edge lines of the surrounding grass. The footpath is the third route leading directly to the ducklings, and it has the ability to draw our attention because it is intentionally unfilled ground space, called "negative shape" in art. In a busy composition, empty space can be intriguing.

All of this was necessary to point out the ducklings, not just because they are so tiny in the distance, but also because McCloskey chose a complicated underlying structure for this composition. First he focused on the interplay between Michael in the foreground, cars in the middle ground, and townscape in the background. Then he imposed strong horizontal lines for the middle ground and verticals in the background. Now we will see the forcefulness he used in diagonal lines for Michael that create the action in the foreground. We must return to the whistle again.

When the bulky figure of Michael was initially traced with the fingertip, visible diagonal lines most certainly appeared down his back, legs, and nightstick. Now imagine the free-spirited whistle as the uppermost left point of an invisible diagonal line that extends down through Michael's arm, stomach, and leg to his left foot, which is almost off the page. Begin a second invisible diagonal line from his right shoe up his back, across the shoulder and head to his hat. The instability of the first imagined line has been neutralized by the second as it crossed over; although the symmetry is not perfect, the X we have imagined does impose order on Michael's superficial disarray.

This is not to imply that peaceful stability has been established. Quite to the contrary, invisible diagonal lines are the underlying structure in art upon which motion and action are built. With the intrusion into our consciousness of a large X sweeping broadly from left to right and right to left, we feel momentarily off balance, just as Michael himself must feel with his foot practically out of the picture. This imbalance, in contrast with the staid horizontal road and upright vertical townscape, is undoubtedly why some children, when asked about the illustration, will reply that "Michael's too big" or it is a "crazy picture." The children are instinctively attracted to "Michael Rushed Back" because they love its action, but they also need reassurance that the "craziness" is well-planned, intentional use of the dynamic quality McCloskey knew exists in strong, diagonal, invisible lines.

A more subtle diagonal X can be found in the townscape; it is needed to balance Michael asymmetrically. The policeman occupies the entire space to right of the gutter, and so the left side needs repetition of diagonals that also help us find the ducklings—the main characters in this melodrama after all. Rooftops in the townscape have visible diagonal lines as do the street and the footpath, and even the minute spots on the sidewalk are lined up diagonally. On closer inspection a gentle, wavering invisible X can be discerned from left rooftop to right automobile and from right rooftop down to left automobile and trailing away down the footpath. This second crossing of invisible diagonal lines is a delicate, intricate path and finding it may be difficult for youngsters' untrained eyes. However, it asymmetrically balances the compositional weight of Michael himself.

As in the asymmetrical balance in "Looking for a Place," here one part of a large subject (Michael) is equal in weight to three parts of smaller subjects (buildings) added to three parts of even smaller subjects (cars). However, one factor that makes artistic analysis of weight difficult is the quality of the parts themselves, in other words their worth in the composition resulting from such factors as size and shape. To simplify the difficulty perhaps the following generalized statements may clarify the balance between Michael and the townscape: (1) Michael carries compositional weight because he is *large* and *isolated*, a figure of *solid volume* and much *eye appeal* (due to his implied motion). In addition, he is the *darkest* shape and the *nearest* to the audience. (2) The townscape carries equal weight because it covers a *large* area with much *depth*, is a *cluster* of strong *vertical* shapes in contrasted *light* and shade, and has much *eye appeal* (due to the surprise of finding the ducklings).

Replace any or all italicized words above with an antonym, and neither Michael nor the townscape would be said to carry the weight needed to balance the other.

As an appropriate postscript to a discussion of weight, we note that perfect balance has been achieved for the "negative shape" of the empty footpath, which needs an equally weightless area where nothing is going on visually. McCloskey has placed the text to act as a counterpoint to the opposite corner—another accomplishment in this fine piece of illustrative art.

Art Appreciation of *Time of Wonder*: Visible Line Effects

Juxtaposed with the representational art in *Ducklings*, McCloskey's second Caldecott winner invites a dramatic comparison of the uses of impressionistic *visible line effects* and pencil-perfect lithographed *line drawings*. With absolute control of the watercolor brush, the artist this time creates an entirely different atmosphere while still exhibiting all the artistic properties attributed to uses and effects of line. But *Wonder's* pictures have been painted with colors, and shaping of images has been accomplished with color itself, as opposed to pictures whose images are formed by lines alone or by outlines within which colors have been added. The intent here is to present reality through use of colors rather than through drawn lines, and the artistic difference can be pointed out to children by the example on pages 38–39. The painted images of gulls here can be compared with drawn images of ducks in *Ducklings*.

Turning to one of the children's favorite illustrations in the book, the beach scene on pages 22–23, one quickly discovers that all the lines previously identified in *Ducklings*—fat curved ones and thin straight ones, continuous diagonals and broken shading—can indeed be found, but this time all edge lines and contours are seen as subtle line effects of colors of paint. Where one thing stops and another begins in this picture is shown primarily through gradations of color, an exception being the cracks in the weathered rock. Any of the illustrations in *Wonder* make excellent study of line effects in paintings where color is used to imply texture, contour, and depth.

Numerous seascapes demonstrate the artist's use of the invisible horizontal baseline as an underlying structure, with obvious implications for known terrain off the pages to left and right. However, vertical points of interest, noted in *Ducklings*, are few in *Wonder*. Those that exist lack the strength to persuade us to linger overlong in these lovely, but rather monotonous, aerial views. Tiny sails on the boats, a minute figure in a red shirt, a beacon of yellow light from a distant window—too often these dabs of color are the only vertical lines with the eye appeal to hold even brief interest. The beach, garden, forest, and boatyard scenes painted from normal eye level definitely have more points of interest in their foregrounds, middle distances, and backgrounds, as in the sunflower picture on pages 58–59. This is also one of the best examples of exquisitely rendered asymmetrical balance of artistic weights large and small. The illustration on the next double page can be said to have symmetrical balance, person for person, color for color, suitcase for suitcase.

Another favorite picture is the rowboat in the evening on pages 26–27, worth lingering over in large part because of its invisible circular framework. This structure is more subtle, perhaps, than that of "Swim and Dive" in *Ducklings*, but it is nonetheless very much evident despite the unfortunate slice made by the vertical line of the gutter. Within the darkest shadow where boat meets water is the composition's center point, from which radiate the visible line effects of the boat itself and also the oars—in intersecting diagonals to the boat's lines—pulling our attention around and around in this picture much as the boat itself bobs around in the still water. McCloskey reinforces his intent that we stay awhile to enjoy this picture by attracting us with circles within circles of ripples from an oar and by spotlighting another round spot on the ocean's green floor.

An excellent use of the invisible diagonal structure in composition is found on pages 46–47, in which the latch gives way during the hurricane. All visible line effects are at conflicting angles except for the sturdy desk and stubborn door that Father strains to close, and a strong center point occurs at the tip of an upraised little hand that almost beseeches us to come to the family's aid in this dramatic picture.

Effects of Line

In "Looking for a Place" from *Ducklings*, the artist combined uses of visible and invisible line to create the audience's viewpoint "up with the ducks," as the children put it. We know we are at bird's-eye level because of the size of the Mallards, the bolder fat lines of their forms, and the dark shading of Mr. Mallard, all of which draw them closer to us than the wee houses barely sketched or the distant blurred line effects of the rolling hills. Bright, empty space behind the Mallards accents their nearness to us; indistinct smudges indicate faraway valleys bathed in shadows cast by light from beyond the right of the page. We cannot see what lies beyond the hills, nor can we see what lies to the left or right off the pages, but because of the horizontal line bleeding off the pages, we sense that the landscape does indeed keep going to either side. This is only part of the landscape we are looking at, and we are high above it—as if taking a snapshot from an airplane.

Humans have always wanted to fly with the birds, and here's our chance, through participating in McCloskey's illustration. How do we feel about it? Serenity and security are the strongest sensations here because the horizontal orientation overall is associated in art with the stability of the earth. This firm anchoring to a "ground line" is intended to provide a stable link to the earth and to the horizon. A review of all the horizontal lines in this picture—far shore of the lake, curved contours of the Mallards' bodies, the foreground edge of road with telephone wires, and layer upon layer of rolling hills—all combined with the dark shadows that pull us into the invisible but strong horizontal center line—reinforce McCloskey's intention that we feel secure. Even placement of the text itself (in hardbound edition) adds to the horizontal framework: it is like a floor beneath the scene and figuratively beneath our feet as well.

The stability that exists in this first double page of *Ducklings* is not as apparent in the other illustrations shown from an aerial viewpoint. In fact, "Looking for a Place" can be considered so relaxed as to be dull compared to the activity depicted in the others, and the sense of action in the subsequent bird's-eye illustrations can now be understood as having been created by a use of diagonal framework similar to that employed in "Michael Rushed Back." But in "Looking for a Place," the concentration on visible and invisible horizontal lines for composition is the main reason for the picture's peaceful feeling, which most appropriately reflects the content of the text.

Still and all, we might not feel so relaxed—out of normal human position, "up with the ducks"—except that McCloskey's representational style gives us images that are true-to-life, and scenery that meets our expectations with comfortably real and familiar sights below. The effect on the audience is well suited to this first scene in the story when, although they do not realize it, the Mallards are seeing the last of open countryside.

We as the audience participate in the picture "Swim and Dive" because we are close and because we are being watched. Such texture of pinfeathers, each one made up of many small lines and exquisite shading, and those ever-mistrustful stares tell us we are as close to a family of ducks as we can ever be. We are at their own eye level (ground level or "worm's-eye" level), and the only visual clue that we are not in the water itself is that we have a full view of the mother's back. Knowing what we know of shyness in wild creatures, perhaps we might prefer to label our viewpoint as a telephotographic one (implying that we are observing the scene through a telephoto camera lens from a great distance), a pleasant declaration that we have not invaded the family's privacy.

The entire lot seems contented enough with our presence, no one skittering off to spoil the tranquil scene. The firmly anchoring shape of Mrs. Mallard and the underlying circular frame composed of her brood—all achieved by lines visible and invisible—have brought order out of what might have seemed twisting, splashing chaos, and "Swim and Dive" is one of the gentlest, most harmonious illustrations not only in *Ducklings* but in the history of picture books. The picture has such grace that we want to pause and reflect, which is exactly what the artist intended us to do. The horizontal structure in "Looking for a Place" has been said to lead our eyes off the page to see what will happen in the next page; the intent behind a spherical structure in "Swim and Dive" is that we comfortably stop awhile to look enjoy, learn, and grow.

The audience is allowed a normal eye level in "Michael Rushed Back," as in all the pictures of the personable Michael. The viewpoint intensifies our participation in the immediacy of the situation, as if we are there for the fleeting moment even if Michael himself does not notice. The audience is so very close to the policeman that we can almost feel the rhythm of his stride: he seems to lean toward us due to the angle of his back and shoulders and a foreshortening of his back leg. His shadow seems rather too small and incomplete—might not it extend into our space as well?

The interplay between the diagonal, vertical, and horizontal lines in "Michael Rushed Back" has the desired effect of suspense and uncertainty. The audience is first alarmed by the urgency intimated by Michael as he heads off the page, by the weight of the figure, and by the dynamics of the invisible diagonal structure that brings him close and demands our concern. Then one feels the stabilizing influence of the horizontal road line and is calmed by the resolute quality of vertical, upright buildings. Still, some nagging feeling of omission remains. But once the Mallard family has been found, attention can shift back to Michael; we are free now to perceive him with more understanding and humor.

Thus the suspenseful stillness of the townscape and the perilous posture of Michael keep youngsters oscillating within this "crazy picture." The contrast is a major reason why they keep coming back for more in *Make Way for Ducklings*.

For Further Study

Adults who wish to pursue with children the study of artistic elements in illustration may find the following exercises useful. Their hands-on approach and moderate activity level should make many of them valuable learning aids.

1. A majority of illustrations in *Make Way for Ducklings* have a stable underlying horizontal structure, although statues, towers, buildings, and the figure of policeman Michael himself provide vertical interruptions. To reinforce the concept of a stabilizing base, a child may lie down on the floor to demonstrate to other children that both the child and the floor represent horizontal "lines." Next, the child stands up straight and tall, forming a vertical line perpendicular to the floor. Then as the volunteer's arms are stretched out

to the sides, another horizontal line appears; it intersects the vertical of the body and is parallel to the floor. For an art exercise, folding a piece of paper along a center horizontal line, then folding again along a center vertical line, will divide the paper as a field of action into four equal sections in which four objects can be drawn as points of interest for each of the areas.

2. The right and left sides of a person form a very familiar symmetry. The two sides of a standing volunteer can be compared with the artistic symmetrical balance between figures of Mr. and Mrs. Mallard in "Looking for a Place." Children can gain additional reinforcement of the concept by drawing a circle around capital letters that are symmetrical. (*Bisymmetry*, or mirrored halves, occurs in *A H I M O T U V W X*; *lateral symmetry*, or a reversal of halves, occurs in *N S Z*.) Further study of symmetry is reinforced by illustrations with similar distributions of weights and balances, as in "Michael Rushed Back."

3. Six other illustrations in *Ducklings* are drawn from a bird's-eye viewpoint but with a diagonal framework as discussed in "Michael Rushed Back." For now the simple concept of an aerial view is important to reinforce through photographs and pictures in magazines or books. Another volunteer might be helped to stand cautiously on a table or chair so as to describe aloud an object or person sitting on the floor. The child should be asked what can be seen from this viewpoint: "Is there a part in Harold's hair?" "Can all sides of this chair be seen clearly?" "How tall does this book appear to be?"

4. An artistic circular pattern is found a few times in *Ducklings* (see pages 23–24 for the nest, 25–26 and 31–32 for formations of ducklings, and 57–58 for the shape of the island home). Help the children find circular "framed" compositions in old magazines and use Magic Markers to draw around those that have a similar effect of unity and tranquility. Discuss a bicycle wheel to show the interdependent structure of the hub, spokes and rim, an example of radial symmetry. For an art exercise, compose family portraits within a drawn frame, placing in the center spot or "hub" an important member of their own choosing (perhaps themselves).

5. Artistic line that implies texture can best be compared to actual texture through tactile experiences. Have the children touch real fur, real feathers, real silk, and then touch realistic drawings or photographs of these things. Few youngsters can resist the urge to "draw like McCloskey," and the exercise with least frustration may be to attempt a simple drawing of a feather itself. Older children or younger

ones with long attention spans can be encouraged to exercise the right side of the brain by turning "Swim and Dive" upside down to copy line for line one of the ducklings on a separate sheet of paper. Drawing with India ink or brushing with watercolors directly on to sandpaper is a distinctive technique used by Wanda Gag to imply texture. Her many poses of kittens in *Millions of Cats* rival McCloskey's studies of ducklings.

6. No other illustration brings us as close to the ducklings as "Swim and Dive," but a few in *Ducklings* approximate this ground-level viewpoint (see pages 11–12, 35–36, 55–56). To reinforce this concept, call on a volunteer to lie on the floor and describe from this perspective someone or something that previously was described from the bird's-eye viewpoint. Call attention to the possible effects of this "worm's-eye" view in the dramatic tension of a story, especially such a story as this, in which "worm's-eye" and aerial viewpoints are both seen as the positions of the ducks themselves.

McCloskey often lowers his normal eye-level viewpoint to accommodate the angle children usually have (see pages 49–50, for instance). In other pictures, encourage youngsters to identify foreground, middle ground, and background and to experiment with drawing this illusion of depth.

7. Many details in the chaotic activity of "Swim and Dive" connote paths of look and gesture, and children enjoy looking through the rest of the illustrations for ducklings whose attitudes could be described as excited, angry, attentive, playful, worried, startled, proud, curious. Point out to the children that these attitudes are often caused by something or someone's actions. Then call on a volunteer to simply stare silently and without gesture at things around the room while the children guess what the objects are, or call on students to think up gestures they can pantomime for the group.

In other illustrations Michael's paths of gesture are fun to find as he offers food, signals "halt," points and motions the Mallards forward. Suggest to the children that perhaps the ducks also "gesture" in a few pictures (see pages 11–12, 15–16, 23–24). Bring in books on body language from the library/media center, or invite an expert in sign language to demonstrate for the children.

8. The figures of Michael are the best examples of McCloskey's skill in imposing a strong diagonal inner structure upon a more stable horizontal framework to create tension (see also pages 39–40, 45–46), but in the aerial viewpoint on pages 51–52 the X takes over completely as layout for the composition itself. This design is most appropriate for the anxious moment when the police hold back the

traffic. Other illustrations with a bird's-eye viewpoint also are angled slightly askew—as a tilted camera might take a picture, rather than the steady viewpoint of "Looking for a Place." The invisible structure in these oblique shots turns out to be a $\vee$, which should be understood to be half of an $\times$ and still an intersection of invisible lines upon which to build action. Provide the children with sheets of clear plastic that they can position over illustrations in *Ducklings*, and then have them actually draw the invisible compositional lines with washable markers. Look through magazines and other books for examples of pictures depicting veritable flurries of activity to compare to previous circular portraiture and horizontal aerial viewpoints they have gathered. This time a volunteer can assume a frozen running position, demonstrating for others the diagonal lines implying motion.

9. The balance between townscape and Michael can best be explained through the metaphor of ounces and pounds, using a balance scale and a series of graduated weights. The balance scale is leveled when an equal amount of weights is placed in the dishes either side. In art, though, balance involves quality as well as quantity. Through another metaphor: an ounce of gold is worth more than a pound of beans.

Asymmetry can be demonstrated by circling the lower-case letters of the alphabet that are different in design from side to side or top to bottom (circle all but *c, l, o, s, v, w,* and *z*).

Looking Ahead: Color, Light and Dark, Shape, Space

It is important to note in *Ducklings* that McCloskey chose to ignore use of color in preference for brown ink on off-white paper. In reality only the male mallard is very colorful; so it stands to reason that pictures full of vibrant reds, blues, and greens would pull attention away from the comparatively drab little ducks and their mother. However, these are the very subjects the artist wants us to pay closest attention to. By omitting color, he can more easily achieve this goal. An interesting comparison for children can be made between *Ducklings* and Leonard Weisgard's color illustrations for *Mrs. Mallard's Family* by Clelia Delafield, another picture-book title from approximately the same time period.

In "Looking for a Place," contrast between light and dark was seen to create an illusion of solid form or to imply a source of illumination by showing dark shadows. In "Michael Rushed Back," shadows added to the implication of depth in the townscape. But generally speaking, McCloskey has not greatly emphasized this element in *Ducklings:* except for the last double-page spread, all scenes have been portrayed in the same anonymous diffusion of sunlight—apparently on a beautiful summer's day.

A large part of the charm that *Ducklings* still holds for young children is due to the artist's inclusion of both natural and manufactured or geometric shapes. Children feel more comfortable with a combination of free-form and geometric shapes than with a concentration of one or the other, and in McCloskey's book their interest is held equally by figures of cars, buildings, and bicycle and by the people and the ducklings themselves. Youngsters also respond favorably to representational shapes that imitate real life. The illustrator's use of idealized proportion gives us perfect little mallards indistinguishable one from another, whereas artistic use of natural proportion offers individualistic touches for some of the people and all of the buildings. It is crucial to notice once again that formation of all shapes is accomplished solely by McCloskey's control of lines of all kinds to imply texture, contour, and depth. The power of lines to create deep or shallow space must be reiterated as well, for without the strong horizontal, vertical, circular, and diagonal frameworks used in *Ducklings*, the audience would not be so openly invited into many of the pictures.

In Time of Wonder, McCloskey demonstrated most profoundly his interest in color's ability to create moods. His watercolor paintings were reproduced by the lithographic process, which afforded him rich variations in color tones, their tints and their shades, for modeling, shading, or highlighting. Incredibly subtle transitions, especially in blues and greens, are accomplished by *line effects*, as one color tone's tint or shade blends into another tint or shade; there is little stark contrast of opposites or even triads on a color spectrum. Except in bedtime or beach scenes, Sal is dressed in a shirt of a primary red tone and pants of a primary blue tone. The use of primaries is known to attract the eye, and her figure is sought by the audience in all scenes where she is present. Interesting, however, is the variety of tints and shades for Sal's clothes as the source of light changes in different illustrations. McCloskey was very interested in colors' dependence on a source of light in painting, and almost every illustration displays remarkable visual sensations created by light or dark—foggy mornings, salmon pink sunsets, high-noon heat, and even the heavy stillness of gray sky before the storm.

The different lights as sources of illumination (lamplight, flashlight, moonlight, sunlight, starlight, and the primary yellow of a light in the window) should be pointed out to children: they contribute to the desired effects of serenity, suspense, lightheartedness, mystery, coziness, or splendor in these paintings.

Boats, the airplane, and finally the McCloskey's house itself are the only artificial figures in this book, which otherwise heavily depends on children's appreciation of organic shapes. Just as photographs of scenery without people can effectively capture the beauty of nature but fail to hold youngsters' attention for very long, the addition of children's faces on the beach, in a boat, under a tree, or among the sunflowers contribute greatly to seashore pictures that are in themselves static and uninvolving. Deep space is created through atmospheric perspective in all the outdoor scenes in *Wonder*, effectively communicating the artist's invitation for the audience to enter. But a picture-book audience is more eager to meet the McCloskey family itself, to join in their activities, to come closer to the attitude of wonderment they experience. The result is that young children today can still find much to enjoy in the pictures of rowboats and sailboats, Parcheesi games and flashlights, wheelbarrows and suitcases, and little Jane and Sal in *Time of Wonder*.

Looking Around: *Mei Li; The Little Island; A Tree Is Nice; Always Room for One More; One Fine Day; Baboushka and the Three Kings*

Another Caldecott Award winner inspired by personal experiences of its author-illustrator is *Mei Li* by Thomas Handforth. This 1939 Medalist shows the new year's fair adventures of a small girl and her brother in China long ago. Since childhood, Handforth had been fascinated by the Orient, and in the 1930s he lived for six years in Peking. During that time, he drew children, animals, actors, and other performers who later appeared in his book. One who came to pose was Mei Li, an orphan left with missionaries and adopted by a rich American, and Handforth chose the little girl, her friends, and pets to be central characters in his story. Much as McCloskey's fictional *Make Way for Ducklings* was based on real events observed in Boston, so also did Handforth's book reflect actual people, costumes, activities, and architecture he saw around him in the ancient walled city. In many other ways as well, *Mei Li* offers excellent comparisons with *Ducklings*. Similarities include book size and shape, formality of text placement, sensitive planning around the gutter in a double-page landscape format, and the exquisite tonal qualities of black-and-white brush and lithograph pencil used masterfully to imply delicate texturing and subtle contouring. The audience's viewpoint changes dramatically, from normal eye level to worm's-eye close-ups and even to bird's-eye level in the endpapers' map of the city. Handforth's pictures also have invisible horizontal, circular, and diagonal frameworks that are strikingly similar to McCloskey's. Although names of characters are Americanized in *Mei Li* and by today's standards the book includes examples of sexist and cultural stereotyping, it still offers a fine example of traditional narrative picture-book art. Its reproduction by early letterpress using copper plates and hand-set type adds a further note of interest.

The Little Island, illustrated by 1947 Award winner Leonard Weisgard, offers equally apt comparisons with McCloskey's *Time of Wonder*: both books have poetic texts inspired by real experiences on islands not far from each other off the coast of Maine, and both are collections of expressionistic paintings, one executed in watercolor and the other in watercolor's opaque form, gouache. McCloskey's illustrations are somewhat less static, since they occasionally include people engaged in activities. *The Little Island*, on the other hand, has the advantage of horizontal-rectangular book design, which, as mentioned earlier, is well suited for presentation of paintings entirely on right-hand pages without interference by the gutter. The island pictured by Weisgard belonged to the illustrator's good friend and frequent collaborator, author Margaret Wise Brown, writing here under the pseudonym Golden MacDonald (as she had for *Little Lost Lamb*, Weisgard's 1946 Honor Book selection). The artist's frequent visits to Brown's island enabled him to depict it from personal remembrances. As in *Wonder*, so also in *The Little Island* are foggy scenes and stormy scenes, distant viewpoints of the ocean interspersed with intimate close-ups of the island's flora and fauna, and masterful use of line effects as luscious blues meet sea greens to define watery depths and ever-changing sky.

Brown in her text rather abruptly personified her little island, giving it the magical ability to enter into a metaphysical dialogue with a kitten about the creation of the world. The kitten not only leaps into the air to imitate the detachment an island must have, but he also pursues the conversation with a fish, who tells him a secret of the deep: all land is one land under the sea. This brief fantasy episode of only a few pages in *The Little Island* ends as abruptly as it begins and is more perplexing than satisfying in its eclecticism. The situation is not improved by Weisgard, who gives this episode literal illustrations in the middle of an otherwise formal series of artistic nature studies. The kitten's leap into the air is more exaggerated than seems required by the text, and the illustration brings to mind artist René Magritte's famous painting *The Castle of the Pyrenees*, in which a castle built on a rock hangs suspended over an expanse of rolling sea. *Rain Drop Splash* with illustrations by Weisgard was an Honor Book choice the same year his pictures for *The Little Island* won the Medal itself.

The 1957 Award winner, *A Tree Is Nice*, is yet another nature study. It appeals to the very young a quarter of a century later because its text is brief and simpler, for instance, than that of McCloskey's *Wonder*. Unlike *The Little Island*, it has pictures that include people involved in playful, busy, or humorous activities—another point of interest. The poetic text by Janice May Udry is so fundamental and uncluttered that, when illustrator Marc Simont first read it, he said he wondered why he had not thought of it himself. He designed all illustrations with a firm horizontal baseline and a tall vertical-rectangular book shape. Within this framework, he mounted tall trees as points of interest beneath which and in which little visual stories expand on the author's simple ideas.

The interior book design unfortunately alternates between four-color reproductions of vibrant watercolors and black-and-white drawings. The illustrations are individually attractive in themselves but, seen as a collection, they offer a wide diversity in stylistic uses of line, line effect, paint added within lines, and line added to painting. A few illustrations could have been better planned to avoid the crease of the gutter, and continuity of book design suffers when the last pages abruptly employ informal text placement between vignettes instead of the panoramic double-page spreads with text formally positioned along the bottom. In 1950 *The Happy Day* with illustrations by Simont was an Honor Book selection; in 1967, for David McCord's *Every Time I Climb a Tree*, the artist portrayed trees and climbing children much like those in *A Tree Is Nice*.

Nonny Hogrogian, like McCloskey, won the Caldecott Award twice, in 1966 for pictures in *Always Room for One More* by Sorche Nic Leodhas, and in 1972 for her own adaptation of an Armenian folktale, *One Fine Day*. In addition she was an Honor Book winner in 1977 for *The Contest*. *Always Room* is a fine example of the difference between drawn line itself and a use of color line effects. The wee house in the heather and the characters in this old Scottish rhyme are all defined by pen-and-ink edge lines for faces and silhouetted by a most dramatic use of *hatching* (a set of short parallel lines) and *crosshatching* (a set of lines crossed over by another set at a different angle and in differing amounts to imply texture and contour). In contrast, the tonal background of the heather itself, the hillside, and the stormy sky are purple, green, and gray chalk and wash dabbed on with paper napkins. Hogrogian studied photographs of the people, traditional costumes, and cottages of Scotland and listened to Scottish music while she illustrated *Always Room* and personally preseparated the art. This is one of the smallest of the Caldecotts; it should be used as a lap book for best enjoyment of its numerous and minuscule figures. The art, dialect, and humor are usually best appreciated by older children.

One Fine Day, however, is a cumulative or sequencing tale in the tradition of "The House That Jack Built" and "The Tail of the Mouse"; such books are most enjoyed by smaller children, who join into the fun of a repeated refrain. *One Fine Day* was illustrated by oil painting and is a further example of line effects when color meets color and of occasional use for additional drawn lines as outlines or contour lines. The fox who lost his tail seems presented deliberately as artistic cliche of the fox motif in folk literature, stylistically simple and idealized in vivid red-orange. Other figures, though, are individualized with humorous, smug, nagging, or flirtatious facial expressions. The fox begins his journey unobtrusively through the forest in the book's front matter itself; this early entrance prepares the audience for the humor of his exit in the last illustration. In all double-page spreads a strong, visible horizontal baseline leads the audience quickly from page to page before the final pages, in which the entire path is retraced in capsulized format and the fox himself beats a hasty retreat off the page.

Smallest of all the Caldecotts is the 1961 *Baboushka and the Three Kings*, a Russian folk version of the Santa Claus story adapted by Ruth Robbins. The decorative illustrations by her collaborator Nicolas Sidjakov feature drawn lines and outlined figures colored with tempera and four hues of felt pen. Hand-set type in an obsolete typeface is positioned informally above, opposite, or within illustrations, masterfully incorporated for maximum balance in small fields of action.

Sidjakov was born in Latvia and traveled all over Europe after losing his family in World War II; he felt in tune with this story from his homeland and sought authenticity in his illustrations, putting peasant shoes on Baboushka even though his young son thought they looked like tennis shoes, and convincing Robbins to change the text so that a peasant carrying a basket was described with a sack instead, since a peasant would want her arms free for work at all times. His main objective, however, was to create a Russian mood, achieved by illustrative experimentation that took liberties with reality. Bold lines outline geometrical representations of colorful figures, expanses of landscape and cityscape, and cold, wintry night skies. After experience with these illustrations, children will feel more comfortable with cubism in fine art, such as that by Pablo Picasso or Juan Gris. Different artistic uses of line can be demonstrated by comparing the outside of Baboushka's small hut with Hogrogrian's wee house in *Always Room*. Sidjakov's hut interior and onion-shaped domes can be likened to Uri Shulevitz's illustrations for another Russian folktale, *The Fool of the World and the Flying Ship*.

Works Cited

Brown, Margaret Wise. *The Little Island*. New York: Doubleday, 1946.
———. *Little Lost Lamb*. New York: Doubleday, 1945.
Delafield, Clelia. *Mrs. Mallard's Family*. New York: Lothrop, 1946.
Gag, Wanda. *Millions of Cats*. New York: Coward, 1938.
Grahame, Kenneth. *The Wind in the Willows*. New York: Scribner, 1908.
Handforth, Thomas. *Mei Li*. New York: Doubleday, 1938.
Hogrogrian, Nonny. *One Fine Day*. New York: Macmillan, 1971.
Krauss, Ruth. *The Happy Day*. New York: Harper, 1949.
McCloskey, Robert. *Blueberries for Sal*. New York: Viking, 1948.
———. *Burt Dow, Deepwater Man: A Tale of the Sea in the Classic Tradition*. New York: Viking, 1963.
———. *Centerburg Tales*. New York: Viking, 1951.
———. *Homer Price*. New York: Viking, 1943.
———. *Lentil*. New York: Viking, 1940.
———. *Make Way for Ducklings*. New York: Viking, 1941.
———. *One Morning in Maine*. New York: Viking, 1952.
———. *Time of Wonder*. New York: Viking, 1957.
McCord, David. *Every Time I Climb a Tree*. Boston: Little, 1967.
Nic Leodhas, Sorche. *Always Room for One More*. New York: Holt, 1965.
Ransome, Arthur. *The Fool of the World and the Flying Ship*. New York: Farrar, 1968.
Rey, H. A. *Curious George* and other titles. Boston: Houghton, 1941– .
Robbins, Ruth. *Baboushka and the Three Kings*. Berkeley, Calif.: Parnassus, 1960.

Sawyer, Ruth. *Journey Cake, Ho!* New York: Viking, 1953.
Tresselt, Alvin. *Rain Drop Splash.* New York: Lothrop, 1946.
Udry, Janice May. *A Tree Is Nice.* New York: Harper, 1956.

3
Color: *Drummer Hoff* and *The Rooster Crows*

A simple rhyme and cannon's blast "KAHBAHBLOOOM" in *Drummer Hoff* have delighted children for almost two decades. The humor and colorful imagination of Ed Emberley's illustrations won the 1968 Caldecott Medal for this book, based on Barbara Emberley's adaptation of an old verse. *The Rooster Crows* by another husband-and-wife team, Maud and Miska Petersham, was the 1946 committee's selection; it is subtitled "A Book of American Rhymes and Jingles" and consists of illustrations for over six dozen nursery rhymes and children's games.

Maud and Miska Petersham

No other Caldecott-winning artists are more easily recognized as having reflected the political climate during certain periods of American history than are Ed Emberley in his illustrations for *Drummer Hoff* and Maud and Miska Petersham in their pictures for *The Rooster Crows*. The latter book exemplifies the ethnocentrism and patriotism that swept the United States immediately following World War II; over twenty years later, the antiwar statement in *Drummer Hoff* was equally popular with many Americans, coming as it did during the country's disquieting involvement in Vietnam. As important artistically is the comparison of styles expressed in these two books, one rooted in the accepted tenets of representational, idealized art so popular in the 1940s and the other, years later, epitomizing the abstract cubist movement that struck at the very heart of those representational traditions in picture-book illustrations. Each of the books offers well-crafted beauty and a great deal of fun to their widely differing audiences, and the fact that Emberley's career as published illustrator began just as the Petershams' was ending makes an interesting study for children in society's influences on artists during different periods of our nation's history.

The remarkable collaboration of Maud and Miska Petersham as children's-book illustrators and author-illustrators spanned almost forty years, producing from 1920 to 1955 illustrations for some forty anthologies, textbooks, and children's classics, and from 1929 to 1958 over forty of their own titles in five nonfiction "Story Book" series, Biblical stories, and picture books. This outpouring of highly skilled talent and diversified interests ceased over a quarter of a century ago; Hungarian-born Miska died in 1960, and his wife Maud, one of four daughters of a New York minister, died in 1971. However, many of the Petershams' contributions can still be found on library shelves today. Such books as *An American ABC* (Caldecott Honor Book in 1942), *The Story of One Hundred Years of U.S. Postage Stamps, The Box with Red Wheels, The Circus Baby*, along with pictures for Margery Clark's *Poppy Seed Cakes* and their own *The Rooster Crows*, will demonstrate for years to come their love of literature, history, and children.

Miska as a child in his birthplace near Budapest wanted dearly to be an artist and walked miles each day to attend art school. In 1911 at age twenty he went to London, where he changed his name from Petrezselyem Mihaly to Miska Petersham. Later, he found his way to New York, where he worked in the same advertising firm as Maud Fuller, whom he married. They were given *Poppy Seed Cakes* as their first book to illustrate, followed by numerous titles written by others over the next two decades before their own first book, *Miki*, was published with their young son as the main character. Husband and wife worked simultaneously on illustrations, since she was left-handed and he was right-handed, and they made color separations for their pictures themselves.

Many of the Petershams' books were of historical or religious nature, necessitating extensive research and travel. Miska particularly was interested in portrayal of American history—"I expect to see him wearing a three-cornered hat one of these days," Maud once said—and several of their titles served as vehicles for that devotion. Publication in 1945 of *The Rooster Crows* came at the height of their popularity; they enjoyed a well-deserved reputation for their artistic representation of Americana for children.

Inspiration for *The Rooster Crows* was said by Maud to have come from a sleepless night during World War II, when she eased her concern about young Miki, then a navigator on a B-24 in the Pacific, by reciting to herself rhymes remembered from her own childhood. The authors later decided to collect these verses in a book, and the illustrations that followed reflected the pride in the American way of life that was prevalent during and after the war. Although other collectors of folk verse, such as Ray Wood in *American Mother Goose* and *Fun in American Folk Rhymes*, may present a better sampling of pure American invention, the Petershams' illustrations give their volume a superior American flair. Colonial boys and pioneer girls, small-town kids and 1940s city kids, farm boys or sailor boys or Yankee Doodle boys, all are there for children of today to find. At their best (and many are quite charming), the pictures are reminiscent of Norman Rockwell's sentimental portrait of Americans.

Romanticism regarding childhood and portrayal of an idealized child with prettiness, good health, and cheerful disposition—in the case of *The Rooster Crows* the perfect white American youth—had artistic roots in the nineteenth century. The bourgeois sentimentality in much of Victorian English art itself followed Eastern, primitive, and Renaissance traditions of idealized form. No penetration of character is shown in the Petershams' depictions of children—Lazy Mary is as easily seen to be "the darling daughter" who's gone out to swim or Tuesday's child "full of grace." Just as George Washington is pictorially glorified frozen as a statue on his horse, so are all these childish characters basically frozen in time as one child, "blythe and bonny and good and gay." Rockwell could imbue his characterizations with some complexity and humor, but the Petershams did not exhibit psychological insight in their work. They are seen today as folk artists to whom face and figure were primarily decoration on the page.

Mother Goose and other children's rhymes, however, are known for their portrayal of action without introspection, so the Petershams' lack of individuality for their characters does not in itself detract from children's pleasure in the beauty and fun found in *The Rooster Crows*. Girl characters are not pictured in any dominant roles; this point may be discussed with students as sexist stereotyping prevalent in many children's books of the 1940s. Generally speaking, though, the parts played in the various illustrations are acceptable as befitting the rhymes. Throughout the history of children's literature, the best illustrators of Mother Goose rhymes have recognized that the challenge in picturing these short nonsense verses lies in the ability to present art that has a life of its own; the Petershams' book has a lasting quality due to its touches of Americana.

One reason these verses continue to attract children is the age-old appeal of learning something "by heart" (one of the loveliest phrases in the English language). The Petershams have collected some of the most popular old rhymes to have come down to us over the years. A Mother Goose or calling-out rhyme is for the very young one of the first exercises of language, and the brevity, repetition, and surprises inherent in them appeal to youngsters' limited attention span. These light-hearted introductions to poetry are unburdened by the bewildering formalities of instruction. Once children get the idea of onomatopoeia and other sound patterns in words, they usually demand the opportunity to immediately recite the whole piece on their own. The strong cadence and dependable rhythm of Mother Goose rhymes entrance children and speak to their sense of movement, dance, and music, inviting them to participate. Although they may sit quietly at the beginning, they will spontaneously join in as the rhyming helps to record the sequence of characters and/or events necessary to get through the verse. For the very young, learning by heart a favorite rhyme in *The Rooster Crows* is a large part of the fun, and for older children an additional benefit lies in the bits of weather lore and the early versions of verses they may know in more modern forms.

Of interest also to older students is the history behind some verses; this may be pursued in *The Annotated Mother Goose* by William and Ceil Baring-Gould. Finding background information for some of the Petershams' patriotic scenes often indicates the care with which these two artists researched their pictures. For instance, the "Yankee Doodle" rhyme reprinted here was originally written by a British army doctor to mock the ragged American colonialists as silly Yankee "do-littles" during the French and Indian Wars, and it is this militiaman rather than the more commonly pictured Revolutionary soldier that the Petershams' illustration depicts. In the verse George Washington is referred to as a captain, the rank he held during the French and Indian Wars, and he is portrayed as such rather than the general he later became. And on page 31[1] appears the best-known verse for the song with picture of an indisputably ragtag Yankee "do-little," complete with his outlandish feather "Macaroni" (an eighteenth-century slang term for an English dandy who put on Continental airs). Such is the historical precision

---

[1]Pagination beings on the first page with text in 1966 hardbound edition.

with which illustrations were fashioned in *The Rooster Crows* by Maud and Miska Petersham, American patriots and beloved artists for America's children.

Ed Emberley

Ed Emberley, with his special style of storytelling in pictures, has made a unique contribution to the world of children and art. After spending the 1960s perfecting his own flair for design and imaginative brand of exaggerated humor in *picture books for children* such as *Drummer Hoff*, he began in the 1970s drawing instruction itself in his *children's books about pictures*. From 1961 through 1968, this artist participated in the production of an astounding twenty-seven trade books—and he has been known to participate all the way through to page layouts ready for the engraver. In some he was illustrator for such well-known children's authors as Franklin M. Branley and Paul Showers; some were done in collaboration with his wife, Barbara, and in some he was both illustrator and author. A variety of artistic approaches appeared in this potpourri of nonfiction as well as fiction, and in the same year that Emberley won the Caldecott for *Drummer Hoff* he published *Green Says Go*, in which the artist himself elaborated on color creation and intended effects of color on the audience. In 1967 the sole Caldecott Honor Book was *One Wide River to Cross*, for which Emberley used background colors that are mostly the same hues as in *Drummer Hoff*.

Thus the artist's interest in color is well documented, but additionally important are his bold figures created by use of circles, triangles, and rectangles that have firmly established Emberley as a children's art instructor ever since his first book, *The Wing on a Flea: A Book about Shapes*. In his eleven very popular drawing books for children published from 1969 through 1980, he created what he calls a "graphic vocabulary" for the kind of geometrical artistic style used in *Drummer Hoff*. Included are step-by-step visual instructions for drawing hundreds of objects from simple shapes and few lines. Creation of this "graphic vocabulary" has enabled him to communicate in refreshing and exciting ways through illustrations in books, but he is the first to admit that the idea of a geometric artistic language has its origins in the early twentieth-century cubism that grew out of the efforts of Pablo Picasso and Georges Braque, with Robert Delaunay as an important disciple.

For geometric shapes and primary colors themselves as subjects for paintings, Piet Mondrian can be studied, and for a most direct line of influence for *Drummer Hoff* the work of Paul Klee should be examined for its combination of bold colors with a breakdown of form into its parts. Through such studies in art history Emberley can be seen to have employed a style in *Drummer Hoff* that is, as he puts it, "subtle resurrection of the culture of one generation to the enrichment of a later one." Fortunate indeed for children is the fact that he chose the picture book as the vehicle for that resurrection.

In *Drummer Hoff* the illustrations have taken an old folk verse, "John Ball Shot Them All," and lifted it from its relative and perhaps rightful obscurity into the limelight of children's literature. The original rhyme was about the making of a rifle and was taken from *The Annotated Mother Goose:*

> John Patch made the match,
> And John Clint made the flint,
> And John Puzzle made the muzzle,
> And John Crowder made the powder,
> And John Block made the stock,
> And John Brammer made the rammer,
> And John Scott made the shot,
> But John Ball shot them all.

An additional line, "And John Wyming made the priming," can be found in the *Barnes Book of Nursery Verse*, edited by Barbara Ireson. This source demotes the folk verse to a "jingle" defined appropriately as repetitious nonsense of a superficial character. Whether "John Ball" was initially a chant for marching or a verse Papa recited to children gathered around his knee as he cleaned his gun, the rhyme had not survived the years to be found widely in print until the Emberleys singled it out. The story was adapted by Barbara Emberley, who added General Border and turned the rifle into a cannon, the name *John* into military titles, John Ball into Drummer Hoff "because of its rich sound," and the shooting of everyone at the end into a more "appropriate ending to the tale," the firing of a cannon.

The revisions lend themselves to a better reading, just as they surely inspired more fun to emerge in Ed Emberley's woodcuts. Only in the last instance—the firing of the cannon as substitution for John Ball shooting them all—can one even question the effectiveness of the Emberleys' reworking of an obviously antiquated piece of nonsense. The *intent* of the reworking was admirable as well as judicious (one doubts whether the Emberleys could have gotten anywhere with Prentice-Hall or any other publisher if the original ending had remained as a mass murder), but curiously enough the new ending, in which no one has "shot them all," is ineffective for a surprisingly large number of children. Despite Ed Emberley's use of a theatrical device that places his characters safely upstage in the illustration "FIRE!", many youngsters still insist the cannon has "shot them all" at the end—even though the phrase itself has been expurgated. A hint of personal violence must somehow exist in the underlying framework of this story. How else can one explain the youngsters who prefer to believe, declare they believe, or indeed truly believe that such mayhem occurs when the very mention of it has been removed? Bruno Bettelheim, who discourses on the effects of fairy tales on young children in his book *Uses of Enchantment* and other writings, would say this is a result of the child's need to put back into stories the fears and aggressions adults have eliminated with the good intention of protecting the child. Perhaps Emberley might have effectively cleansed the verse even more thoroughly of its taint of violence by adding after "KAHBAHBLOOOM" yet another illustration that would show "happy warriors" leaving the field intact.

Children continue to enjoy this remarkable book because the very spirit of the poem as well as its content is reflected in the pictures. Just as the rhyme follows the predictable form of a cumulative tale, so are the soldiers visually added in turn to the scene before us. Each occupies a page alone before falling in with the others on the next page, in illustrations and in verse. And last, in pictures as in poem a rhythm exists like a counting exercise or a march, as the whole group is added up. Thus text and illustrations are inseparable for children right up to the order to "FIRE!"—but not through to the end by any means, since the last pages are Emberley's own surprises.

"You might be interested to know how 'we' (Prentice-Hall, Barbara and I) felt about *Drummer Hoff*," Ed Emberley said in a postscript to his Caldecott acceptance speech. "We had no idea that it would ever become a popular book. It was designed for a very few special (unknown) children. We thought the story line was too simple and naive and the art work too complicated and sophisticated to interest more than a very few. We were wrong. We still don't know why, even with the Caldecott, so many have found it interesting."

Be that as it may, lasting popularity has been won by this "simple and naive" cumulative tale consisting of only seven lines (thirty-six words) extended into twenty-eight pages of uncannily expository art. The verse appeals to children as a work story that tells how something was done: first the building and then the firing of a cannon by a group of soldiers. The intended audience knows very little about such a task, and so everyone watches closely as each piece of equipment is named as it is brought forward. One is to understand that there is a proper sequence for these pieces, and when the thing is finished—it works! On the adult level we find enjoyment in *the way* Emberley shows it works (never to work again); the children find additional satisfaction in now knowing *how* it was put together to work—at least just this once. An interest in knowing how something is done is a facet of human nature, and so we sympathize with the child's plea to start again from the beginning so he or she can get it right.

In addition to satisfying the fascination with the use of tools and accumulated parts needed to make something go, this work story specifies which members of the group are required to accomplish the task at hand, from the general down to the drummer. The rhyme says who does what. And young children who are just beginning to broaden a concept of self to include emotional commitment to a group are gladdened by the evidence that sometimes the lowest-ranking member of the group can get the best job. When it is Drummer Hoff who fires it off, they see hope for their own fledgling experiences in group activities at home, on the playground, or in the classroom. Another advantage of group involvement is demonstrated as well. Blame for the ultimate destruction of the cannon is not laid on any one member of the gun crew (probably the powder was in excess or the shot itself was too tight for the muzzle—but still, whose fault would either be?). Thus, one "naive" but vital message in *Drummer Hoff* is that group membership can not only hold reward for success, but can sometimes also deflect responsibility for failure.

Many students readily enter into discussion about Emberley's creation of "two endings," the last being the final wordless page showing the wrecked *Sultan*, as described by the artist himself in his speech:

> Many people prefer to stop at the "KAHBAHBLOOOM" page. And for some purposes that is where the story should end. But others prefer to go on to the next page, which shows the cannon de-

stroyed. The men have gone, and the birds and flowers that appear to be merely decorative through the first part of the book are in the process of taking over—again. The picture of the destroyed cannon was purposely put on a half page to keep it in its proper place as a minor theme.

Neither the "KAHBAHBLOOOM" nor the "cannon destroyed" pictures are really implied in the verse itself; one should address the ambiguity they present to children, whether in preschool or junior high. Once again the illustrator himself provides helpful interpretation:

> The book's main theme is a simple one—a group of happy warriors build a cannon that goes "KAHBAHBLOOOM." But, there is more to find if you "read" the pictures. They show that men can fall in love with war and, imitating the birds, go to meet it dressed as if to meet their sweethearts. The pictures also show that men can return from war sometimes with medals, and sometimes with wooden legs.

Children are known to search for symbols in art, and Emberley surely intended that his viewer "read" the pictures to find examples of the pomp and ceremony with which men often play at deadly games. His exemplary artwork presents for youngsters a concern over the folly of humankind to build only to destroy, and a faith in nature's endurance to reign triumphant in the end.

Book Design

Top-quality binding and durable paper in the Prentice-Hall hardbound edition contribute to *Drummer Hoff*'s ability to stand up to constant rereadings when children plead "Do it again!" The dust jacket is dramatically attractive with its eye-catching illustration in bright red, blue, and yellow, so well designed around the drummer and the cannon that even placement of a Caldecott sticker itself seems to interfere with the overall composition. The large size and bold simplicity of illustrative style make the book easy to share with an audience of one or many youngsters.

The shape of the hardbound edition is a horizontal rectangle that, when opened, extends wide into a panoramic double-page field of action for all but the last of the illustrations. The binding's gutter is used to advantage as an invisible vertical center line that emphasizes simple compositional balance between left and right pages. A storyteller holding up the book with one hand at the binding should be careful, however, to avoid covering up one of Emberley's little ladybugs, which often are placed too near the crease of the gutter.

Two paperbound editions are both somewhat smaller but identical in shape; they can be recommended for certain uses when the hardbound is unavailable. But experience with these paperbounds should be limited, since color reproduction from the original has not always been successful. Color lacks intensity, overprinted colors are slightly askew of the outlined figures, and sometimes colors are downright distorted. Since all of these complaints deal directly with color—which is the subject of our chapter here—we will explore the specifics behind the criticisms later when we demonstrate that these same printing errors can actually be helpful in a discussion with children about the creation of colors themselves.

However, one serious complaint about a printing error must be lodged now because it has been proliferated throughout hardbound, paperbound, and filmstrip versions of *Drummer Hoff*. On page 21,[2] General Border's coat and hat as well as his horse's mane and tail are different colors compared with those items on the next two pages. Although the color printing has been improved somewhat in the Treehouse Paperbacks edition by Prentice-Hall, the Young Readers Press edition, published by arrangement with Prentice-Hall, and the Weston Woods sound filmstrip compound the errors by adhering faithfully to illustrations in the original edition. Only in the Weston Woods motion picture version are the general and horse set aright in a film additionally pleasurable due to its sound effects, explosive colors, and ability to bestow appropriate personalities to the soldiers. The only criticism of the fast little six-minute animated film is that the word "KAHBAHBLOOOM" does not appear on the screen to tickle the children's funny bones as it does when the book is read aloud.

From the beginning title page itself, the design of the book sets the stage for *Drummer Hoff* as the briefest of one-act plays. All the action in the story takes place in one spot, a military position somewhere in a green field. This place is identified along the bottom of each page by a visible, horizontal grassy baseline upon which all the actors gather, each a strong vertical figure. Each of them is also in glorious costume, with much eye appeal to hold our attention on

---

[2]Pagination begins on first page with text in hardbound edition.

the page. The grass line repeated from page to page acts as the edge of an imagined proscenium stage, and the audience's viewpoint is that of a front-row theater seat slightly below what could be called normal eye level. Adding to the theatrical effect, blue front and end papers of the hardbound edition give the impression of curtains drawn to the sides.

On page 1 Drummer Hoff is already onstage in a permanent position down left (to be understood as the actors' left), and as the little playlet unfolds other actors enter to perform center stage before retiring stage right. In another theatrical device applied to page design, the row of soldiers is seen only from the shoulders up, as if they were far upstage and almost hidden from the line of vision of the audience, "seated" as it is below the stage's apron. This position upstage for the general and his men is important to note, since it places them all out of the line of the cannon's blast and does well to negate some children's insistence that everyone's been killed in the end!

Last, placement of text stands to the actor's right of center stage, balancing action going on elsewhere. This device finds its parallel in the old theater tradition that has a monologist recite downstage as a pantomime is played out beside him. Except for the last two illustrations, which are Emberley's own inventions, the pictures convey only the exact story as told in the text. When the time comes for the general to speak, speech ballons as script are imaginatively used within the illustrations themselves, effectively separating the command of "Ready! Aim! FIRE!" both literally and artistically from the verse. When the moment arrives for the cannon to perform, sound effects also are provided right in the pictures: first a small "click" followed by a full-page, hand-carved, mock-Lydian Cursive typeface for "KAHBAHBLOOOM" so forceful that Drummer Hoff himself is tilted to one side and the cannon barrel is destroyed.

The last scene is the only single-page illustration and, with blue endpaper acting as curtain closing from stage left, our final glimpse is of the birds and bugs onstage merrily taking over. Our applause grows into a standing ovation for Ed Emberley as impresario exceptionale in his design for *Drummer Hoff*.

The book-jacket illustration for *The Rooster Crows* is from a rhyme that ends "The rooster crows and away he goes" and pictures a child jumping from a barn loft down into a haystack. The illustration sets the tone for the book as a compilation, not only of nursery rhymes, but also of the short verses children "call out" in their games or other amusements. The contents are sorted accordingly into categories concluding with six verses for "Yankee Doodle" added as a story poem at the end. Macmillan's hardbound edition has a vertical rectangular cover that opens up into single-page illustrations for which the audience's viewpoint is always a comfortably normal eye-level position—even when an elephant jumps so high "He reached the sky / And never came back till the Fourth of July." The numerous illustrations are equally divided among full-page scenes, partial-page scenes, and small vignettes that form simple decorations beside some rhymes. Verses are in formal arrangements above, below, or beside the illustrations, with only a couple of more informal placements within the pictures themselves. Especially for the games, the pictures are needed to additionally elucidate exactly how the verse was intended to accompany an activity. Some of the smaller pictures, such as illustrations for finger games, are difficult for everyone in a large group to see, and in this respect *The Rooster Crows* can be better appreciated by an audience of only a few children. The book's length and variety of rhymes make it an unlikely choice for a reading in one sitting, but a general introduction can be accomplished if desired by reading aloud only those verses with illustrations large enough for everyone in a group to see. This skimming leaves out some two dozen shorter rhymes, but more than twice that many remain to be enjoyed during a single reading.

The paperbound edition by Collier-Macmillan is smaller but roughly the same shape and cannot be recommended for use in art appreciation because of inexplicable changes in coloration from the original: inaccuracies randomly result in a brown sky, blue geese, and a red colt (yet when one verse distinctly calls for "pretty horses" of red and blue, the discoloring perversely presents white and brown in the picture). This 1971 paperback edition is also the only known instance in which a Caldecott Award winner has been drastically abridged; nineteen of the verses and almost as many illustrations from the original have been removed entirely. Collier's juvenile paperback line was just beginning in the early 1970s, and books in each category were standardized as to format, size, and price. A few of the Petershams' illustrated rhymes cut from the original are a real loss. One wishes that the "pretty horses" lullaby called "Hushabye" on page 28 had been removed rather than some others, such as a very pretty valentine. Not only is the "Hushabye" picture discolored, but also this verse is generally recognized as a folk song rather than a "rhyme or jingle" and as such does not seem appropriate in this collection. In addition, "Hushabye" is known to have a bitter background: it was a southern slave song sung by a black nurse or "Mammy" to white children while her own children were left alone and unprotected. To ignore the concluding verse in which the "bees and butterflies are peckin' out the eyes" of her own "poor little lambie" leaves the first verse to stand as a seemingly pretty little song and denies the tragic situation from black history that prompted the lullaby itself.

Definitely a dramatic improvement in the paperbound edition is the removal of the two racially stereotypical illustrations lamentable in a Caldecott winner: black dialect rhymes "Cold, Frosty Morning" and "Old Mister Rabbit." By the fifteenth printing in 1966 they had also been removed from the hardbound edition. A later edition of the hardbound, then, is the only edition seriously recommended for use with youngsters today, unless the desire is to conduct a study of stereotyping in pictures from past children's books. By 1966, "Cold, Frosty Morning" and "Old Mister Rabbit" had been replaced with six traditional Mother Goose rhymes and an illustration for "Little Jack Horner." These substitutions, as well as several other verses in the collection, cannot be called American in origin, but their presence is not disagreeable. On the contrary, publisher and illustrators are to be commended for altering their Award-winning work in order to remove the two blatant instances of racial derogation, and their example should stand for others less sensitive in the field of children's literature and educational materials for the young.

Art Appreciation of Drummer Hoff

In his Caldecott Award acceptance speech, Ed Emberley began an explanation of the color printing process for Drummer Hoff with this statement: "Although only three inks were employed—red, yellow, and blue—we were able to create the impression of thirteen distinct colors." Use of red, yellow, and blue is one of the oldest theories of color creation, and the picture book Drummer Hoff offers a vividly unique opportunity for primary-age children to become acquainted with this theory of color harmony and order.

Those adults who desire to expose children to artistic study more sophisticated than a fundamental exploration of standard color harmonies will find the book is additionally a splendid introduction to the complexities of color printing. For Emberley had much to say about the making of Drummer Hoff, and his remarks can lead to new discoveries about color for youngsters of all ages.

Two illustrations have been chosen for extensive study in order to provide reference and vocabulary needed for color criticism of other books in the Caldecott collection. Beginning with "KAHBAH-BLOOOM" (pages 26–27), then turning back to "FIRE!" (pages 24–25), children will find in *Drummer Hoff* a thoroughly enjoyable way to study colors, theories of color harmony, and the intended effects of colors on an audience. Exploration of the tonal qualities of color will be reserved for study of *The Rooster Crows* by Maud and Miska Petersham. Having both Caldecott winners before you for inspection will be indispensable to our discussion of elemental concepts that can be applied to other colorful picture books on the shelves.

PRIMARY COLORS

Ask a group of kindergarteners (all of whom are likely involved with classroom exercises in the naming of colors) to identify the colors they see in "KAHBAHBLOOOM," and most of them reply with confidence, "Red and black and yellow and *blue!*" Asked to inspect the illustration more closely for colors, many will point out that there are actually two reds, two blues, and to the left of the yellow letters that spell out "KAHBAHBLOOOM," a few youngsters will find with amused surprise a brown and black half-circle—the cannonball itself as it exits stage right. Required further to describe the differences in the colors they see, the children might say that one red is "bright purplish pink" (magenta) and the other is "more orange" (red-orange), that one blue is "a light greenish blue" (turquoise or cyan) and the other is really not a blue but rather a "dark purple" (violet). Even the kindergarteners who may not have the vocabulary yet for all these discriminations can easily recognize in conclusion that the yellow of "KAHBAHBLOOOM" itself is very "bright or light" compared to the very "dark" brown of the cannonball next to it.

Total agreement on these descriptions within the group would be unusual, for no two people see the same color exactly alike. For instance, some children in this same group will declare that the red-orange is not that at all but is a "true red" or crimson, and only perhaps if a sample of crimson itself is placed beside this illustration will those children see any difference, and some will not see it even then. (An appreciable number of children, especially boys, are partially color blind, though total color blindness is uncommon.) Even experts in the field admit there is no agreement on what is the reddest or "purest" red or, for that matter, what is the purest of any other color in the artist's spectrum. The intent here is not to frustrate children by demanding they "see" exactly what the majority see but that they observe and listen for commonly accepted differences and definitions for colors so that they can better appreciate the intriguing processes Emberley and many other artists employ for their illustrations in picture books.

Colors, then, are not so much the properties of the page but a matter of personal perception and emotional response. To expect children to develop the skills for translating their visual experiences into words requires that they be offered refinements for clarification as they build onto the beginnings of an art vocabulary. For the children who described Emberley's magenta in "KAHBAH-BLOOOM" as a "bright purplish pink," the time has undoubtedly come for some additions to their vocabulary, for the enjoyment we all find in learning there's a single, precise word as substitute for a multitude of descriptive, less-precise ones. Although choosing a vocabulary that will please everyone is impossible when discussing color, we will use terms here that find common usage in art education.

Names for hues in "KAHBAHBLOOOM" should now be understood to be widely known as magenta (ma-jen'-ta), red-orange, violet (often called purple), cyan (si'-an), yellow, brown, and black. Artists prefer to call a color a *hue*, since this term distinguishes essential pigments that establish colors of paint or ink. In contrast, the word *color* is also used by the scientific community to refer to all visual sensations and might thus lead far afield into an exploration of diffraction gratings to disperse light or other such esoteric discoveries dealing with color as science. In art, however, we can say that rose (the color) has a reddish hue, and it will be understood that the origin of a rose color lies in the artist's use of red pigment. Following the example of most other books about art appreciation, however, we will use the words *hue* and *color* interchangeably when we speak of an artist's choice of pigment or ink.

Although adults as well as children disagree as to the appropriate identification for hues, differences in hue are easier to spot. When the kindergarteners were initially asked what colors they saw in Emberley's illustration, their answers "red, black, yellow, and blue" indicate that even the very young can quickly identify greatly contrasting hues. This picture has strong appeal because its underlying composition is based on principles of contrast between red, yellow, and blue, called in art the *primary colors*. Primary colors are the hues an artist uses to mix other hues, and the theory of red, yellow, and blue as original pigments to make other hues is one of the most respected of color traditions taught by American art educators. In reality it is almost impossible to create a vivid spectrum through the use of three colors only, as witnessed by the fact that violet can theoretically be made by mixing red and blue pigment but is actually difficult or impossible to create this way.

There are as many arguments about abilities of primary colors to create others as there are ways of thought, whether from the viewpoint of the artist, the physicist, or even the psychologist who concentrates on the effect colors have on people. The term *primary color* is in reality a misnomer since original colors that have the ability to create others vary considerably according to whether the artist is working with paint, ink, light, or even prisms. For instance, the commonly held opinion that pure red as a primary is scarlet or crimson and that pure blue is cobalt or ultramarine may prove workable when one is creating other colors in painting. But in the printing process for books, use of scarlet and cobalt results in dull, murky third colors because transparent inks blend differently with paper than paints do. These impure third hues can be avoided in the graphic arts by substituting magenta as primary red and cyan as primary blue on a color chart for process printing.

Magenta and cyan as primary colors are an abrupt departure from the crimson and cobalt commonly taught to children. Knowing this can work wonders in freeing young minds from early restrictions on color usage, unintentional or otherwise. To discover the hues Emberley and other illustrators use in their books is exciting for youngsters, since they are not the usual hues found in ten-hued crayon boxes or most eight-hued watercolor trays intended for children's uses.

The creation of other colors in "KAHBAHBLOOOM" was accomplished by a process called "overprinting"—the printing of one transparent colored ink over another to make a third color. As Emberley himself explained in his acceptance speech:

> By printing one ink over another, or "overprinting," a third color is made. For instance, if blue ink is printed over yellow ink, the yellow ink shows through and turns the blue ink green. Blue ink printed over red makes purple, and so forth. A separate drawing has to be made for each of the three colors, to show which color went over which color to make what color.

Overprinting, rather than simply mixing inks, is a complicated approach to coloring, and when asked "Why bother?" Emberley replied, "The sharpness and brilliance of the color in *Drummer Hoff* cannot be duplicated by any other practical printing process."

All the hues in *Drummer Hoff* were created from overprinting primaries of magenta, cyan, and yellow. Use of these primaries is a color mixture scheme represented on a color wheel many years ago by the American colorist Herbert E. Ives. On the Ives color wheel nine other hues—red-orange, orange, yellow-orange, yellow-green, green, blue-green, blue-violet, violet, and red-violet—are created by combining various amounts of the primaries.

Many color circles or color wheels have been devised since Sir Isaac Newton charted the first one in the 1700s. Wilhelm Ostwald was a colorist who recognized a sea green as a fourth primary and Albert H. Munsell added violet as a fifth. Arguments about color wheels abound but are generally thought of as rather meaningless, since any well-planned diagram of the spectrum gives a basic idea of color relationships. Different charts are used for different purposes, and to educate children in the theory behind only one or another does not fairly present an understanding of intelligent color usage. Young students of art need to become aware that choosing a certain color system is a decision each artist makes.

In color reproduction of book illustrations, however, the use of magenta, cyan, and yellow as primaries is a standard procedure and is demonstrated perfectly for children in *Drummer Hoff*. In "KAH-BAHBLOOOM" primary yellow is obvious as spelling out the word itself, magenta is the color of Drummer Hoff's face (compared to the red-orange of his hat), and cyan is the farthest background hue (compared to the violet knots of smoke). As we proceed in this chapter, the other hues that result from use of these primaries will be pointed out as they appear in illustrations themselves. Far better that a child explore Emberley's color creation through a study of pages in his book than from a lesson that begins, "Today we will learn about a color wheel." Only in the next section when we discuss color harmonies will a modification of the Ives's chart be necessary to clarify possible confusion about use of colors to provide contrast.

COLOR HARMONIES

Harmony in art can be compared to harmony in music, and like the musical composer, the graphic artist can take great liberties in composition to produce pleasing, harmonious arrangements. But like octaves, keys, and chords, certain rules and propositions of art regulate expression through color. "Chords" and "keys" exist most certainly in art as well as music, and figure 1 can simplify a discussion of color harmonies that form the foundation for the dynamic visual appeal of "KAHBAHBLOOOM." In this one illustration can be found demonstrated three of the six long-established principles of color contrast: the harmony of triads, the harmony of adjacents, and the harmony of opposites.

A *harmony of triads* is accomplished through the equal use of the three hues at the points of a triangle superimposed on the Ives color circle. Such a triangle may rotate around the circle; each *harmony of triads* thus indicated has its own distinct artistic appeal. The triad harmony of primary colors, however, is felt to have the most straightforward appeal of all triad possibilities, and such is the case with magenta, yellow, and cyan used so effectively in "KAHBAH-BLOOOM." This illustration has smaller amounts of the three primaries than of its other two hues, red-orange and violet, but the force of the first three is recognized because they are lighter (more "light-giving" of the five hues here) and so they require less area to balance the heavier red-orange and violet.

The light cyan in the background stands out nicely next to the darkness of the violet, but the magenta may seem lost in the overall impression of red-orange. The latter phenomenon is a good example of *harmony of adjacents*. On the color wheel, cyan and violet have one step between them (blue-violet), and so they offer more contrast than magenta and the adjacent red-orange. Adjacent hues are sometimes called *analogous colors* or *chords* when found in groups of three. One main appeal in such a *harmony of adjacents* is that whatever the chord, it usually gives emotional weight to either the "warm" region of the spectrum (yellows, oranges, reds, associated with the sun and fire) or the "cool" region (greens, blues, violets, associated with water, sky, and trees). The adjacents magenta and red-orange are appropriately "warm" here; a good example of "cool" adjacent harmony is the predominantly blue cannon barrel as it is pictured on many of the pages preceding "KAHBAHBLOOOM." The contrast accentuates the steely coldness of the cannon compared to its fiery blasting.

The imposition of the yellow letters "KAHBAHBLOOOM" upon the magenta and red-orange combination is warm and attractive. Within the cooler background is violet, which lies opposite yellow on the wheel and forms a *harmony of opposites*. Because primary yellow is so brilliant, its force in composition is quite strong even in a relatively small area. A larger area of violet is usually needed to balance its strength. Colorists feel that opposite harmony is an

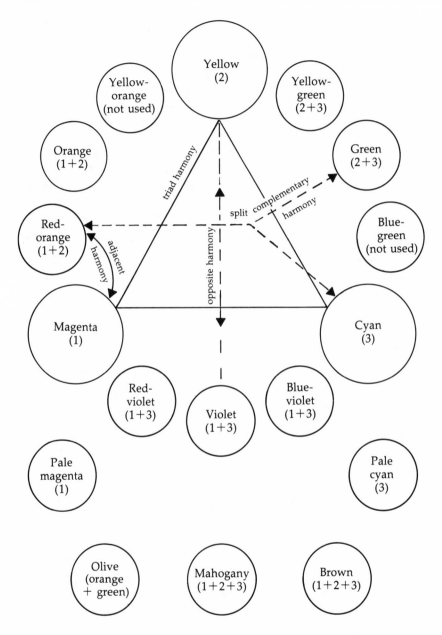

Fig. 1. Color Scheme for *Drummer Hoff*. The twelve-hue color circle is based on magenta, yellow, and cyan.

emotionally satisfying visual sensation, for the eye is believed to seek an opposite for every color it perceives.

For the *harmony of split complements*, we must turn in *Drummer Hoff* to pages 13 or 14 for a look at the debonair Captain Bammer as a full figure. The colors for the uniform of this dashing gallant— right down to his eye patch—are considered unabashedly sophisticated because they are based on the split-complement theory: a dominant or *key hue* (here blue-violet) is combined with two hues (yellow and orange) found on either side of the key hue's direct opposite (yellow-orange). A modicum of refinement is associated with the beauty and variety found in split-complementary harmony; the posture of the captain would indicate that he (and Emberley) might well be aware of that fact. Of the other split complements, red-orange with green and cyan is evident to varying degrees in the full figures of Private Parriage, Sergeant Chowder, and Drummer Hoff himself.

SECONDARY AND TERTIARY COLORS

In the illustration called "FIRE!" is a resplendent display of all but one of the thirteen hues Emberley used in *Drummer Hoff* and created from the primaries magenta, yellow, and cyan. The outline of the carriage is yellow, the barrel's firing mechanism is cyan, the stripes on General Border's uniform are magenta. Centers of the flowers are orange, the general's coat and hat are violet, and the star on the cannon barrel is green. The speech balloon is red-orange, grass is yellow-green, Captain Bammer's hat is blue-violet, and the general's top feather is red-violet.

The darkest hue in the barrel is an olive green (created by a combination of orange and green) and Major Scott's hat is brown (created by combining the three primaries). Mahogany as the thirteenth hue is created by a different combination of the three primaries and is used for Sergeant Chowder's keg of powder on pages 9 and 10 but is not included here in "FIRE!" Faces of the men are pale magenta, and the carriage is pale cyan; these are not be considered separate hues but as lighter primaries. (Emberley explains the "pink" as being "an illusion created by the printer by printing the *same solid red* of Drummer Hoff's jacket but in far lesser amounts of tiny dots of red," with the result that more of the white paper shows through. The same is true of the "powder blue" of the cannon's carriage, which has been printed with fewer dots of cyan. "An interesting classroom investigation," continues the artist, "would be to observe closely under a magnifying glass the Sunday funnies in the newspaper. Even less dots of color are used and the process is easier to understand.")

On the Ives color wheel orange, green, and violet, usually called *secondary colors*, are derived from primaries and offer another example of triad harmony. Their potential for strong contrast is considered by some to be less than that of the primary hues. Areas of orange, green, and violet can be found, seemingly at random but actually quite methodically balanced, across Emberley's double-page spread "FIRE". The place where they lie in close proximity is in the figure of Drummer Hoff, where bits of orange and green appear with the violet of his drum. This secondary triad adds to the dominant effect of red-orange, yellow, and cyan (a combination just one step removed from the primary triad).

Remaining hues on the Ives color circle—red-orange, red-violet, blue-violet, yellow-green, blue-green, and yellow-orange (the latter two not used by Emberley for *Drummer Hoff*)—are called *tertiary colors*, generally considered the most difficult to name and the least able to offer strong contrast. An example is found in the low contrast between the red-orange of the speech balloon and the red-violet of the feather on the general's hat.

The process of overprinting used to create all these hues can best be understood by some children through study of the Young Readers Press paperbound edition published by arrangement with Prentice-Hall. There, errors in reproduction offer an unintended opportunity to see some underlying hues. Experience with this paperbound has shown, for instance, that on page 23, where General Border gives the order of "Ready! Aim!" youngsters can readily identify cyan and magenta exposed to the sides of his red-violet top feather, can find yellow and cyan that contribute to Private Parriage's green helmet decoration, and can discover in Major Scott's hat a most graphic example of the creation of brown—cyan, red-orange (magenta plus yellow), and green (yellow plus cyan), all evident to the sides of the intended brown of the hat! Very few and minor indeed are errors in printing to be found in the Prentice-Hall hardbound edition or in that publisher's Treehouse Paperbacks edition, but the latter edition is guilty of distorting colors, especially for the cannon's barrel, whose vivid blue-violet, olive green, cyan, and green become washed-out violet, yellow-green, tint of cyan, and even *brown*. The relative paleness of coloration in both the paperbound editions does lighten the hues for easier differentiation; for example, some youngsters do not notice the green star on the cannon's barrel in the hardbound edition but spot it in the paperback.

COLOR FOR IMPLIED TEXTURE, CONTOUR, AND DEPTH

The textural appearance of "FIRE!"—what touching the pages is *thought* to feel like—is above all else consistent in its implication of smoothness and hardness. With its repetition of brilliant hues—primaries yellow and cyan in the carriage and its wheels, and the tertiary red-orange of the speech balloon that seems as if it might even be hot to the touch—the implied texture in this illustration is one of colored glass or bits of glazed tile or semiprecious stones. No feathery feel here, no coarseness of grass, no softness of cloth, or velvety flower petals. Like the other pictures in *Drummer Hoff*, the impression is of bright jewels spread upon the page: all colors are set inside black lines, are straightforward and unsophisticated, with no shades or tints or changes in intensity.

At first glance, all figures appear to be paper-flat shapes that lie two-dimensionally on the surface; this is certainly true for instance in the case of the flowers. Black lines around a hue tend to intensify that color and heighten contrast by preventing one hue from "borrowing" the tone of a second. So the lines increase the colors' boldness, flatness, and two-dimensional quality. A pulsating or vibrating effect is created as attention jumps from form to form. Additional vibrancy is achieved by "backlighting" the scene in white, as if a strong light were directly behind the figures.

Only the slightest implication of contour exists, and this is found in the patternlike lines within the shapes themselves. The cannon and men have been broken down into their pieces by these contour lines that move inside the shapes to delineate folds and creases in pants, coats, and hats and to plot the workings of an apparently crazed gunmaker who fashioned this particular cannon. Occasionally more than one side of an object is implied, but no modelling exists to give any true three-dimensional effect. Still, the artistic intent has been to provide some semblance of shapes as other than mere silhouettes upon the page.

The only illusion of depth comes from the theatrical design throughout the book. The grassy "floor," blue endpaper "curtains," and bold white "backdrop" suggest compact, shallow depth as on a stage. Although Emberley positions the gun crew upstage before the command "FIRE!", sizes and brilliant hues of their figures imply no more depth than before. These clear, vibrant colors tell the audience quite plainly that little middle ground (and no background except for white "sky") exists, since none of the hues lose intensity, appear to recede, or become blurry as they would from a distance. If anything, the red-orange speech balloon visually projects toward the audience, an illogical illusion since the general would be the farthest character away. From this example, children can learn that color is perhaps the most dramatic element in such graphic arts as posters and advertisements as it calls attention to key words, ideas, or parts of an illustration. Emberley, who has a background in the commercial arts, wanted brilliant colors in *Drummer Hoff*, and his picture book has often been called the most radiant of the Caldecotts.

Art Appreciation of *The Rooster Crows*: Tone and Other Color Forms

Comparison of the jacket illustrations for *Drummer Hoff* and *The Rooster Crows* gives children an excellent opportunity to identify similar uses of primary colors for composition. In *The Rooster Crows*, the placement of red in the girl's shirt, blue in the boy's trousers, and bits of yellow in the hay above and below have visual attraction and lend a basic sense of color balance to the entire scene. And just as Emberley's secondary and tertiary hues were derivatives of the primary colors, so on close inspection can the brown of the Petershams' barn be discovered to have underlying red in dark shadows, occasionally orange for highlights, and a yellowish glow on the door. The green hay is pale yellow over which light strokes of blue have been applied in a methodical fashion. The barn's strong vertical visible lines lead our eyes downward, just as the girl's path of look and gesture indicates where the main point of interest is to be found in this picture—a brave fellow below who has indeed just taken quite a leap.

The nine full-color illustrations in *The Rooster Crows* present good examples of how the continuous-tone artwork afforded by lithography can simulate reality. The modeling of shapes and figures by gradations of hues implies contour and texture. The naturalistic distribution of shades and highlights implies some source of illumination for many scenes. This modeling, shading, and highlighting is achieved through use of lines both visible and invisible and through use of color *tone*.

Some children may readily discern that the red, yellow, and blue in the cover illustration for *The Rooster Crows* are not the same as the magenta, yellow, and cyan in *Drummer Hoff*. And indeed the Petershams' choices are not pure primaries but are instead tones of these same hues. They are used as the predominant colors throughout *The Rooster Crows*. Every hue has its tone, produced by mixing the hue with its complementary color, and every tone has its shade, produced by adding black, and its tint, containing white. The gradation of a hue from its tone into its tints or shades can subtly model a figure, for example in the illustration of the girl and the mountains in "I have a little sister" on page 37 of the hardbound. In this picture are no visible lines for the mountains as they stretch out "high, high, high"; rather, line effects are created as the cyan tone meets its tint or shade, the lighter or darker version of the same hue. The results lend contour to the mountains and shade those areas not highlighted by the moon shining overhead. The child's nightgown and even her hair are also modeled in this manner, with very little use of visible lines at all.

Gray is naturally created through a combination of black and white; it is seen in various gradations along with black and white themselves throughout *The Rooster Crows*, often with the striking addition of just one of the color tones. Since variations of gray contain the elements black and white, considered by artists to be lacking in hue as such, gray has come to be thought of as the antithesis of pure color; in fact, it seems to clash or appear garish when used with pure color. However, tones, tints, shades, grays, black, and white are called *color forms* and in combination may result in pleasing combinations. This effect is called the *harmony of color forms*. In addition to the full-color illustrations easily recognized for use of all these color forms, many of the other illustrations stand out for their creative use of a more limited selection, such as the shade of brown with black and gray in "Wake up, Jacob" on page 14 or with black and white in "Entry, kentry, cutry, corn" on page 47. Once the children begin to train their eyes to seek out such harmonies, they can better appreciate the tinting and shading of a single hue that implies contour and texture and lends a sense of balance when many other hues are used as well.

Sometimes one color form can be felt to control a picture's effect on the audience, as exampled by the still serenity unmistakable in "I see the moon" on page 29. A gentle wash of blue tint imposes a lovely sense of quiet as the entire scene is flooded with moonlight, an unearthly cast over wagons and canvas tops and the little girl's gown, face, and hair. Even the slight addition of pink has a blue tinge. This ability of a tint to envelop a scene with one pervading visual sensation is called the *harmony of a dominant tint*. A dominant tint draws all other colors or color forms together and mellows them. The Petershams use the technique most appropriately for several illustrations in *The Rooster Crows*.

In its use of the tonal qualities of color, *The Rooster Crows* offers children a dramatic comparison with *Drummer Hoff*. In *The Rooster Crows* a three-dimensional effect is achieved as rounded shapes gain contour and texture from softened lines and delicate color tones, tints, and shades. *Drummer Hoff* has flat, largely two-dimensional patterns of vibrant colors, a hard, gemlike texture, and bold black lines to provide what little contour there is.

Effects of Color

The bright colors and their arrangements in striking harmonies lend a festive, almost carnival air of fun to the activities portrayed in *Drummer Hoff*. This "group of happy warriors," as Emberley has said, is gathered onstage in brilliant array for the purpose of entertaining, and so they have and will yet for generations of children to come. The colors themselves are the main reason the book has succeeded as Emberley intended; the dour expressions and arrogant postures of the figures are no ingredients for a light-hearted tale. The fact that the cannon barrel is the only dark, heavy, and somber figure is no accident, since this malevolent thing is a tool of war and will make its presence known with unleashed fury in the end. Without the colors, *Drummer Hoff* would hardly be a happy little story at all.

Children enjoy the illustration "FIRE!" They tingle with anticipatory excitement as the command is finally given and find in this one picture the most glorious display of Emberley's colors all together. One is torn between wanting to linger awhile to take in the array and to turn the page fast to see just exactly what will happen. A great deal of children's delight in "KAHBAHBLOOOM" results not only from what *did* happen, but also from the outrageously gaudy primary, adjacent, and near-adjacent colors that blast off the pages to all sides. The courageous interplay among three color harmonies produces a resounding *boom*! for our eyes as well as our ears. Youngsters can tell there is violent force expended in this picture because as the flames and smoke spread and the cannonball is shot off the page, Drummer Hoff himself is precariously thrown to one side—the only instance in which this character is allowed to express through an invisible diagonal line that he can move at all. The fire-red glow of the magenta and red-orange envelops the whole scene, and, with the brilliant yellow, these colors appear to advance from the page, as warm colors are considered to do. The effect is dramatized by the only dark background in *Drummer Hoff*; the violet and cyan as cool colors appear to recede.

"KAHBAHBLOOOM" in the hands of another illustrator might have been a terrifying portrayal. But Emberley continues with his audacious, almost comical uses of colors. Children feel the sudden "noise" from the pages and experience a release from the restrictions of structured verse and art used up to then. They accept—as the artist intended—that "KAHBAHBLOOOM" is all in good fun. This larger-than-life composition bursting with energy can be compared in its effect on young audiences to the "wild rumpus" pages that likewise produce fits of giggles in Maurice Sendak's *Where the Wild Things Are*.

Use of color forms throughout *The Rooster Crows* elicits a quieter, calmer response, which is appropriate for a compilation of many rhymes, as opposed to a cumulative tale that builds to a climax as in *Drummer Hoff*. For children of today the book provides a glimpse into the past, not only because of its historical figures and scenes but also because of the illustrators' coloring itself. Some of this artwork can have an effect on the audience that may or may not have been intended by the Petershams forty years ago. For example, of the different color schemes used for major illustrations occupying half- or full-page layouts, the harmony of color forms in which tone of brown is combined with gray and black is by far the most common. The dominance of brown in these pictures is reminiscent of the daguerreotype, rather a dull color usage in a picture book even in the most pleasing compositions. In these cases, the activity depicted in the scene itself is usually all that truly engages the attention of modern-day young viewers accustomed to brighter hues. Of the illustrations in which blue plays a major role, by far the most effective still today are those that exhibit harmony of a dominant tint to create atmospheres for weeping Sally Waters, baby bunting wrapped up on a blue-cold frosty day, seeing the moon and the moon sees me, or climbing up the mountain high, high, high. Addition of red or green to combinations of blue and gray results in a bit more appeal for youngsters in illustrations that are less than full color.

The eight full-color pictures, however, have survived the years to remain understandably the most attractive to children of today. Whether of historical, commemorative, imaginative, or 1940s contemporary significance, each stands out in *The Rooster Crows* as a prime example of the Petershams' abilities to create exquisite tonal variations when, despite high costs of color reproduction in the forties, they were allowed to work with a full spectrum. Addition of green to the triadic harmony of magenta, cyan, and yellow tones along with black, gray, and brown lends just the right richness to the color scheme for such classic representational art from the period. Many children today react most favorably to this straightforward, simple, and idealized portrayal of color as well as of figure.

As a final observation, one cannot help noticing that, in all the full-color illustrations, important figures for storytelling purposes are colored red and blue, and an area of white space is always included to provide a pleasing contrast and sense of balance. Children now might not think this a particularly significant or intentional detail in picture composition until one turns to the book jacket design and points out also the frame of red, white, and blue that surrounds the "rooster crows" illustration. In the historical context given this book, the patriotic effect was surely not a total accident on the part of Maud and Miska Petersham in 1945.

For Further Study

1. Playing a simple game helps young children recognize basic primary colors of red, yellow, and blue. Assign as a first task that a child (or a group of children in a class) find in the room as many examples of red as possible; as a second task, another child is to find examples of yellow; and as a third task another child is to find examples of blue. Then look through magazines and packages of colored paper to find similar examples to cut out and glue onto oaktag to make three hue charts. Tones and different variations of hues become apparent as well as the ability of various textures (glossy magazine pages, rough fabric of a chair) to alter the appearance of a hue.

2. Many experiments in mixing red, yellow, and blue to achieve other hues can be tried, using crayons, watercolors, and felt-tip pens. Results will be differing and often frustrating. Truly the most successful of such experiments will be done with magenta for red and cyan for blue, as Emberley has done with his inks. His overprinting

process can be remarkably well duplicated using a sixteen-color watercolor tray that includes magenta and cyan or a tray that features these choices as primaries themselves, such as those produced by American Crayon (Prang) or Binney and Smith (Crayola). Keeping a container of water nearby for frequent brush cleaning, one can mix the watercolors right on the tray or on the paper itself to produce close likenesses of every hue in *Drummer Hoff*. For experimentation in creation of tones as in *The Rooster Crows*, one color is mixed with its complementary color; for making tints of pure colors or of tones, white is added, while for making shades, black is added.

3. Examples of kinds of color harmonies can be found in full-color pictures in both books. Have the children look across an illustration in search of only one color at a time, noting its frequency of occurrence. Next, have them refer to figure 1 in order to identify the triad, opposite, adjacent, or split complement of this color. Then ask them to find these color combinations in the picture.

To set up culminating experience in this study of color harmonies, a large piece of white paper can be laid out on the floor. Have the children take turns adding other pieces of paper that have been cut out in various sizes and shapes and that represent as many hues as desired. This composition should at first be formed by a random use of colored pieces, then rearranged into more thoughtful interplay of varied harmonies to produce an extravagant "symphony" of hues deemed most satisfying by the children themselves.

4. Designating color "temperatures" as warm or cool should be approached with caution, but to help children see the general idea behind colors' ability to affect us in this way, a good resource is a comparison of the advancing "warm" oranges and receding "cooler" greens in the jungle paintings of Henri Rousseau. Children can be encouraged then to take out their crayons or watercolors to create "hot," sunny, or explosive scenes with reds, oranges, and yellows, or "cold," rainy, or quiet scenes with violets, blues, and greens.

5. To expand color identification beyond the primary colors, have the children look around the room for secondary colors as well. Also make hue charts from orange, green, and violet found in magazines and construction paper. Many children will quickly realize that some colors remain in the room that have not been directly identified. These tertiary hues like yellow-green can be seen to belong to both yellow and green charts. Taking the hue charts outside to the parking lot, children have fun identifying colors and tones of cars. When time permits, youngsters can watch for the changes in

natural colors outdoors that occur during the morning, noon, and evening.

6. The concept of color mixing can also be reinforced by filling glass jars with water that has been colored to approximate the primary, secondary, and tertiary colors from any twelve-hued color wheel. As light shines through these twelve jars, they can be arranged to demonstrate various color harmonies, or they can be placed one behind another to show color mixing itself.

7. One of the more intriguing color exercises involves *afterimage*, the eye's tendency after long exposure to an intense color to see that color's opposite. Afterimage can be demonstrated using the illustration "FIRE!" Instruct the children to stare intently at one point in the red-orange speech balloon for several seconds, then blink their eyes as they look at blank white paper. A pale blue afterimage replaces the original red-orange, slowly for some children. Blue can be found on a color wheel opposite red-orange, and this afterimage can supplement a discussion of complementary hues.

8. The addition of black outlines around colors can best be demonstrated through an art project for young children in creating a "stained glass window." Have them cut an openwork design from black construction paper and fasten colored construction paper to the back of the black paper frame. Use colored cellophane or tissue paper if light is to shine through. An interesting variation of this project is to use white for the frame. Colors outlined in white tend to be lighter or less intense. This tendency for colors to diffuse when juxtaposed with white is called a *spreading effect*. Like afterimage, a spreading effect is purely a visual phenomenon but effective artists are aware of it. In contrast, the brilliance of Emberley's hues in *Drummer Hoff* can be attributed in large degree to his use of black outlines. Other demonstrations of color intensified by black outlining can be found in works by Fernand Léger, Georges Rouault, Pablo Picasso, and Paul Gauguin.

9. Other children's picture books with incidence of comical misfortune on the battlefield are *The Duck in the Gun* by Joy Cowley, in which a duck builds her nest in a general's only cannon, and *War and Peas* by Michael Foreman, in which a selfish king's army tanks plow a field where suddenly a neighboring country's crops begin to grow. Many children from an early age are interested in weapons, battles, and even military history, and for them some background about *Drummer Hoff* might be in order. For instance, the artist's choice of headgear and uniforms for the gun crew represents a variety of classic military wardrobe styles found around the globe since

the Middle Ages. Seven different styles of hats are seen; each have provided identification of rank and/or duties in the field. The bear-skin hat of Major Scott was once worn by French Grenadiers in Napoleon's army. The helmets and the conical and classic com-modore hats can be found in various military corps. The tricornered hat has been made famous to America's schoolchildren by pictures of George Washington and the Continental Army. Drummer Hoff's exotic, Arab-style "bloomers" are a direct reference to the pictur-esque "Zouave" trousers Emberley felt were appropriate for the servant of a cannon the artist had chosen to name "SULTAN." As late as the American Civil War this distinctive Oriental uniform was popular, states Emberley. "A number of Zouave-uniformed units joined the Northern cause dressed in bloomers, short jackets, and little pillbox caps (perhaps even fezzes)."

Children's appreciation for historical detail in *Drummer Hoff* can be enhanced by looking through such books as *Warriors in Art* by Nancy Forte. The intricate design of metalwork on the cannon raises the interesting historical note that some of the first cannonmakers had originally been bellmakers, and so cannons were often as ornate as church bells. (This is also an early example of career change due to advances in technology.) The sun motif Emberley placed on the cannon's carriage was a deliberate reference, verified by the artist himself, to the French royal foundry at Tours, where the gunmakers often embellished their work with the flaming-sun insignia of the French royal family. As to the cannon's name, "SULTAN," which is throughout *Drummer Hoff* an intriguing point of interest, Emberley states that the word "merely seemed the sort of grand impressive name that could be assigned to a mighty cannon (so much better than 'BUTTERCUP' or 'FRED')." In the history of military hardware, many pieces of ordnance have been given such dignified names. For example, the seige guns "Peter" and "Paul" on display in the Krem-lin were named after the princes of Moscow, and the field gun "Napoleon" was used by the U.S. Army until the 1880s.

Cannons as seige guns have always been assembled, it seems, on the field. Often twenty horses (unseen in *Drummer Hoff*) were required to move the barrel alone as one load on a wagon. Then the firing carriage was sometimes delivered as a second load (hardly pushed by one private). Both were then delivered using a simple crane (obviously under the command here of Corporal Farrell). Such seige guns as Emberley has illustrated were used in military cam-paigns until they were destroyed or so worn they could no longer fire. In either case they were abandoned on the field as in *Drummer*

Hoff, and pieces perhaps might be gathered up, remelted, and cast into a new cannon for some future campaign. So might the battle be over but wars continue.

These historical footnotes can be important as reinforcement for the fact that, despite Emberley's cartoonlike style and artistic sense of outrageous fun, the setting for *Drummer Hoff* is indeed the real world. Sad but true, wars and battles exist in other than a child's make-believe realm of fantasy.

10. Emberley himself suggests that a worthwhile classroom project would be to proceed from research into the backgrounds of other objects given names, such as "Big Ben" and "Big Bertha," into the naming of things like boats or ships, summer homes or camps, that the children themselves choose to draw. This naming he considers an interesting assignment because "having named a number of boats of our own, I have noticed that a name cannot only describe the 'personality' but can also *create* the 'personality' of an inanimate object." A most striking example of this phenomena would be the personification of "Hal" the computer in the classic film *2001: A Space Odyssey*.

11. Few elementary-age youngsters have the manual dexterity required for fashioning figures by woodcuts as the artist in *Drummer Hoff* has done, but some of them might be satisfied with experiments in linoleum-block printing. A reversed image is traced from paper onto a linoleum block, the background area is cut away as in woodcuts, and ink is rolled across the raised design on the block. To avoid the need for using any cutting tools, an even simpler kind of block printing can be accomplished by gluing design shapes from chipboard onto a larger piece of board, then rolling the ink onto the raised shapes. Styrofoam meat trays from the supermarket can also be used satisfactorily to demonstrate the idea of block printing. Pressing firmly with pencil or ballpoint pen into the Styrofoam makes the background for a design or simple drawing, and the raised area is then rolled with ink for printing. Or to make the reverse (background inked and design or drawing white), simply draw firmly with the pen or pencil, then roll with ink to print.

12. Students enjoy looking through different Mother Goose books to note in what ways the same rhyme has been illustrated by such divergent artists as Kate Greenaway, Arthur Rackham, Gyo Fujikawa, Raymond Briggs, and other Caldecott Medalists Barbara Cooney, Feodor Rojankovsky, and Berta and Elmer Hader. Several nursery-rhyme collections have been named Caldecott Honor Book

selections, including those by Tasha Tudor in 1945, Marjorie Torrey in 1946, Marguerite de Angeli in 1955, and Phillip Reed in 1964.

For background to many rhymes in *The Rooster Crows*, refer to *The Annotated Mother Goose*, and for other American rhymes, turn to Ray Wood's collection with foreword by John A. Lomax. John and Carol Langstaff have collected today's city children's street games and calling-out rhymes in their book with photographs, *Shimmy Shimmy Coke-Ca-Pop!*, which interestingly enough has a new version for "Engine, engine, number nine" found in *The Rooster Crows*.

Looking Back, Looking Ahead: Line, Light and Dark, Shape, Space

Visible line effects play a major part in modeling, contouring, and shading of figures in *The Rooster Crows*, as has been pointed out in our discussion of color tones and their tints and shades. Outlines for figures are also noted, within which hues and all their subtleties have been added. Invisible lines for composition present an interesting and revealing study into the formality with which the Petershams viewed many of their subjects in illustrations for the rhymes. A static and posed attitude seems to have been felt appropriate for almost two dozen characters depicting certain rhymes, as evidenced by the characters' flat-footed vertical stances, most often right in the center of the field of action. Note the staunch vertical postures of groups of children in "One, potato" and "All around the buttercup" for instance, and then turn to other rhymes such as "Lady bug," "Star bright," "Red at night," and a dozen others to see the same postures. A few illustrations are composed with invisible diagonal lines to imply more action, such as "How much wood would a woodchuck chuck" and "I climbed up an apple tree," and some have a circular structure, such as "This little pig" and "Ring around a' rosies." All in all, there is enough variety to capture children's attention.

All colors in the illustration "FIRE!" in *Drummer Hoff* are confined by visible edge lines. Patterns of contour lines are uniformly bold and continuous but diverse in direction and angle. Colors rather than lines are seen to balance this picture, as the underlying forcefulness of certain color harmonies draws the audience's attention from left to right across the double spread. But this side-to-side visual reaction to the presentation results also from the artist's use of horizontal visible lines as a base and horizontal placement of one character beside another. The staunch vertical posture of Drummer Hoff to the right, as in many other illustrations in the book, makes us pause before we turn the page.

Visible lines go off in every direction in "KAHBAHBLOOOM," unable finally to confine the explosive colors as the fire and smoke expand every which way off the pages. Bold, continuous lines all of the same width make geometric patterns for tongues of flame, swirls and knots of smoke, just as they have patterned the cannon and Drummer Hoff and all the soldiers that have gone before. Use of black for all patterning lines provides stronger contrast among the bright colors, similar to the effect of mosaic decoration or stained glass.

Edge lines and configurations of lines within shapes were achieved by a woodcut technique reminiscent of early book illustrations. After drawing the pictures onto ordinary pine boards from the lumber yard, Emberley explains, "all the white areas were cut away, ink was rolled on the remaining raised areas, and a set of prints was pulled on rice paper." When asked why he didn't use a faster method like pen and ink, Emberley replied that the reason "is hard to explain in a few words, but I suppose the most important reasons are that the picture looked better and the method pleased me." He has often varied his style in books to make sure the technique suits the text and is experienced with pencil, felt-tipped pen, crow quill, photography, printing by offset and letterpress, and hand lettering, in addition to the woodcuts used for several of his books. In the woodcut technique for *Drummer Hoff*, outlines around the colors result in illustrations not properly thought of as paintings.

"KAHBAHBLOOOM" is dominated by bombastic lines rather than the horizontal, stable baseline of grass, which here is barely visible. But Emberley has not abandoned his invisible horizontal structure, for the cannon's blast is forcefully directed from right to left, and the horizontal is accentuated by not only the letters of the sound-word "KAHBAHBLOOOM" lined up in strictest order but also by the cannon shot as it leaves the field. Ascending smoke and the posture of the drummer are on the diagonal, leaving not a single vertical line as stabilizing influence on this dynamic scene.

Spatial orientation in all of *Drummer Hoff* has been described as the shallow depth of a theater's stage, accomplished by orientation for objects along an edge line likened somewhat to children's own use of a baseline in drawing. The naive appeal of *Drummer Hoff's* flat figures against a flat background spans the centuries, as witnessed by wall paintings from 1400 B.C., fifteenth-century frescoes, and work of cubists in this century. This perspective is based on shallow planes for figures, broken down into their pieces, with no vanishing point for lines to create any illusion of deep space.

In all illustrations except "KAHBAHBLOOOM" the white of the page serves as light background that gives an open, sunlit appearance to the scenes as the soldiers build the cannon piece by piece. In "KAHBAHBLOOOM," however, the brilliance of red-orange and magenta advances toward the audience just as the smoke and flame would seem to do, while dark violet against farthest background of cyan recedes to create more implication of deep space than was found in pages with white sky. Space to left and right on previous pages has always been alluded to by the horizontal baseline, but in "KAHBAHBLOOOM" the fiery blast extends not only to the sides but also up, down, and even off the stage toward us. Most assuredly this is the absolute core of activity, but it is also part of a much larger scene.

The geometric shapes in *Drummer Hoff*, each one broken down into its planar parts that imply a modicum of contouring, can also be appreciated as being rooted deeply in art traditions of the past. For example, ancient Mexican masks of wood decorated with turquoise, colored shells, and corals, or the highly stylized patterns on ceremonial shirts of the northwest coast American Indians demonstrate such use of mosaic patterns of lines. Simplified shapes made from triangles, circles, and rectangles are perhaps best explained by Emberley himself in his own series of drawing books, almost a dozen titles found in most media centers and bookstores. Emberley has also experimented with drawing on an Apple computer using the KoalaPad Touch Tablet and Micro Illustrator software, demonstrating that his well-known techniques are remarkably suited to computer graphics as well.

By the time the viewer reaches the illustration "FIRE!" shapes of the cannon, General Border and all his men—especially Drummer Hoff—are very familiar and known to remain unchanged throughout the story. And in "KAHBAHBLOOOM" this predictability of shape is very important, for in the wild explosion the recognizable figures of Drummer Hoff and the cannon are all that anchor the scene on the page. They remain seemingly as stolid and unmoved as ever despite the destruction they have caused, a slight tilt in the drummer's stance the only hint that he is shaken a bit. Their size and mosaic design give weight on the right page needed to balance the unleashed fury on the left. The audience knows them to be the main characters, after all, in this little drama, and their figures are as familiar signposts in an unfamiliar land.

Idealized shapes in *The Rooster Crows* present a romanticized notion of perfect American children from the colonial past up to the 1940s, when the book was published. Except for fantasy illustrations with pigs, bears, rabbits, and even some angels, all in idealized proportions, the book could be seen as a representational portrayal of an ideal United States. A sense of depth is accomplished in many of the full-page illustrations, while shallow space creates a cozy closeness in partial-page pictures, and there is no semblance of depth at all in decorative vignettes around some rhymes. Interest in a source of illumination is demonstrated by formal motifs for sun and stars in several illustrations, and hauntingly lovely are the pictures in which the harmony of a dominant tint bathes the scenes in blue- or gray-tinted moonlight.

Looking Around: *May I Bring a Friend?; Madeline's Rescue; Finders Keepers; Chanticleer and the Fox; Cinderella; Many Moons; Song of the Swallows*

All but a handful of books in the Caldecott collection are in color, and any of the color illustrations could be studied for identification of hues, types of color harmonies, illustrators' intended effects on the audience, and differences in quality of color reproduction over the years. Only a few of the Award-winning titles have been selected for discussion; they exemplify illustrators who use color as an artistic element in book design itself, whose books would not have had the same effect if other color choices had been made, or whose work further demonstrates concepts introduced in *Drummer Hoff* and *The Rooster Crows*.

Emphasis on color as an artistic element can be seen most dramatically in *May I Bring a Friend?*, the 1966 Award winner written by Beatrice Schenk de Regniers and illustrated by Beni Montresor. Montresor came to the United States from Italy in 1960 as a set designer in film and theater. In *A Friend* he brought to picture-book design the magic and glitter of a full-fledged stage production of fantasy: costumes, sets, scenes, lights, and implied action, all emphasized by choices of colors in theatrical page layouts. Alternating pages present a simple patterned rhyme about a boy who visited a king and queen each day of the week; the royal couple's invitations in the text are each time illustrated in black-and-white vignettes set like minor scenes before the curtain on a stage's apron. Each of the boy's arrivals at court is pictured on double-page spreads in vivid full color as if the curtain were opened wide to reveal different sets inside and outside the castle. All the boy's unorthodox friends entertain their royal hosts in black line drawings on single pages with backgrounds of solid pink, yellow, or orange, just as if the scenes were theatrically spotlighted through colored filters. Colors and tones used throughout are predominantly warm hues created by use of primary yellow, pink (light primary magenta), orange (pink and yellow combined), and black, all controlled by acetate overlays in printing, and the pulsating vibrancy and gaudy interplay of adjacent and opposite harmonies in *A Friend* result in an artistic celebration of color itself.

More flexibility in book design and less monotony of rhyming text are evident in an earlier Caldecott-winning title by an author/ illustrator who also demonstrated a preoccupation with color, artist Ludwig Bemelmans, in *Madeline's Rescue*. Here also are alternated full-color illustrations with black line drawings on a yellow field of action bordered in white, but there is no consistent pattern in use of one over another except a rhythm dictated by Bemelmans himself. Bemelmans was Austrian by birth and American by citizenship but Parisian by artistic influence, a self-styled gypsy who professed to know no ordinary people, a painter and writer whose works were colorful transformations of characters, events, and architecture found wherever he went. All these facets of the man came together in 1940 Honor Book *Madeline* and again in 1954 Medal-winning *Madeline's Rescue*, suggested by daughters of American writer Phyllis McGinley as a sequel. The project sent Bemelmans back to Paris to find a dog and a plot. As he painted along the Seine one day, a dog retrieved an artificial leg floating down the river, inspiring the story line and the first few illustrations in *Rescue*. In the Fauvist tradition of crude and impulsively bright colors by such turn-of-the-century artists as Maurice de Vlaminck and André Derain, Bemelmans's river Seine is bright yellow or dull green or even red (on the cover of early editions), and his sun-drenched sky in the first watercolor paintings is likewise red or yellow. Later full-color illustrations of Parisian scenes exhibit the same use of vigorous drawn line added to paintings or bold line effects of colors red, yellow, blue, and green. Compositionally these street scenes demonstrate influence as well from

Impressionists such as Camille Pissarro, who also evoked the city's quiet lanes and bustling boulevards in many of his paintings.

No other Caldecott Award-winning artist used color in quite the same expressive way for intended effects on an audience as did Nicolas Mordvinoff in the 1952 selection *Finders Keepers*. From sinister outlines of ghostlike figures on a black double-spread title page to a skull motif on the back of the book's blood-red jacket, the artwork throughout *Finders Keepers* conveys an appropriate artistic message that the book should not be viewed superficially as another cute or funny dog story for children. Will Lipkind's text about Nap and Winkle and their dispute over a bone is a tale of ignorance and selfishness that leads to trickery, greed, and violence through a series of events that is reminiscent of fairy tales of old but disturbing in a twentieth-century fantasy. *Finders Keepers* is commendable only if Mordvinoff's art is fully appreciated as intentionally fostering a negative attitude toward what is, after all, a very ugly story. Heavy use of black is combined oppressively with feverish red and dull ocher (earthy yellow), the latter two used more often for backgrounds than is the white of a page itself. In several illustrations a red road appears as a river of blood, and red is also used like woodcut texturing for bloody horns, bodies, and clothes. This necessarily grim interpretation of *Finders Keepers* is supported by grotesquery of figures, use of hierarchical proportions for menacing characters, the repeated savagery with which the dogs are twice pictured biting and slashing Longshanks at the end, and the chaos underlying the entire book design with its crude page layouts, various sizes of illustrations, and differing audience viewpoints.

Mordvinoff left his native Russia as a child to escape the violence of the Russian Revolution. Later, like Paul Gauguin, he studied in Paris before living in Tahiti for many years. His picture-book art after coming to America was aggressive and uncompromising. His 1951 Honor Book *The Two Reds*, for example, was characterized by use of color and form as expressions of experiences in themselves, much like the work of fine artists Vincent Van Gogh and Ernst Ludwig Kirchner. Mordvinoff's first love as a young man had been for horses, and he often rushed home to draw them after watching them on the streets of Paris. Perhaps it is no coincidence that the only illustration in *Finders Keepers* with compositional grace and lightheartedness pictures a farmer's horse-drawn cart.

The same red, ocher, and black that Mordvinoff used so somberly combine quite cheerfully with brilliant cobalt blue, vivid green, and rich red-brown in varying harmonious combinations by Barbara

Cooney in the first of her two Award winners, the 1959 *Chanticleer and the Fox*. Once again an alternating system was devised for book design, this time with black-and-red illustrations interspersed with five-color pages. In fact *Chanticleer* exhibits the most artful of all such systems discussed here and also has some of the best total page design among all the Caldecotts. Double-page spreads sensitively accommodate informal text placement, and color is used to best advantage as a point of interest and as a balancing element in itself, especially when only red is used with black for moments of danger in the story. Cooney's crisp style is reminiscent of decorative folk art that includes the right amount of detail in costumes, household, and plants. In addition, all these elements were researched and are correct for a fourteenth-century English setting of a story that is an adaptation of Chaucer's "The Nun's Priest's Tale" from *The Canterbury Tales*. The necessary formality of text makes *Chanticleer* usually more successful with an older picture-book audience. It is interesting, though, that this morality tale dating back to Aesop is often given a modern-day interpretation by even the youngest children, who often see it as a kidnapping or child-molesting fable.

Award winners *Many Moons* (1944) and *Cinderella: Or the Little Glass Slipper* (1955) are more correctly thought of as illustrated storybooks with pictures by Louis Slobodkin and Marcia Brown, respectively. *Cinderella* by Charles Perrault is probably the most beloved age-old fairy tale; comparing it with *Many Moons*, a tale written in the twentieth century by American adult humorist James Thurber, offers an interesting study not only in the use of color but also in the subtlety with which the genre itself can be used. For instance, fairy tales traditionally establish good versus bad characters. We assuredly recognized these types in sweet Cinderella and her mean stepsisters. In *Many Moons* they are modified as spoiled Lenore versus only foolish wise men. Fairy tales tend to employ repetition by threes. Three adversaries are foiled by Cinderella's fairy godmother's gift of three things; *Many Moons* has only three foolish opinions about the moon and three even funnier suggestions about how to hide it. The feats of magic common in fairy tales are incredibly real in *Cinderella* but only incredibly clever in *Many Moons*. Illustratively, both books are dated by the artistic mannerisms of their times: a highly ornamental style popular in the 1940s graces *Many Moons*, and a frivolous and frothy style considered appropriately French is used by Brown in *Cinderella*. However, both books graphically support basic uses of primaries magenta, cyan, and yellow. Bedroom and staircase scenes from both are also alike with their simple lines and colors that define familiar shapes and give a satisfying closeness of shallow space or expanse of deep space.

Slobodkin, who was illustrator for Eleanor Estes's 1940s Moffats series, worked on *Many Moons* without contact with Thurber. He imagined palace, king, and little princess as he thought they would be envisioned by a child uncontaminated by preconceptions. Unintentionally, he added to what has become an overburdened storehouse of visual stereotypes. For six out of seven years preceding *Cinderella*, Brown had titles chosen as Caldecott Honor Books: *Stone Soup, Henry-Fisherman, Dick Whittington and His Cat, Skipper John's Cook, Puss in Boots,* and *The Steadfast Tin Soldier,* most of which have not been as frequently illustrated and offer more unique experiences in art appreciation than the artist's Caldecott Medalist itself.

A title that children enjoy comparing to *Many Moons* is Theodor Geisel's *Bartholomew and the Oobleck,* one of several 1950 Honor Books the year Leo Politi won the Medal for *Song of the Swallows.* Politi himself had twice before received Honor Book awards, for *Pedro, the Angel of Olvera Street* in 1947 and *Juanita* in 1949. Over many years he would continue to contribute illustrations that repeat similar artistic elements for characterization or plot. Typically, small Latin American children involved in traditional activities gave color and charm to customs of the past, and simple images were lovingly rendered of animals, birds, and flowers as the earthy things of life. Little Juan and his experiences with old Julian at California's Mission San Juan Capistrano in *Swallows* is an excellent example. *Swallows* is an illustrated storybook with overlong text for a picture book, but the soft, warm earth tones in Politi's illustrations provide lasting impressions of a boy, an old man, and an even older mission where twice each year occurs the miracle of the swallows.

Works Cited

Andersen, Hans Christian. *The Steadfast Tin Soldier.* New York: Scribner, 1953.

Baring-Gould, William S., and Ceil Baring-Gould. *The Annotated Mother Goose.* New York: New American Library, 1962.

Bemelmans, Ludwig. *Madeline.* New York: Viking, 1939.

———. *Madeline's Rescue.* New York: Viking, 1953.

Bettelheim, Bruno. *The Uses of Enchantment: The Meaning and Importance of Fairy Tales.* New York: Knopf, 1976.

Brown, Marcia. *Cinderella: Or the Little Glass Slipper.* New York: Scribner, 1954.

——. *Dick Whittington and His Cat.* New York: Scribner, 1950.

——. *Henry-Fisherman.* New York: Scribner, 1949.

——. *Puss in Boots.* New York: Scribner, 1952.

——. *Skipper John's Cook.* New York: Scribner, 1951.

——. *Stone Soup.* New York: Scribner, 1947.

Clark, Margery. *Poppy Seed Cakes.* New York: Doubleday, 1924.

Cooney, Barbara. *Chanticleer and the Fox.* New York: Crowell, 1958.

Cowley, Joy. *The Duck in the Gun.* New York: Doubleday, 1969.

de Regniers, Beatrice Schenk. *May I Bring a Friend?* New York: Atheneum, 1965.

Emberley, Barbara. *Drummer Hoff.* Englewood Cliffs, N.J.: Prentice-Hall, 1967.

Emberley, Ed. *Green Says Go.* Boston: Little, 1968.

——. *One Wide River to Cross.* Englewood Cliffs, N.J.: Prentice-Hall, 1966.

——. *The Wing on a Flea: A Book about Shapes.* Boston: Little, 1961.

Estes, Eleanor. *The Moffats* and other titles. NewYork: Harcourt, 1968– .

Foreman, Michael. *War and Peas.* New York: Crowell, 1974.

Forte, Nancy. *Warriors in Art.* Minneapolis: Lerner, 1966.

Geisel, Theodor S. *Bartholomew and the Oobleck.* New York: Random, 1949.

Ireson, Barbara, ed. *The Barnes Book of Nursery Verse.* New York: Barnes, 1960.

Langstaff, John, and Carol Langstaff. *Shimmy Shimmy Coke-Ca-Pop!* New York: Doubleday, 1973.

Lipkind, William. *Finders Keepers.* New York: Harcourt, 1951.

——. *The Two Reds.* New York: Harcourt, 1950.

Petersham, Maud, and Miska Petersham. *An American ABC.* New York: Macmillan, 1941.

——. *The Box with Red Wheels.* New York: Macmillan,1949.

——. *The Circus Baby.* New York: Macmillan, 1950.

——. *Miki.* New York: Doubleday, 1929.

——. *The Rooster Crows.* New York: Macmillan, 1945.

——. *The Story of One Hundred Years of U.S. Postage Stamps.* New York: Macmillan, 1947.

Politi, Leo. *Juanita.* New York: Scribner, 1948.

——. *Pedro, the Angel of Olvera Street.* New York: Scribner, 1946.

——. *Song of the Swallow.* New York: Scribner, 1949.

Sendak, Maurice. *Where the Wild Things Are.* New York: Harper, 1963.

Thurber, James. *Many Moons.* New York: Harcourt, 1943.

Wood, Ray. *The American Mother Goose.* Philadelphia: Lippincott, 1938.

——. *Fun in American Folk Rhymes.* Philadelphia: Lippincott, 1952.

4

Light and Dark: *The Little House, Where the Wild Things Are,* and *Jumanji*

The transformation of peaceful countryside into urban sprawl in *The Little House* by Virginia Lee Burton is as timely a theme for children today as when the book won the Caldecott Award in 1943. More than two decades later, in 1964, another winner featured a different sort of transfiguration: in Maurice Sendak's illustrations for *Where the Wild Things Are*, a boy's room changed into a forest with an ocean tumbling. And almost another twenty years later, in 1981, Chris Van Allsburg's Caldecott winner *Jumanji* transformed two children's boring afternoon at home into a bizarre adventure some might call a nightmare.

Virginia Lee Burton

Virginia Lee Burton is recognized as one of the great American designers of picture books, an artist who considered placement of both text and illustration to be crucial to the book as a whole. Specially shaped areas for typesetting were balanced with different sizes of illustrations on single pages, double-page spreads, decorative borders, and endpapers. Even inobtrusive placement of page numbers played a role in her books.

With publication in 1939 of *Mike Mulligan and His Steam Shovel*, and three years later *The Little House*, she demonstrated her insistence on tight control over length and placement of text. As she herself once said, as "illustrator/author" she was more deeply interested in the pictures than in the text. That the latter must complement the former is exemplified in Burton's full-page shaped text on page 37[1] of *The Little House*, where meandering indentations for the lovely prose poem correspond in shape as well as content with the long journey along winding road in the illustration on the opposite page. Original printer's dummies for *The Little House* show that text was cut out as a shaped block and placed precisely in its designated area on each page. Similarly, the halolike arches of sky in the pictures were painted separately, cut out, and imposed upon the field of action.

Burton also excelled in clarity of detail that delights young children, as witnessed recently by one preschooler's discovery in *The Little House* of a favorite Burton motif—what she called the "Swing Tree." Early in the book the child noticed to the right of the house an apple tree that had a swing attached to a limb; although the swing and tree itself both disappear during the city scenes, the swing reappears attached to another tree on the left in an illustration near the end of the story. "Things are fun again," explained the child with satisfaction, testifying that this bit of detail contributed as much to her understanding of the story as did the text recited to her during story time.

The "Swing Tree" can lead children to the pleasant discovery that the family pictured in the last daytime scene is Burton's own family: she often said that inspiration for her books came from her own family and friends. The children playing in the trees at the end of *The Little House* are Burton's sons, Aris (short for Aristides, her older son who became a sculptor) and Michael (the model for the little boy in *Mike Mulligan and His Steam Shovel*). She wrote the story for them when they were in the picture-book age. Pushing the lawn-mower is her husband, George Demetrios, reknowned sculptor and teacher of life drawing, first at the Boston Museum of Fine Arts School and later at his own studio, and of course seated beneath the tree is Burton herself, holding a drawing tablet.

It is well known that the idea for *The Little House* came from the family's experience of moving its own house from its position near the street to a more congenial spot "in the middle of a field with apple trees growing around." The house in the book has an overly simplified shape, but the orchard, meadow, woods, and brook clearly reflect the actual appearance of the land around the Demetrios home, situated with curved driveway and fenced barnyard in the area of Folly Cove in the seaside city of Gloucester, Massachusetts. Burton's studio was also on the premises, and there she

---

[1]*The Little House* has its own pagination, which will be used here.

worked tirelessly on her illustrations for children's books and also taught her own theories of design in the art of linoleum-block printing. Her students became known as the Folly Cove Designers, a group that began by designing block printings for fabric and wallpaper used in their own homes. Later, they opened a shop offering hand-printed textiles and exhibited their work at the Cape Ann Historical Association in Gloucester. Burton's other work was influenced by this experience in design. Textiles and block printing emphasize pattern, repetition, decorative shapes, and the spacing of areas into parts; this interest may be detected in Burton's picture books and illustrated storybooks, including the 1948 Caldecott Honor Book *Song of Robin Hood*. Her painting style might be likened to early-nineteenth-century naive painting, such as that of Henri Rousseau, who deviated from visual realism in order to present a more arresting, simplified image than was then offered by academic painting.

One of Burton's favorite decorative motifs, the "Swing Tree" seen in *The Little House*, showed up in other books and block prints; once she even reproduced the pattern repeatedly in her living-room curtains. Of almost thirty carved designs she perfected, she chose the "Swing Tree" as her theme for a Horn Book Calendar in 1965, three years before she died. The smiling sun was also a much-used motif and offered testimony that Burton as illustrator/storyteller was comfortable with simple symbolic representations in her work. She often chose the personifications of inanimate objects for her characters. For example, the little house "who watched and wondered" in the country was later "very sad and lonely" by herself in the city. Burton herself described the impetus for her books in an autobiographical sketch in *Illustrators of Children's Books: 1946–1956* (Viguers et al.):

> An engine on the Gloucester Branch of the Boston & Maine is the heroine of *Choo Choo*. "Mary Ann," Mike Mulligan's steam shovel, I found digging the cellar of the new Gloucester High School. *The Little House* was inspired by the moving of our own house . . . and Katy (of *Katy and the Big Snow*) is the pride and joy of the Gloucester Highway Department . . . . *Maybelle, the Cable Car* I did in memory of my own childhood and love of San Francisco.

By giving objects magical gifts of speech and emotions, Burton turned real encounters of her life into gentle fantasies in which impossible things happened. The active fantasy life of young children makes them a most receptive audience for the imagined inner spirits of a steam shovel, a train engine, a cable streetcar, a snow-plow, or a little house who could "settle down on her new foundation [and] smile happily." This appeal to the child's imagination ("What if *my* house could talk?" or "What if ordinary things are not as they seem?") couched within simple ideas in Burton's books makes the world of the impossible come alive for children. At the heart of the charm of *The Little House* lies both artistic sensitivity to children's book design and the breath of life given the house itself.

Maurice Sendak

The potential for charm was on the other hand hotly contested in literary circles twenty years later, when Maurice Sendak's Caldecott winner *Where the Wild Things Are* upended many notions about children's sensibilities. Controversy surrounded the two questions of whether Sendak should have portrayed monsters—one reviewer said he would not like to have the book left about where a sensitive child might find it to pore over in the twilight—and whether he should have depicted Max's behavior as so uncivilized—"Sendak's books have no room for the tidy, the obedient, the adorable . . . . Max indulges his fury at being punished with an anarchic fantasy," reported another source. The author-illustrator replied that children sent him "their own drawings of Wild Things: monstrous, hair-raising visions . . . [that] make my Wild Things look like cuddly fuzzballs," and that only through fantasy could Max vent his anger before returning "to the real world sleepy, hungry, and at peace with himself." But decades later, the controversy persists: some primary-grade teachers still do not want the book in their classroom.

Sendak's portrayal of an unreal world of wild jungle fantasy has been said to have changed the way the real world of childhood is viewed by adults. *Wild Things* stands unique in its time for appealing to more sophisticated sensibilities in children, whom Sendak felt to have a higher level of appreciation for complexity in plot and in art than was then explored in picture books. Before this the status quo in children's literature had stressed prettiness, wholesome attitudes, gently decorous humor, and a strong reliance on adult authority—"the great nineteenth-century fantasy that paints childhood as an eternally innocent paradise," as Sendak put it. Sendak had begun to break with this prevalent view in earlier illustrations for titles by Ruth Krauss: *A Hole Is to Dig* and *I'll Be You and You Be*

Me, which presented children having day-to-day problems. In *Wild Things*, he said, many of his ideas finally came together as one.

For the most part, children themselves have accepted Sendak's deviation from the picture-book norm with glee. Many adults in 1963, and indeed a few today, simply could not and cannot share the children's positive reaction toward Max's problems. Another reviewer's tongue-in-cheek note perhaps sums up the ongoing differences of opinion about *Wild Things*: "Boys and girls may have to shield their parents from this book. Parents are very easily scared."

Worldwide recognition has most certainly come to Sendak, the first American recipient of the Hans Christian Andersen Illustrators Award in 1970 and the 1983 recipient of the Laura Ingalls Wilder Award for his overall contribution to children's literature. He has illustrated seven Caldecott Honor Books: *A Very Special House; What Do You Say, Dear?; Moon Jumpers; Little Bear's Visit; Mr. Rabbit and the Lovely Present; In the Night Kitchen;* and *Outside Over There.* The last two along with *Wild Things* make up the Sendak trilogy about "how children master feelings and come to grips with the realities of their lives." This illustrator of some seventy titles is often thought of in a category by himself as a mad genius or eccentric visionary. Whatever Sendak himself thinks of such quaint praise, the children surely consider it rubbish, for most of them have welcomed this eccentric as one of their own. After all, he gives them his best and they think—as he does—that they deserve it.

If there are truths about childhood in *Wild Things*, then what might those truths be, and how has Sendak presented them in his artistic vision for young children? The truths are quite simple ones: primary-age youngsters are intellectually intrigued by creatures from the wild, are fascinated by dinosaur and monster books, and often develop an early interest in exotic environments unlike their own. Socially they set a great deal of store in surprises, birthday wishes, and daydreams that hold heartfelt hope for their own lives. They enjoy games, like to win, and to be boss. They can be sassy and become resentful over imagined injustice when punished. They need love and security but often don't show it. Most play "pretend"—not always wild or scary pretending, but if someone else's pretending isn't as interesting as their own would be, they can get bored. In case this paints too sweet a picture of childhood, it is also important to point out that these same children can ruthlessly break all the rules to win, boss siblings and pets to the breaking point, throw red-faced tantrums when punished, scare each other so badly that nightmares develop, act most unlovably in a crowded supermarket, and if *too* bored, have been known to amuse themselves with peeling off wallpaper. In short, children are not little adults, but like home-made wine, most improve with age.

Little wonder, then, that so many of these normal children have loved *Wild Things* in much the same way that they love Halloween night. Sendak's book relates directly to the good and the bad, the comfortable and the scary, the known and the unknown, the realities and the fantasies they have experienced in their own lives. Since the book appeared, children's picture books and Saturday morning TV cartoons have become more flamboyant, even surrealistic, so that today's children are not nearly as impressed by the illustrator's monsters and Max's behavior as were children in the 1960s. In fact many youngsters today do not think of the Wild Things as really fearsome at all but instead rather homely, absurd in a couple of instances, and downright pathetic when unloved and left behind.

However, *Wild Things* is one of the few titles still remembered by young adults who were elementary-school children when the book first appeared. They remember because the Wild Things were indeed scary in 1963 and were unheard of in their other books. Sendak gave form to the nightmarish unknown these young people recall being frightened of: there were "The Monsters," and if "They" were pictured in a book, then just maybe other people thought about "Them" too, and perhaps "They" need not be so feared. After all, as naughty as Max was, he did have the bravery to stand up to "Their" bluff and win as "boss of Them All." People in their twenties may articulate for us what children have been trying to tell us all along but have lacked the vocabulary to express: *Wild Things* in a very real way assuages childhood's fears and pains by labeling as universal the inner monster we all have known, a monster that must be controlled if we are to survive emotionally.

Sendak himself has described how his book ideas came about. As a young man in Brooklyn he spent hours at his apartment window, filling notebooks with sketches as he watched children at play. These sketches later showed up in his illustrations for fantasy worlds like that in *Wild Things*. The author/illustrator now feels that his art has roots in his own childhood, when a long series of illnesses overalarmed his mother, who kept him in bed. During this time his father told beautiful, imaginative tales from his homeland in Poland that brought alive the rich past of the Old World to Sendak, his brother Jack, and his sister Natalie. "I think I had to find self-reliance at an earlier age . . . isolated from other children . . . . It stimulated being an artist," Sendak has said.

Schooling was a miserable experience for the young artist; so he did not continue after high school, working instead at designing window displays and attending the Art Students League in New York. "There was no question as to my profession . . . . I wanted to be an illustrator very early in my life . . . to make books. . . . Feelings come to me, and then I must rush to put them down . . . build a house around them, and the house is what you call a story, and the painting of the house is the bookmaking."

"Truthfulness to life—both fantasy life and factual life—is the basis of all great art," Sendak has said, and he identifies nineteenth-century English illustrator Randolph Caldecott as his favorite teacher of truthful drawing. Musicality is another aspect of Caldecott's work that Sendak admires. He professes infatuation with "the musical accompaniment Caldecott provides in his books, for I have reached for that very quality in my own. In fact, music is essential to my work." This quality is seen in Sendak's "wild rumpus" scene in *Wild Things* and "goblin dance" in *Outside Over There*, which have their own kinds of implied musical accompaniments.

For the crosshatched drawings in *Wild Things*, Sendak studied the work of artists George Cruikshank and Wilhelm Busch. "What I take, I transform," he says, "but basically, borrowing is how you learn. . . . what you do is fall in love with other artists, past and present." Sendak also loves the paintings of William Blake and the music of Mozart, who not accidentally is shown as the pianist in *Outside Over There*. Comic books, radio, Walt Disney, and other early movie makers have also influenced his styles and even his subjects over the years.

The Weston Woods motion pictures *Maurice Sendak—1965* and *Sendak*, produced in 1986, can give children valuable insight into the varied work of this prolific and versatile artist. In 1975 Sendak worked on sets and lyrics for the televised animated special of his *Really Rosie*; in 1981 he was the set and costume designer for the Houston Grand Opera production of Mozart's *The Magic Flute*; and in 1980 he produced sets, costumes, and libretto for the operatic stage version of *Wild Things* premiered in America by the Minnesota Opera and the St. Paul Chamber Orchestra in October 1985. His 1984 illustrations for Ralph Manheim's translation of E. T. A. Hoffmann's *Nutcracker* were full of costume and set designs; an inside joke is "Main Guy" from *Wild Things* pictured peeking from behind the clouds in a sea scene.

A comparison of illustrations in *Wild Things* with the paintings of Henri Rousseau, a forerunner of the surrealists in the twentieth century, would be of interest to children. Rousseau's fantasy worlds of exotic images set in mysterious, tropical landscapes remind us hauntingly of the combination of reality and dreaming that Sendak has given in his Award winner. The controversy that surrounded Rousseau when his work first appeared was similar to the dispute over *Wild Things*. Luckily Sendak continued to picture for children his own version of truthfulness to life, however unsettling that may be. "It seems to be the gift I have . . . catching hold of those moments that are the experiences of all human animals when they're small children. I don't stifle the child in me. I hear it loud and clear." Children will be listening to the child's voice that comes from Maurice Sendak for years to come.

Chris Van Allsburg

When Chris Van Allsburg's *Jumanji* came out in 1981, the book was hailed in reviews as a masterpiece of light and dark and a diabolical exercise in eye-fooling angles. The artist himself was called a consummate draftsman whose extraordinary multiplicity of gray tones displayed a subtle intelligence beyond the call of illustration. That Van Allsburg created such a startlingly realistic-looking setting for a world in which the utterly impossible happens results from use of artistic perspectives that force the audience to join in as participants. The mood is ominous from beginning to end and reality is imitated solely through incredible mastery of black-and-white drawings. This twilight fantasy, as *Jumanji* has been called, has very dramatically given children a new way to see the inner world of an imagination gone berserk.

The element of surprise in stories is another of Van Allsburg's contributions to children's literature. Like Sendak, he delights primary-age youngsters by requiring that they listen carefully to the words and look closely at the pictures to get the point. Van Allsburg's *Ben's Dream* and his 1980 Honor Book, *The Garden of Abdul Gasazi*, have ambiguous twists at the end implying that the plots are indeed more than just dream sequences. For his first full-color book, *The Wreck of the Zephyr*, the author-illustrator suggests, just as in *Jumanji*, that the fantasy adventure need not be entirely over just because the book itself is closed. The only text for his 1984 book *The Mysteries of Harris Burdick* is in the introduction found before a collection of totally unrelated illustrations with mysterious captions that leave interpretation to the viewer—"in hopes that children will be inspired by them to tell stories" of their own, said Van Allsburg. In the 1986 Award winner, *The Polar Express*, the first gift of Christmas from Santa is lost by the young hero of the story, only to be found at the end underneath the Christmas tree that morning. And the sleigh bell's sweet sound can only be heard by those who truly believe. Mystery, suspense, and magic are marvelously combined in all these Van Allsburg titles to exploit the storyteller's age-old tactic of surprise.

As illustrator for his own tales, the artist included details in both pictures and text that hint that what follows is not as it may seem. In *Gasazi*, flowered wallpaper and the landscape painting hanging over the sofa as Alan takes a nap are suggestive of the garden and bridge in the next illustration, when the boy embarks on his excursion into the traumatic land of magic with Fritz the dog. An open geography book sets the stage for a flood in *Ben's Dream*. In *Jumanji*, the solemn blank stare of a toy dog and a dollhouse with dark empty windows and an open door like a startled face mutely accuse Judy and Peter: they have not only made a mess of the house, but they now appear likely to make things even worse. The topiary garden (inspired by a visit to the famous "Green Animals" garden in Portsmouth) from *Gasazi*'s book cover is pictured on the lid of the game box in *Jumanji*; the magical flying boat from *Zephyr* is shown mounted on the wall above a bed in *Harris Burdick*; the white bull terrier pops up in all the books after Fritz's debut in *Gasazi*; and a toy locomotive in *Jumanji* turns up as a full-sized steam engine in *The Polar Express*. Most droll is the self-portrait of Van Allsburg himself that appears in illustrations for *Zephyr*, *Express*, and *Harris Burdick*, like Alfred Hitchcock's brief signature appearances in his own movies.

In addition to picture books, Van Allsburg does sculpture and drawing; he teaches at the Rhode Island School of Design. This illustrator's career in sculpture was evident to one child, who remarked after long study that a picture in *Jumanji* looked like "a photograph of clay people"; indeed for centuries the monochromatic gray paintings called *grisaille* were intended to look like sculpture from a distance.

Van Allsburg's designs for clothes, toys, and interiors in *Jumanji* are reminiscent of the 1930s, but the impetus for the story itself came from the artist's own 1950s childhood, as explained in his Caldecott acceptance speech:

> In writing and illustrating *Jumanji*, the inspiration was my recollection of vague disappointment playing board games as a child.

Even when I owned Park Place with three hotels, I never felt truly rich, and not being able to interrogate Colonel Mustard personally was always a letdown. Another motivating element for *Jumanji* was a fascination I have with seeing things where they don't belong. The pictures in newspapers of cars that have run amok and crashed into people's living rooms always get my attention . . . .

Elsewhere in his speech the illustrator named all those to whom he has been indebted in his work, a list about which he later elaborated as follows. Seventeenth-century Dutch master Jan Vermeer has been called "the enchanter of Delft" for his compositional uses of light and dark. Edgar Degas, nineteenth–century impressionist, captured subjects in a fleeting moment. Max Klinger, late–nineteenth-century printmaker, produced drawings charged with strange qualities of light and perspective; his Glove Cycle tells "stories fraught with Freudian symbolism." Italian filmmaker Federico Fellini's movies rely visually on the juxtaposition of events as well as emotional response. Andre Kertesz, pioneer in photography as an artistic tool, takes "surreal pictures of things having no surreal context." Turn-of-the-century American newspaper cartoonist Winsor McKay drew the comic strip "Little Nemo" (also an animated film), which showed exacting use of perspective, superb draftsmanship, and an imaginative way to "create giants from midgets." The late sculptor H. C. Westermann produced works that are "frightening but not scary." Early–twentieth-century furniture maker Gustav Stickley believed that life is shaped by objects around us; he originated mission style oak furniture. In the children's book *Harold and the Purple Crayon* by Crockett Johnson, Harold has an "illusionary power to make things" that Van Allsburg related to his own childhood feelings about being an artist.

Other artists that children find interesting to compare to Van Allsburg are Joseph Wright and Edward Hopper for their refinement of composition in light and dark, Andrew Wyeth and Gustave Caillebotte for their capturing of the fleeting moment, Grant Wood and Picasso for similarity of modeled form in two-dimensional art, and most of all René Magritte for his fantastic juxtapositions of things that do not belong together.

Book Designs

Hardbound editions of all three titles are the same horizontal rectangular shape, just an inch or so wider than they are tall. *Wild Things* and *The Little House* are identical in size, and *Jumanji* is a bit larger. All three may be seen by a large group of children during storytelling.

The three titles offer excellent examples of types of book design that contribute in different ways to ideas behind the stories. Discussing the books together provides an interesting comparison in use of the artistic field of action and of text placement in picture books. The opening page of *The Little House,* for instance, is a perfect presentation of text designed to fit within an illustration or the imposition of words into a field of action to balance the overall composition. On page 31 Burton is seen to have repeated this design technique with equally attractive results. The curved text on page 1 is repeated on many of the pages that follow, interspersed with and finally replaced by shaped text with a more angular form. Both styles fit very well the phrasing necessary as the book is read aloud. In the beginning, text occupies a formal position on the left page as balance for illustrations on the right. However, soon little decorations around words become an extension of the picture on the other page, until finally all the crowding in the city that the text describes has literally spilled over into the design of crowded double-page spreads.

The audience's viewpoint for illustrations in *The Little House* is bird's-eye level, and enjoyment of the action in double-page illustrations is never spoiled by interference from the book's gutter, although single-page illustrations would have benefited from reproduction shifted to the right to avoid the binding's crease. Country scenes in the beginning are all on single pages; double pages depict city scenes, and single pages reappear once the city is left behind. The shape of text changes from meandering curves beside country scenes into irregularly blocked text that often accompanies city scenes and back again to the gently curved text for concluding country scenes. Such meticulous attention to book design has contributed greatly to the aesthetic pleasure provided by *The Little House*: we see the tranquility of the country "slowly changing with the seasons" as opposed to the disorder of city life where "everyone seemed to be in such a hurry." Often the illustrations and overall design convey even better than words how horse-and-buggy days were taken over by automobiles and streetcars, and Burton especially enjoyed creating this visual history of transportation for endpapers of the hardbound edition.

The only disappointment in an otherwise masterful demonstration of book design is the last page, an ending surely worthy of the previous sense of artistic balance from left to right but abruptly presented on one page as only a small illustration with brief text. Both artistically and textually, the more appropriate ending would have been the page before, a lovely full-page illustration with text "Once again she was lived in and taken care of." These words give the same powerful satisfaction in closure that twenty years later were recognized in Maurice Sendak's "and it was still hot," ending *Where the Wild Things Are.*

Sendak certainly surprised readers in 1963 with his little unillustrated postscript, and many of today's children know it so well they anticipate it long before the page is even turned. Along with other surprises, "and it was still hot" has contributed to recognition of the phenomenal *Wild Things* as a landmark in children's books. Another surprise from Sendak in 1963 was his unique style of book design, which can make here a striking comparison to *The Little House,* indeed to most other picture books that went before and many that have come after.

The design of *Wild Things* is one foundation block upon which the book's well-deserved success with children is built. The brilliance of this book design is that the figures seem to grow upon the pages, enlarging or diminishing as suits the telling of Max's story. At first Max is seen as a very unruly little boy with an awfully big hammer in a small illustration precisely centered like a photograph in a scrapbook on the right page with text placed very formally on the opposite page. The little picture is framed by over two inches of white border; throughout the next few pages this border shrinks and disappears, until finally, a forest occupies the entire right-page field of action. The audience realizes this exotic forest scene extends beyond the confines of the page—"walls" are gone, both the white border and those of Max's room. In the final scene in this short sequence of pages, the walls have become "the world all around," limited only by a child's imagination.

Next Sendak designed a shorter sequence of pages in which the forest is left behind for the ocean. Illustrations begin to invade the left-hand pages, which up to now have been reserved for text. First a tree and then a sea dragon are ingeniously posed as dramatic points of interest at the book's gutter; the artist has employed this invisible vertical line rather than ignore it or illustrate around it. This second sequence of only three double pages concludes with Max's arrival scene, which now occupies a full two-thirds of a double-page spread *horizontally,* with text moved down to white space across the lowest remaining third. This first double-page spread is appropriate as introduction to four Wild Things, for only in their land will Sendak use the panorama offered by a spread of both pages.

In the next sequence of pages, illustrations for the land of the Wild Things expand to take over the remaining white space "floor" previously reserved for text. Finally in the three explosive "wild rumpus" scenes, text is totally absent. Here Sendak the artist defines the "rumpus" superbly in pictures alone, and when young children are asked to relate any comparison to behavior in their own lives, they equate these unrestrained scenes to jumping on the bed, running through the house, slamming the screen door, swinging from the porch railing, hollering and dancing and banging on the lid to the garbage can, hopefully not all at the same time.

When Sendak's words for the story resume, white space is reestablished below and then once again on the left-hand page for the final sequence as Max heads home. The forest even reappears briefly as another tree positioned at the vertical line of the gutter. Significantly, the illustrator chose not to reverse the design process totally, since an air of ignominy might be attached to our returning hero if Max were shown at the end confined within a tidy snapshot as in the beginning. Max may be a very little boy, but he has had one large adventure; so he is shown returning triumphant in a full-page picture of his very own room. Of course in the picture he discovers his supper, but the description of it as "still hot" is not found until one has turned the page.

The audience has watched this story unfold as on a proscenium stage, always from the same normal eye-level viewpoint. Horizontal lines of floor, ocean, or wild land stretch out of sight side to side, and the only ceiling or walls are those in Max's room itself. But Sendak as stage manager has regulated our responses to the various acts in his play by opening and closing the "curtains" of white space and by enlarging or telescoping the "backdrops" of forest, ocean, and wild land. His book design has been used to build toward the climactic rumpus scene, and the subsequent denouement is emotionally satisfying not only because Max does come home in the story but also because his homecoming is pictured equal in size—implying equal in importance—to his adventure out in the world. The careful planning behind such unique artwork lies at the heart of the remarkable *Wild Things*. No artist before had designed a book quite like this one, and admiration can only grow over the years for this most significant effort to bring exciting new direction to the world of art in children's books.

Almost twenty years after *Wild Things*, another book arrived that some considered again a departure from standard picture-book illustrating. In Chris Van Allsburg's *Jumanji*, however, the startling difference in approach is not the variety of text design, as in *The Little House*, or the variety in sizes for the fields of action, as in *Wild Things*. Quite to the contrary, *Jumanji* is comprised of over two dozen illustrations, all with the exact same dimensions, all framed exactly the same on right-hand pages like large photographs, and all with accompanying text placed in the same formal position on left-hand pages. (Unfortunately this arrangement sometimes spoils the fun in a tale of suspense by stating after the fact what the audience already has seen.)

Van Allsburg chose to explore new ground by couching unnerving pictures within this rigid formality. Viewpoints assigned to the audience include a variety of exaggerated and maddeningly informal angles, more often from below or above the action than from a normal eye level. Our view from the floor, from above the bookshelf, or from behind a chair intentionally makes us participants, willing or not, while the story unfolds. This technique can be seen as variation on another theatrical device, the thrust stage that breaks through the confines of a proscenium to join with the audience itself. In picture-book art, this approach catches the viewer off guard, and Van Allsburg intensifies the effect by inhabiting his scenes with increasing numbers of objects foreign to the environment. In contrast to the detachment resulting from a distant viewpoint in *The Little House* or the constant observer's stance in *Wild Things*, *Jumanji* gives us good reason for concern, alarm, and finally relief—our involvement, after all, is implied in the very space on the page. Van Allsburg has imposed a clever deception on his audience by accommodating uniquely informal viewpoints within a handsomely formal but rather pedestrian choice of book design. His approach seems superbly appropriate for a story about a game of chance full of unexpected surprises literally at every turn. The artist's craftsmanship in use of light and dark will be discussed in the section on art appreciation.

Jumanji at this writing is available only in a hardbound edition, but paperbound editions of *The Little House* and *Wild Things* have been published for years. Printed by Houghton Mifflin and Scholastic respectively, both are faithful to the originals in size and shape, art and text.

Jumanji is available as a cassette read-along by Random House/ Miller Brody. Many years ago the Walt Disney Studios produced an animated cartoon featurette called *The Little House* that is now avail-

able both as a sound filmstrip and as a cassette read-along to accompany the Disney version of the book. However, the Disney art
is so loosely based on the original as to be unrecognizable; it is not
recommended for art appreciation. The sound filmstrip of *The Little
House* by Weston Woods is an acceptable adaptation that highlights
plot development by extending the original twenty illustrations into
over twice that many still frames. Interesting in this filmstrip is the
creation of two scenes not found exactly as such in the book and
the use of endpaper designs when needed for one part in the story.

Variations on the art from the classic *Wild Things* include au-
diovisuals, posters promoting children's reading, and dolls designed
in 1981 by Sendak himself. A sound recording by Caedmon has
music by Mozart, and, for appreciation of the book's illustrations,
both an eight-minute animated film (also available in videocassette)
and an even shorter sound filmstrip by Weston Woods are excellent,
not only in their devotion to original artistic intent but also in their
creative interpretation of the story on screen and soundtrack. The
motion picture is a masterpiece of animation; both the movie and
the filmstrip impart the larger-than-life presence of Sendak's monsters. In the latter presentation, one does not object to the division
of an original double-page spread into separate frames, for only by
so doing can the overwhelming immensity of the Wild Things be
communicated. Indeed curious, however, is the impulse that has
attempted to embody the spirit of these beasties in a line of stuffed
toys called "Bull," "Monster" or "Main Guy," "Bird Lady," and of
course Max. Sendak's Wild Things will always be loved best as seen
from the illustrations in the book itself, rolling their terrible eyes
and showing their terrible claws.

Art Appreciation of *The Little House*

The use of light and dark in a work of art may be incredibly subtle,
like the soft shading of a duckling's down in *Make Way for Ducklings*,
or it may be dramatically dazzling, like the shimmering reflection
on an ocean's surface of the night sky, as in *Time of Wonder*. Also
called value, the artistic element of light and dark is inextricably
woven into an artist's uses of lines and choices of colors. In fact,
many art theorists require that this element be discussed along with,
if not before, a study of the other two. Very young children, however, are better able to deal with lightness and darkness after they
are comfortable with discriminations regarding line and color, which

they find easier to identify. Most certainly, after an appreciation of the *contrast* of light and dark in *The Little House* and an exploration of *gradation* of value in *Wild Things* and *Jumanji*, the children should return to books by McCloskey, Emberley, and the Petershams for new insights.

Children can think of light and dark simplistically as involving two concepts: the difference between night and day and the difference between black and white. In art the simple difference between night and day is demonstrated when the artist shows an interest in a scene's source of illumination, such as sunlight for daytime and dim moonlight or perhaps lamplight for nighttime. The difference between black and white simply points to stark *contrast* or subtle *gradation* of colors or color forms for modeling, shading, and highlighting of figures. The analogy between day or night and black or white would carry little weight with experts in explaining the uses of light and dark by certain artistic movements. With children, though, the easy comparisons have been found to properly set the stage for fundamental investigation without intimidation. Beginning the study of light and dark by discussing night and day, we draw on illustrations from *The Little House*, called here "Very Happy" and "Not So Quiet" (pages 2–3 and 20–21). The study includes identification of illumination sources other than sunlight. The difference between black and white as an introduction to contrast of value is seen in another pair of illustrations, "In the Winter" and "More Roads" (pages 12–13 and 18–19). Exploration of tonal scale in gradation from black to white is best reserved for studies of several illustrations in *Wild Things* and *Jumanji*.

SOURCES OF ILLUMINATION

Children can easily identify obvious daytime or nighttime in pictures, and so the difference between two such compositions makes a logical introduction to light and dark. Thus, whether the artist has indicated a source of illumination *within the composition itself* is the first idea to stress with children. This point is graphically made in the illustration "Very Happy" in *The Little House*. The "sunlight" for this picture is formal; the sun symbol is repeated within a decorative arch across the double-page spread as the stages from dawn to sunset are strictly confined within a vaulted curve. Burton's compositional interest in this light source must be viewed as purely structural, for the sun sheds onto the scene below no more sunshine than what we assume. The trees give no shade, and the house has no shadows. The artist has given us flat forms clearly seen in overall tones, and we must assume it is broad daylight. Softly contrasting greens, browns, and grays combine to imply delicacy in substances, but these subtle shifts in tone do not seriously model the forms and so do not really tell us where light is coming from.

Since an even distribution of lightness makes all shapes in this picture clearly evident, even the youngest of children, when asked if this scene is set during day or night, can reply with absolute confidence, "Daytime!" although no sunshine is used directly within the composition itself. On the next page, they can be equally delighted to identify "Nighttime!" They easily spot within the darkness the lights switched on inside the house, the black shadows, the glow of moonlight, and once again a formal arch that confines specific light—this time the halo of the city and star-filled sky complete with the Big Dipper framed at the top of the page. This night scene is perfect as immediate juxtaposition for "Very Happy," but a later night scene, "Not So Quiet" (pages 20–21), has been chosen for further study here because it presents a unique opportunity to study a wider variety of light sources at night and their influences in composition.

In "Not So Quiet" the now familiar "Burton arch" of lights and sky is seen as a formal frame at the top of the picture. Now, however, white moonlight from above is joined by subtle hints of yellow from the city's lights as *backlighting* for the buildings. Backlighting is a technique in art that offers direct contrast between dark and light in that the source of illumination is directly behind the form. As a result, the figures are seen as silhouettes or two-dimensional shapes with little detail. As in Burton's daytime scenes, forms are rendered flat and even-toned, but illumination from behind is used rather than an overall distribution of anonymous light from in front or above.

A half dozen streetlights blaze along the picture's perimeter, replacing as points of interest the yellow light shining in the window in the previous night scene. The blinding light of these streetlamps has also blotted out details in the buildings but this time from the front. This technique is the reverse of backlighting but equally effective in rendering shapes flat and two-dimensional. Using a direct light from the front to erase a surface and leave only the intense sensation of light itself is an effect called *disintegration* of form.

Having seen daylight's all-pervasive wash over a scene, as in "Very Happy," children can study "Not So Quiet" to increase their appreciation of backlighting and disintegration of form. This is an important step toward a deeper awareness of artistic uses of light and dark. *The Little House* makes this step an easier one by providing graphic demonstrations of both simple and sophisticated uses of light.

CONTRAST OF LIGHT AND DARK

Another important concept for children to recognize is choice of light or dark colors or color forms for compositions. Many storytelling picture books have only one set of characters and one or only a few episodes, and the colors throughout the book are limited to the range chosen for the initial illustration. Once again, however, *The Little House* offers a good opportunity to compare a wider variety of compositions.

In this context, a selection of colors considered light would be the pure hues or their light tones and tints and white itself. Dark colors include the darker tones, shades, the other color forms of gray and black itself. For example, Burton's night settings have made appropriate use of darker shades, whereas day settings are composed of lighter tints. The shift from day to night is indicated as much by color choice as by source of illumination.

Within daytime illustrations, however, there is also an interesting change from light to dark colors related to the plot itself. Country scenes in daytime make predominant use of light colors, but city scenes in daylight are portrayed mainly in dark colors. Indeed, as the book's illustrations show the progression from country setting to city and back again, the dominant colors change radically from light tones of red, yellow, blue, and green to browns and grays and back again to light tones. The illustrations "In the Winter" and "More Roads" offer the best comparison for this contrast of light and dark color choices.

The snow-white scene "In the Winter" can easily be identified by youngsters as constructed on a basic principle of lightness rather than darkness. All is bright and clear and unobstructed; the cheerful red of the house and buggy and the decorative brown skeletons of the trees make a clean contrast against the snow tinged with blue. To be noted are two shadows for the trees, an instance of real interest in pale sunlight from the right as source of illumination.

Tints and shades here are dull, weak, or pale, that is, of low *intensity* (also called *saturation* or *chroma*). Intensity deals with relative brightness or strength of a hue. Every hue has a *value ladder* from lightest (called high value or high key, a tint or pastel) to darkest (low value or low key, a shade or muted hue). Similarly, the same colors have an *intensity scale* running from light dull (weak, lightly obscure, low saturation) to bright (strong, pure, full saturation) to dark dull (murky, darkly obscure, low saturation), in which varying amounts of the hue's complementary color have been added to create tones. In *Drummer Hoff*, for instance, pure hues of bright intensity were used, and in *The Rooster Crows* the differences in a tone's value were seen to model shapes by shading and highlighting. But in *The Little House*, the artist has based whole compositions around equal tones of light dull intensity but with variations in value. Since white and black occupy opposite ends of a value ladder (with intervals of grays as transitional steps between the two), the starkest contrast for the snow-covered hills of "In the Winter" has to be again the first night scene in the book, in which those same hills are mysteriously transformed by use of grays and black. Even the very youngest children, when asked what the "main colors" are for these compositions, can recognize the "White!" of snow and the "Black!" of night.

In the "More Roads" illustration, the artist again transformed the scene but this time in daylight, making an even more interesting comparison to "In the Winter." The cheerfulness and cleanness of the snow scene has been replaced with the gloom and griminess of tenements and pavement, accomplished as much by dark color choices of grays and browns as by addition of ominous shapes crowded within limited space. Earlier in the book brown and gray were used as naturalistic earth tones for plowed fields and harvest; only when the steam shovel came to dig the road—a diagonal scar across the rounded hills—were these same tones seen to represent an unnatural invasion of gravel, tar, and sand. By the time the illustration "More Roads" arrives, the darkest tone of brown dominates the composition, just as the buildings dominate the little house; the gray of a pebbled path has now become a dark smear of asphalt, and a mild overcast winter sky has been replaced by ominous dark smog. In "More Roads" and "In the Winter," children can see the most meaningful contrast, for storytelling purposes, of light and dark color choices that refer to a basic difference between black and white. Burton's intent was to maximize the use of this elusive but most emotional of artistic elements—light and dark—to best dramatize the story of the little house.

Art Appreciation of *Where the Wild Things Are*: Gradation to Imply Texture and Contour

The differences between night and day or black and white in *The Little House* have been called contrast of light and dark, just as the concentration on pure, brilliant hues in *Drummer Hoff* can be thought of as stark contrast of colors within composition. *Gradation,* or gradual change from light to dark, offers contrast also but ever so slightly. Subtler use is made of colors, sources of illumination, and visible lines. For example, in *The Rooster Crows* a gradual transition of color tones models shapes; in *Time of Wonder* forms appear soft and out of focus in gradual haziness of early morning sunlight filtered through fog; in *Make Way for Ducklings* delicate and gradated use of light and dark lines form rounded shapes and feathery texture.

Gradated light and dark colors, lines, and illumination are often combined in a systematic approach for implied texture and contour that are quite different from an artist's emphasis on any one of the three alone. When all three aspects of gradation are joined within one composition or within one picture book, time and place can be implied in a most sophisticated way. The haunting and mysterious allure of *Wild Things* can be tied directly to its subtle uses of gradated color tones, drawn lines, and light sources. A study of Sendak's combined applications of light and dark gradation can indeed deepen children's appreciation for the masterful art in these pictures they already know so well.

Page 14,[2] in which Max sails off in his private boat, is a good introduction to the difference between contrast and gradation. Youngsters can be confident in identification of triad harmony of primary colors, the red boat with its yellow sail on the blue ocean, all three presented in the lightest tints used anywhere in the book and offering much contrast. A contrast of light and dark to denote a slight source of illumination is also seen in the shadow of Max's wolf suit ears on the sail. On the other hand, gradation of color is discovered in the light and dark areas of the water, painted in varying shades of blue and green. Gradation of light and dark lines is noticed in the sky, where heavier pen strokes delineate the background and lighter strokes give shape to soft folds in the clouds.

[2]Pagination begins on first page with text.

For further study of gradation of light and dark colors, turn to pages 27-28 for the last of the "wild rumpus" scenes, where Sendak's palette is dark: gradual transitions of brown, ocher, neutral gray, violet, and a blue-green that almost blends in with the dense foliage in the background. The tones are so low key as to offer the least contrast among colors of any illustration in the book, making a good comparison with the high-keyed tints in the picture of Max in his boat. This tonal gradation combined with black and white shows one harmony of color forms. The key for identifying such tonal variations of primary and secondary hues in the book is provided inconspicuously in the endpaper design of leaves.

Yellow in the terrible eyes of the Wild Things is the only contrasting light color here and serves a strategic purpose: those wild eyes and Max's wolf suit are the lightest colors in this dark composition. Spaced at intervals along the top half of the illustration, they pull the audience's attention from one marching figure to another lined up across the double-page spread. The eye appeal of these light areas directs us to Max. In addition, twisting vertical lines and paths of look and gesture lead toward the center of the picture—important because otherwise the boy's small figure might be overlooked in a composition dominated by five creatures so enormous they seem barely accommodated by space on the pages.

Whereas contrast of primary tints resulted in clearly defined shapes in the illustration of Max's boat, gradation of dark tones in this "rumpus" picture results in softer determination of where one figure stops and another begins. Each shape has its own overall tone confined within black edge lines, yet the low level of dull intensity and the equal values give the shades an appearance of blending together despite their outlines. The underlying dull shades are also important as a foundation for gradation of light and dark lines to imply contour and texture.

The middle "rumpus" scene on pages 25–26 has excellent examples of lines imposed upon dark tones for shape and texture. The effect is easier to see here against a lighter background. Readily apparent are the little black lines going this way and that on each figure to imply hair, fur, or contour shading. This technique is called *crosshatching*, the pen-and-ink style that has come to be identified with *Wild Things* and much of Sendak's other work. In crosshatched drawings, one set of short, broken, parallel lines is crossed over by another set at a different angle, producing darker areas where lines are close together and lighter areas where farther apart. The technique is based on the principle that on white paper the eye visually "mixes" the black lines with the white to create an impression of variations on gray. By controlling areas of crosshatching an artist can accentuate the rounding of figures, their seeming projection or recession within a field of action—in essence, their illusion of solid form.

Heavy crosshatching in black india ink on top of the dark shades (themselves created through addition of black) obviously darkened those underlying tones and gave Max's friends density, weight, and seeming movement. Crosshatching constructs tails and hair and soles of the feet and gives contour to crown and trees. This use of visible ink lines over tempera is a different technique than is used for the purely painted portions of grass and foliage in these pictures. Turn back one page to the first "rumpus" scene in which a crosshatched Wild Thing is positioned behind a painted tree on the right for a perfect comparison of the two techniques. Sendak has said elsewhere that his pictures show an interest in "a graphic line that *controls*" because he wants "to put gray into everything. I'm not easy with fat, bright colors." In *Wild Things* he has given children a most useful demonstration of the effect in composition of the gradation of light and dark lines over colors, through his mastery of crosshatching over muted tones.

The third and last aspect of gradation is the subtle transition of light and dark related to a source of illumination. In the first "rumpus" illustration in the book we see the influence of moonlight on darkness already achieved by gradated color tones and crosshatching. In this illustration the Wild Things and their new king are seen cavorting and undoubtedly making a great deal of noise under a beautifully full moon placed in a formal position at the top of the picture. Faces of Wild Things turned toward the moon are not crosshatched but are instead *highlighted* by tones lighter than are found on those snouts anywhere else in the book. Full dark crosshatching over the remainder of their figures here signifies a subtle *backlighting*. The forms seem flatter and have more evenly distributed tones than in the second "rumpus" scene.

Sendak must be praised as a master of nuance throughout *Wild Things* for such sophisticated control of sources of illumination, lines, and colors, and students can enjoy looking at all the other illustrations in the book for gradations of light and dark.

Art Appreciation of *Jumanji*: Contrast and Gradation to Imply Depth

Chris Van Allsburg has a consuming interest in ways to imply depth through contrast and gradation of light and dark, as superbly demonstrated in his Caldecott winner *Jumanji*. The sun has no formal position in these illustrations; no diffusion of moonlight shines anonymously upon a scene. Here rather is a very methodical, precise structuring of late-afternoon sun as source of illumination. For his dim and gray illustrations, Van Allsburg used a black Conte à Paris pencil or crayon (a compressed chalky substance bound by a unique formula that makes it different from charcoal, pastel, or chalk itself). Ground dust from the same kind of pencil was quickly applied with cotton balls and sprayed with matt fixative as background shade on the paper. Then drawing was done with a medium hard Conte, and gray values were the amounts of paper and dust still exposed. The resultant drawings in shades of gray make an interesting comparison for children with the crosshatched lines in *Wild Things* and have basically the same effect as grisaille, or painting in grays, a perfect technique here for the telling of the sinister twilight tale.

To understand implied depth in a work of art, children need to refine further their understanding of contrast and gradations of light and dark in color tones and in sources of illumination for pictures with different perspectives. Van Allsburg's absolute devotion in *Jumanji* to strict geometrical principles of linear perspective is evident in preliminary drawings that exhibit the artist's own ruled lines from corner to corner, which served as guides for placement of forms. Other early drawings exhibit visible guidelines that extend off the pages to an implied vanishing point somewhere across the room.

Guidelines, guide points, scribbled figuring by the artist in the margins of his drawing sheets, and several different versions of the same illustration all attest that Van Allsburg oriented his forms in absolute linear perspective before he ever began to illustrate. Only after adherence to correct perspective could he begin to construct his scenes with implication of depth through gradation of light and dark.

The best example for children to begin with is one of the latter illustrations, on page 24.[3] In this picture it is easy to identify light and dark areas that imply depth. Here the stairway balustrade stands in starkest contrast of black against the white of the door beyond; backlighting forms a silhouette of the banister, and the foreground where the audience sits becomes a neutral, darkly dull area. The glare of sunlight disintegrates details on the door but backlights the form of Peter and intensifies the urgency of his escape. Light areas in a field of action are thought to attract attention and visually advance toward the viewer, while less eye-attractive dark areas are

[3]Pagination begins on first page with text.

considered to recede. A reverse positioning here of darkness close up and light farther away adds to the confusion in depth and to the near-hysterical mood. Our eyes jump back and forth, attracted to the dramatic light in the middle ground, then comprehending the solid, dark balustrade as an obstruction contrasting with this light. Finally we settle our attention right where the artist intended—on the figure of Peter in between.

Peter's implied motion leads our attention outside, where there exists once again a reversal of light and dark areas—black trees in front of gray trees on a background of white. Since the eye is again attracted most by the light area, we seek the farthest background point first. Circuitously, but with careful deliberation in this picture, our visual trip has thus been guided from the black of the balustrade ultimately to the white of the sky outside, from looming dark foreground to open light background. The result is an exhilarating display in a single illustration of the power of light and dark to imply depth. The audience views the scene from a normal eye level, and the only diagonal line, the staircase, accentuates the tension in a picture that would otherwise be rather static in its horizontal baseline and strong vertical lines. Much depth is implied in this picture because it features a center vanishing point in addition to the interplay of light and dark that finally leads the eye out the door with Peter to safety.

Contrast of light and dark contributes immeasurably to the implied depth on page 12, when the monkeys invade the kitchen. The edge of the table's vertical line is in the exact center of the picture and projects toward the audience, effectively dividing the illustration into light and dark halves as illumination from a window shines more onto the right than the left side of the room. Dark gray and black lines imply texture for the long-haired monkeys and also emphasize their close, menacing presence that dominates the darker side of the illustration. The relative lightness on the right balances the heavy thrust of darkness on the left, but our uneasiness grows when we see repetition of dark areas deep within the lighter half—a contrast of white and black that calls our attention to open cupboards where more monkeys lurk. An exact moment has been captured so precisely that a shadow is seen as a can falls from the shelf, implying depth for the room and firmly leading our eye to Judy, who stands in horrified silence.

Another illustration that uses exaggerated angle and value contrast for implied depth is page 8, where the closest white of Peter's shirt leads our eye to the sheet music on the piano in the middle ground, and then up to the lion's teeth before stopping at the farthest point deep within his open black mouth. On page 20, gradation of light and dark in shallow depth contributes to the momentary illusion that the python on the mantle is nothing more than a repeat of the upholstery pattern on the chair. On page 22, the same gradation continues to trick us with the python and chair, but contrast between white steam and Judy's dark hair creates a stifling sensation of depth so shallow that a mere hint of mantle and lamp is all that remains as background for the room. On page 18, gradation contributes to the compositional heaviness of the rhinos as they charge through the dining room. Note both the dark doorway *behind* the rampaging beasts and a chair in the immediate foreground that protrudes *toward* the audience beyond the artist's established field of action. This example of "forward extension" from a picture plane demands the viewer's involvement.

Another interesting illustration for children's investigation of implied depth is the scene on page 6, in which Judy and Peter first spread out the game. Dark tones for objects on the bookshelf imply that the immediate foreground is cast in deep shadow *above* the source of illumination from the left. The audience's viewpoint is from this high, balconylike perch, in close enough proximity to actors directly below to clearly see the part in Peter's hair. Sunshine like a theatrical spotlight spreads across the two children and disintegrates much of the form for their shirts and Judy's important piece of paper. The glare's contrast with the dark bookshelf anchors our attention to this shallow middle ground. However, the background extends into much depth, and here mysterious shadows lengthen dramatically. Shadows as gradations of light and dark play a sinister part in the story, as best evidenced in this illustration and in the final one, where the Budwing boys unwittingly take up the game after Judy and Peter have called it quits.

Van Allsburg's balancing of light and dark through contrast or gradation to imply depth demonstrates mastery of a tonal scale, subtlety of form, variations on implied texture, and unusual perspectives. The work provides a sophisticated conclusion to children's study of light and dark in art.

Effects of Light and Dark

Artists can set a mood for pictures by appealing to the audience's basic feelings about light and dark. The emotional response to a bright, sunlit scene is a positive reaction. We feel secure in seeing forms we know and recognize easily in fullest daylight, as in "Very Happy" from *The Little House*.

Bright light, on the other hand, can produce uncomfortable feelings when the blinding glare erases what we know to be there, as the streetlamps do in "Not So Quiet." These lights have been used to make us feel uncomfortable rather than secure, and they heighten the sense of gloom produced by the tall buildings looming behind the little house. Shapes are here rendered unrecognizable and frightening as night has fallen, and so also do our spirits fall as we react to the grim solemnity of a dark city skyline that crowds in upon the little house. Our reaction to the earlier night scene, showing the house in the countryside, was less negative. In that picture the dim moonlit evening seemed cozy and comforting due to shadows across shapes known to be hospitable during the day. But in "Not So Quiet" the buildings are known to be dirty and ugly even in daylight; so our revulsion for them is merely intensified by the darkness, known for its association with depression and fear of the night.

The change in colors, from the light hues of "In the Winter" to dark in "More Roads," emphasizes the transformation of country into city with unpleasant consequences. We respond to the snow scene as idyllic, clearly defined, spacious, and pretty; we are repulsed by the city scene as murky, crowded, massive, and obscure. Other illustrations in *The Little House* reinforce the progression of these changes, and the overall effect from these contrasts is a feeling of uplifting exaltation in natural surroundings versus subdued depression as urbanization takes over the scene.

From *Wild Things*, the scene in which Max is pictured in his boat has the intended effect of spaciousness and lightheartedness due to the use of primary colors against a pink-tinted sky. The audience shares in Max's obvious pleasure as he starts out on his adventure, and we are as confident as he seems to be that he will be able to handle whatever comes his way. The sky grows increasingly dark, however, as Max continues his journey, until he comes to the land of Wild Things and night falls for the "wild rumpus" scenes. A full moon in the first of these scenes illuminates activities going on below but is intended as a symbol for frenzied abandon rather than as a comforting light cast across an otherwise threatening and unfamiliar landscape. To compare with this dark scene, another intended effect of lightness can be studied in the early morning illustration on pages 29–30, in which Wild Things sleep and Max is lonely. With only dawn's light as source of illumination, this picture has an even distribution of pinkish cast that softens contours and textures of figures, royal tent, and even trees themselves. Just as a dark forest against dark sky was exactly the right mysterious backdrop for the wild dance in the night, so now is the gentle harmony of color tones in a wash of pink the perfect effect for Max's pensive wistfulness in the early morning. One cannot help wanting the terrible yellow eyes to open soon and the Wild Things to come out to play again.

Throughout the book, dark underlying tones for the Wild Things are accentuated by Sendak's crosshatching to communicate to the audience their heaviness and malevolence. In contrast, little Max is highlighted in his white wolf suit to call attention to his vulnerable figure dwarfed by the enormous creatures he plays with. In the first "rumpus" illustration, Wild Things have tones of grays and browns, and added to the heavy crosshatching is an even distribution of darkest night that further intensifies the bulk of their forms. Notice that "Bird Lady's" hair and furry coat are even darker in coloration and implied density than in other illustrations (and inexplicably her feet have been changed as well). Logically, Max himself should be totally in the shadows, but his white figure provides perfect balance of weight for the full moon as point of interest overhead.

In the second "rumpus" illustration the sky is lighter, and to the audience the Wild Things appear to be friendlier as they swing playfully in the trees. The darkest and hairiest Wild Thing is "Bull"; lines are crosshatched on his head and blue-green body as he hangs rather uneasily from a limb and clutches the tree trunk for support. "Main Guy," on the other hand, seems to be having more fun as he imitates Max, and his motion is communicated to us by crosshatching that implies contortion of his form as he swings forward and back. "Bird Lady" appears more hesitant and even a bit vulnerable as she tries her best, and she is shown to have fur much softer than "Bull's," due to some lines crosshatched that are closer in color to the underlying tones. A nappier, shorter fur coat is also suggested for the "rooster man" on the right, who with his stiff posture appears to participate most reticently in this nonsensical mischief. Of all Sendak's pictures, this "rumpus" illustration seems to indicate most to the viewer some differences in personality among the irrepressible Wild Things—differences communicated by facial expressions, body language, and implied motion of differently contoured and textured figures.

Van Allsburg's drawings in black and white for *Jumanji* brilliantly convey the intended ominous atmosphere of a late November afternoon. Part of the chill and thrill of the book is that the formal square format and text placement initially indicate that this is an ordinary tale, and only gradually does the audience discover that the story is anything but ordinary. The book becomes a series of clues to what is really going on—gradual tones that form patterns deceptive to the eye, angles that throw one's perceptions into confusion, seeming reality that is in truth totally unreal. The intensity of plot is deepened by this gradual realization that things are not as we thought them to be. Stark contrasts and soft gradations of tones afforded by use of pencil strengthen the haunting effects of light and dark in a way that color never could have done for this unusual, unnerving story.

To better appreciate the visual impact of the pictures in *Jumanji*, children can be shown that Van Allsburg designed his illustrations using three systems of *linear perspective* in order to heighten the suspenseful effect of the story: stable *parallel perspective* in which lines are parallel to the picture's edges and a center vanishing point generally corresponds to the audience's viewpoint; *angular perspective*, in which vertical lines are parallel to the sides of the picture but more than one vanishing point is implied for other lines, creating confusion; and *oblique perspective*, in which a tilted and unstable composition has lines that do not run parallel with any sides of the picture and vertical lines may converge either up or down.

Superior examples of these three systems of perspective are used to communicate mood in *Jumanji*. For example, when Judy and Peter first spread the game out on the table, the illustration is presented with a bird's-eye level oblique perspective that artistically is a "warning" of impending disaster. Then, when the kitchen has been invaded by a group of menacing monkeys, "danger" is intensified by an unusually low worm's-eye level angular perspective that adds a sense of personal vulnerability for the audience as well as for Judy. And as Peter bolts out the door at the end of the story, the normal eye-level parallel perspective of the illustration aids in establishing stability and "safety" once again.

The three visual impressions of warning, danger, and safety conveyed by oblique, angular, and parallel perspectives from bird's-eye, worm's-eye, and normal viewpoints are repeated throughout *Jumanji*. In large part, the success of the book is due to Van Allsburg's changes in perspective systems for effects on the audience.

For Further Study

1. Study other titles by Virginia Lee Burton, Maurice Sendak, and Chris Van Allsburg for similarities among the three author-illustrators and within their own works. All three deal in transfor-

mations, whether in the real world or the world of fantasy; change from the comfortable into the uncomfortable and back again can be exciting as well as instructive to a picture-book audience. Burton in many of her picture books breathed life into inanimate objects; Sendak has said that he is most interested in confrontation of childhood's deepest fears and guilts; Van Allsburg has presented for the younger child an introduction to bizarre fantasy and the suspense of a surprise ending. Collected works of all three can be an important part of every child's imaginative development through picture books.

2. Children use the symbolic motif of the sun or moon in their own artwork, and they can be introduced to various artists who have also used such formality in paintings. They can be encouraged to experiment with more expressive use of a sun motif and might place it in different positions to reflect its relative importance.

3. Ask students to list places that can be dark because (a) of the weather or the season, (b) night has fallen, or (c) an area has no windows. Discuss possibilities for different feelings about the darkness in these categories.

4. Pass around sunglasses or colored cellophane for the children to look through, or bring a black light bulb to put in a lamp. Identify the changes in coloration that result, and instruct the children to experiment with overall washes of lighter or darker colors in their pictures.

5. Using an overhead projector, cast a silhouette of an object on a screen. Instruct the children to draw the outlined shape and fill it in with a solid color so that it appears flat. Pass around the real object to point out details that are absent in the silhouette.

6. A silhouette in the form of a photogram can be made using Kodalith paper, household ammonia, a tray, a wire screen, and selected small objects. Arrange a few objects on the paper, expose them to sunlight for one minute, then remove the objects and immediately place the paper on the wire screen over a tray containing one cup of ammonia. The fumes will react with the paper and cause the shapes of the objects to appear blue against the white of the paper. (Only an adult should handle these materials and adequate ventilation should be arranged. Cover up the tray of ammonia to hold in the fumes between demonstrations.)

7. Once the differences between two compositions can be recognized as based around contrast of light and dark color choices, then more attention should be paid to contrasts within each picture separately. For instance, "In the Winter" from *The Little House* has a pleasing arrangement of dark trees contrasted against the white

snow. The pink of the house has much eye appeal due to its warmth, whereas the blue intensifies the cold of the snow. Within "More Roads," the changes in brown tones from lighter to darker are deliberate smudges that make the buildings most unattractive compared to the light yellow-green of the grass, and neither the pink of the house (dingier than in earlier illustrations) nor the bits of color along the street can provide enough warmth to overcome the austere neutrality of gray pavement and brown tenements. Contrast of light and dark can thus be seen to play a vital role within a composition itself, and children can be encouraged to experiment with these contrasts in their own artwork.

8. Study more closely the "Burton arches" across the tops of illustrations in *The Little House* (which continue a historical tradition in art as old as such illuminated manuscripts as *The Book of Hours*); look especially in the daytime scenes for different emphases on sunlight, clouds, and smog. To better appreciate the variety of the sky's tints and shades in *Wild Things*, take children outside to observe the sky. Discuss the cloud formations and the tints or shades of sky blue, misty gray, or sunset pink. Note how tree or building shapes obstruct full view of the horizon. If possible, arrange for the children to draw or paint what they see.

9. Display a series of alternate sheets of black and white construction paper to show contrast. Then give each child one small square of black and three of white. Instruct the children to leave one white square blank and use graphite pencils to produce a light gray on another white square and a dark gray on the third. Have the children put their four squares in proper sequence of black, dark gray, light gray, and white, to produce a value ladder as in *Jumanji*.

10. To create dark dull tones of primary and secondary hues, as in *Wild Things*, tempera paint can be mixed in egg cartons. Beginning with cups of yellow, red, and blue, the children can experiment with creation of green, violet, and orange in three other cups, rinsing and drying their brushes often. Next, have them fold a piece of heavy paper into six squares and number them one through six. Square one should have red with an added bit of its complementary green, to create a tone of red. Square two should have a tone of green by adding a bit of red to green. Square three should have a tone of yellow made by adding purple; square four, a tone of purple by adding yellow; square five, a tone of blue by adding orange; square six, a tone of orange by adding blue. When papers are dry, note the variety of tones achieved with different ratios of paint.

Shades of brown, a mixture of all primaries, result when brushes are not properly rinsed.

11. Cover a box with colored paper and set it on a sheet of black paper. Darken the room and direct a floodlight or filmstrip-projector beam toward a corner of the box. Point out to the children that the true value of the color is on the side of the box facing the light; a tint is on the top; a shade is in the shadow. Cover the light with colored glass or cellophane to see a mixture of two colors on the top of the box and the complement of the light's color on the farthest side.

12. Students may enjoy experimenting with hatching and cross-hatching for implied contour and shading of figures. A way to introduce them to the technique is to provide them with magazine photographs that have prominent shading on figures and instruct them to hatch or crosshatch in pencil over the shaded portions.

13. Students can plan compositions in parallel, angular, or oblique perspective by first drawing across their paper a few preliminary lines that imply a vanishing point somewhere beyond the field of action. These analogies may be helpful: (a) by standing between railroad tracks and looking into the distance, one would see parallel perspective with a vanishing point implied at the horizon where the tracks would come together; (b) by standing at the corner of a building and observing walls extending to either side, one would see angular perspective, with vanishing points to left and right; (c) by standing on the roof of a tall building and looking down into the street corner, one would see one kind of oblique perspective; there is no horizon, and if vertical lines are present, they converge downward.

Looking Back, Looking Ahead: Line, Color, Shape, Space

Visible line effects create the contrasts and gradations of colors and color forms in *The Little House*; they emphasize the softness of the countryside and the harshness of the cityscapes. The spreads do not bleed off the pages from side to side but are instead controlled by rounded edges. In addition, circular invisible frameworks concentrate attention to the scenes depicted. As the story progresses, the country scenes with a few delicate verticals for trees or houses and many gentle horizontal curves for hills are replaced by city scenes with many looming verticals for buildings and strict horizontals for elevated trains and subways.

In *Wild Things*, figures have drawn lines and crosshatched contouring and shading, while line effects of color tones depict background trees, mountains, and sky or foreground ocean. Black india ink lines imposed over tones of primary and secondary hues are a hallmark of this book. Only in the beginning are pictures framed within borders. Other illustrations are composed along a strong horizontal baseline which implies a larger scene to left and right. Strong vertical figures with paths of gaze from terrible yellow eyes or paths of gesture from terrible claws command attention on every spread portraying Wild Things.

Subtle line drawings with Conte pencil and even subtler line effects accomplished by gradations of Conte dust contribute to the twilight feeling in *Jumanji*, a book whose successful depiction of a time gone by depends largely on a quality reminiscent of black-and-white photography. Horizontal framework is evident in the several illustrations from a parallel perspective, and all the pictures imply a larger scene than that portrayed in the field of action. Points of interest are discovered sometimes only after second or third readings of this remarkable book, whose author-illustrator has included visual games that depend on discrimination of grays rather than colors. For example, a reader may try to decide how many deceptively subtle floral patterns can be found or how many small reflections of light from a window can be discovered on vases and lamps.

Satisfying combinations of organic and geometric shapes occur in all three titles. It is interesting to note that the main concern in *The Little House* is insidious domination of natural forms by the artificial, while in *Wild Things* and *Jumanji* the reverse is true—the natural invades the artificial world. Simplified shapes are in idealized proportion for the first half of *The Little House* but are replaced by hierarchic and finally even distorted proportions for looming skyscrapers as the city is built up twenty-five stories on one side of the little heroine and thirty-five stories on the other. In *Jumanji* all proportions are perfectly natural, which understandably adds to the audience's alarm when rhinos tangled in telephone cords and a python wrapped around a clock appear in an otherwise normal-looking world inhabited by two highly individualized, realistically depicted children. Fewer geometric shapes appear in *Wild Things*, but they are there nonetheless and can be deceptively insignificant; a hammer and fork are replaced by a scepter in Max's hand, and a bed is replaced by a boat. However, the transformation of the geometric (Max's room) into the organic (the forest) is the core of the plot itself. In the fantasy world of Sendak, to designate proportions for monsters, Max, boat, or room as natural, idealized, or hierarchic seems woefully inadequate. Figures simply are as they must be in *Wild Things*.

Deep space was created for all illustrations in *The Little House* except at the very beginning and end. To accomplish this, the artist used aerial perspective, in which sizes become smaller, lines and colors are blurred, and details are diminished. Parallel perspective was also used; there is one implied vanishing point for lines of houses, buildings, or roads. Beginning and ending scenes imply shallower space with no horizon in order to focus attention on the little house on the hill. In *Wild Things* and *Jumanji*, indoor scenes occupy shallow space confined by walls, floors, and ceilings; outdoor scenes have implication of deep space as horizons meet the sky. However, Sendak's interest in both spatial systems is like that of a stage manager placing sets and backdrops, whereas Van Allsburg pulls the audience in or pushes it back with unusual viewpoints impossible to ignore. All illustrations in *Wild Things* have parallel perspective, but in *Jumanji*, three perspective systems maximize the book's startling effect.

Looking Around: *The Polar Express; Shadow; Sam, Bangs and Moonshine; The Biggest Bear; Ox-Cart Man; They Were Strong and Good; Frog Went A-Courtin'*

In his second Award-winner, *The Polar Express* in 1986, Chris Van Allsburg has written and illustrated an original fantasy about the first gift of Christmas that is destined to become a seasonal classic as well as an exemplary contribution to American picture-book art. His horizontal book design and formal text placement are flawless, and reproduction of the full color art exhibits a mastery of implied texture that is as close an imitation of real texture as a two-dimensional work could be expected to be. Feathery falling snow and Santa's beard and downy mittens are the best examples of implication of texture throughout this book, accomplished, the artist has said, by the interplay between an oil pastel medium and pastel paper itself as support medium. Lights from windows in *Express* shine so brilliantly in the story's cold night air that they seem tangible, visually disintegrating what is behind windowpanes inside train or buildings to form decorative shapes across the page as if they were Christmas ornaments themselves, implying depth and texture through contrast of light and dark that appropriately heightens a festive effect.

Interior scenes throughout are intimate close-ups of bedclothed children portrayed quite rationally participating in what may look like a real-world adventure but is nonetheless a fantastic experience which for one of them will continue into Christmas morning and, in fact, have lingering effects for a lifetime. By comparison to these cozy inside scenes, outdoor scenes are filled with mysterious and surrealistic majesty that inspires wonder and awe in a young audience: a steam locomotive stands waiting outside a boy's front door; the train journeys through stately forest, around mountain peak, and over a Roman aquaduct-like bridge; the Express at last reaches the North Pole, an enormous city suitably industrialized considering its role as manufacturing center for all the toys of Christmas.

For the illustrations thus far and for most that follow, a stable horizontal framework has been used by the artist from a generally normal eye-level viewpoint (some are just below or above normal but none appear as exaggerated as are those in *Jumanji*; perhaps once again an artist can here be said to have painted from the eye level of a young child rather than that of an adult). After the train stops inside the city, however, the artist twice employed the oblique perspective from bird's-eye level that served so well in *Jumanji* to establish a mood of "warning." In *Express* the feeling that something momentous is about to happen is not as strongly one of foreboding because of the textual nature of the story; instead, these two bird's-eye levels are dramatic viewpoints used to announce first the imminent arrival and later the exciting exit of Santa Claus himself. Because of our viewpoint from above when Santa leaves on his rounds, we even get to see inside the sleigh where his foot is holding down the important gift list.

Van Allsburg has said he realized after *Express* was finished that he was thinking of the work of Caspar David Friedrich, considered one of Germany's most gifted artists of the Romantic period in the early nineteenth century, a painter whose landscapes often contained small figures rendered symbolically insignificant in the solemn and silent presence of nature. Also in Friedrich's paintings can the stark contrast of light and dark created by specific sources of illumination be seen to have influenced some of Van Allsburg's illustrations for *Express*. In the first illustration, for instance, light from the Express below in the street serves to spotlight the boy's figure in his bed upstairs; then, as the train journeys north, moonlight from the right implies depth for shapes of trees, mountains, and bridge; once inside the city, the moon shines down between the tall buildings to dramatically backlight Santa as he appears with arms upraised; and last, returning in the story to the Express itself as an important ingredient in the plot, light from the train's windows are reflected on the door to backlight the boy as he waves goodbye at journey's end.

Except for Van Allsburg, no Caldecott illustrator has demonstrated a more powerful use of light and dark than Marcia Brown in her 1983 Award winner *Shadow*, whose text was translated from the French poem by Blaise Cendrars. Using color in double-page spreads, Brown created boldly fantastic images in an African landscape by building up layers of overlapping paper or tissue cutouts blotted with paint and stamped by woodblocks. Although *Shadow*, *Jumanji*, and *The Polar Express* differ in subject matter and artistic style, they all affect the audience profoundly with their creations built around lightness and darkness.

Brown presented her own artistic impressions from research and travel in Africa. Critics point out that by choosing to illustrate only primitive figures in an untamed environment, she presented denigrating and destructive pictures that foster stereotypic thinking and damage black children's racial image of themselves. *Shadow* is defended by others as but one picture book depicting but one aspect of an enormously broad African experience. This defense might have been acceptable if it were not for implications from the text supporting the pictures, the Cendrars poem "La Feticheuse" or "Shadow." It implies that shadows are spiritual symbols of an ancestral past represented by masks and other powerful objects, evoked by dancers and musicians and other storytellers, and found in fire and ghostly light or in ash and slithering darkness. Such sophisticated textual images are beyond the comprehension of most young children, and the book is left to communicate primarily through Brown's visual images alone. These repeatedly use unrelenting darkness itself in pictures of Africa and its people. Questionable backlighting of all figures presents black silhouettes in which human detail is disintegrated except for whites of the eyes. Blackness represents repugnant squirming creatures and staggering inhuman forms; black or translucently white cringing shapes sprawl grotesquely across the earth; black figures against black shadows march or leap or creep menacingly through high grass. All these uses of black and unearthly white have negative connotations as artistic symbols. Thus, in her third Caldecott Award winner, the artist has struck an unfortunate chord with young children—their fear of darkness, of the supernatural, and of the black of night itself.

The element of light and dark is employed most effectively for opposing moods of frivolity and despair in the 1967 Caldecott winner *Sam, Bangs and Moonshine* by Evaline Ness. (Her books *All in the Morning Early, A Pocketful of Cricket,* and *Tom Tit Tot* were chosen as Honor Books during three consecutive years leading up to the Award itself.) When life goes well for Sam in her fantasy world inhabited by lion, mermaid mother, chariot drawn by dragons, and wise old talking cat named Bangs, illustrations in line-and-wash halftones of two colors are crisply clean and filled with lightness of a summer's day by the sea. When Sam's flummadiddling moonshining lies get friend Thomas and Bangs himself in trouble, pictures are covered by darkness just as somber as the gray ribbed curtain of rain that falls outside.

Ness wrote the story from remembrances of her own childhood, adding touches along the way from photographs of fishing boats, Thomas's bicycle cap, and the baby kangaroo. She initially mounted the text onto page dummies, leaving blank spaces for illustrations; contrasting light and dark texturing was created with an inked roller and a wad of string. The resulting informal book design with its varied uses of double spreads and text placements is often more interesting than the rather static illustrations themselves. The pictures are reminiscent of the works of Swiss artist Albert Giacometti in their similar uses of sketchy lines, limited colors, and dramatically light and dark compositional areas.

Gradations of light and dark tones for implied texture and contour is exhibited superbly in *The Biggest Bear*, 1953 Medal-winning title by Lynd Ward, whose *America's Ethan Allen* had been an Honor book selection in 1950. Opaque watercolors in brown and black were used for the collection of single-page illustrations. Text was placed very formally on opposite pages. Pictures alternately showed deep space of outdoor settings and close-ups of solidly modeled figures highlighted on white pages with no implication of space beyond. The latter have an uncluttered simplicity in which light is used, not as source of illumination but as highlighting to direct the audience's attention to specific characters or events portrayed darkly silhouetted in the foreground. This technique is especially effective in three pictures in which the bear returns, always with a little smile for

Johnny Orchard, and in the sequence when the bear takes off through the woods, dragging Johnny behind him into the bear trap.

A strong influence on Ward's art was the Canadian backwoods, where he had spent a part of almost every year since early childhood. Although he once did meet a bear in the woods, he protested that he was not himself Johnny Orchard but rather an artist who could imagine even more clearly the bear never seen face to face, the one that is always the biggest, blackest, fiercest bear that ever lived. He never drew from live models but always from memory, and for *The Biggest Bear* he composed the whole sequence of pictures before adding the minimum amount of words needed to hold it all together.

Barbara Cooney's second Caldecott Award-winning title was the 1980 *Ox-Cart Man* with text by Donald Hall. Executed in an early-American primitive technique resembling painting on wood and in similar style to that of nineteenth-century painter Edward Hicks, *Ox-Cart Man* is a staid and simple cyclical tale given an unusual spark of life by appropriately formal yet imaginative page layouts, delightful richness in coloration, and a pleasantly surprising use of light and dark in a series of three illustrations. Most of the book pictures New Hampshire pastoral and Portsmouth marketplace settings with a keen eye for authentic detail of time and place and always in the flat shapes and blunt colors of primitive style, even for October leaves fallen to the ground or May blossoms on the apple trees. When a wonderfully red sunset appears just as the Ox-Cart Man approaches home from the market, it is something of a surprise. It dramatically transforms sky and hills by implying depth and contour, and after a dozen illustrations it is the first to demonstrate interest in a source of illumination. A turn of the page, and one has the welcoming home scene in warmth of the kitchen with exquisite modeling and highlighting of figures gathered around softening firelight. (This quiet family moment was accomplished by Cooney after changes were made from an earlier drawing on which she notes an intent to make the illustration darker, browner, more dramatic in use of light versus dark, cozier, and with Mother busier.) Another turn of the page, and one finds a barn scene in which the Ox-Cart Man carves a yoke while the winter sun casts across the floor and walls a long low shadow that is stunningly unique for such a work in early-American primitive style. Fire and red sky are repeated in a later illustration, but neither gives off the light or indeed offers the pleasurable surprise that Cooney's pictures of sunset, hearth, and barn offer in *Ox-Cart Man*.

They Were Strong and Good, the 1941 Award winner written and illustrated by Robert Lawson, offers excellent examples of cross-hatching done in fine lines using a brush and black tempera for gradation of light and dark contouring and texturing in figures and backgrounds. *Strong and Good* was an autobiographical account of the illustrator's parents and grandparents, representing both southern and northern lineage of which he was proud, even though his forebears were sometimes presented with characteristic Lawson levity. The story is to children of today an example of early black-and-white picture-book illustrating—as well as one of racial and sexual stereotyping in art and literature of another age. Twice an Honor Book Award winner (for *Four and Twenty Blackbirds* in 1938 and *Wee Gillis* in 1939), Lawson himself in his Caldecott acceptance speech expressed the opinion that book awards should not be given for one particular work but rather for long and faithful service, as in the military. He was perhaps unintentionally supporting a generally held notion that the 1941 Caldecott Committee was actually honoring his *The Story of Ferdinand,* published a few years before establishment of the Award and still beloved a half century later as a classic in American picture books.

Controversial 1940s Golden Book illustrator of *The Tall Book of Mother Goose,* artist Feodor Rojankovsky was awarded the Caldecott Medal in 1956 for his illustrations in *Frog Went A-Courtin',* the ancient ballad about Frog's wedding to Miss Mousie written down long ago in Scotland and retold here by John Langstaff. Rojankovsky from his childhood days in Russia had an unusually strong attachment to nature and to animals; he came to the United States after World War II as an illustrator for the Artists and Writers Guild. When presented with the manuscript of *Frog* to illustrate he began to see frogs everywhere—filling his working hours, haunting his sleep.

Rojankovsky's formality of book design alternates single-page illustrations in four colors with those in two colors (green and black). Placement of rhyming text is always at the bottom of the page except in two wordless double-page spreads, the last illustration and the endpaper decoration, which stand as highlights of balanced compositional accomplishment in a book that otherwise exhibits stylistic mannerisms of its day. Rojankovsky is for children a prime example of picture-book illustrator as folk artist, one who demonstrates artistic disinterest in effects of light and dark or implication of deep space, one whose professional motive and artistic motifs are documentation of a narrative and decoration of text through color and shape. But like Randolph Caldecott himself in his own version of this same story, Rojankovsky could uncannily express humor through color and shape in charming images that live in the hearts of long-ago children long after they are children no more.

Works Cited

Brown, Marcia, trans. *Shadow*. New York: Scribner, 1982.

Burton, Virginia Lee. *Choo Choo*. Boston: Houghton, 1937.

————. *Katy and the Big Snow*. Boston: Houghton, 1943.

————. *The Little House*. Boston: Houghton, 1942.

————. *Maybelle, the Cable Car*. Boston: Houghton, 1952.

————. *Mike Mulligan and His Steam Shovel*. Boston: Houghton, 1939.

————. *Song of Robin Hood*. Boston: Houghton, 1947.

Caudill, Rebecca. *A Pocketful of Cricket*. New York: Harper, 1964.

Emberley, Barbara. *Drummer Hoff*. Englewood Cliffs, N.J.: Prentice-Hall, 1967.

Fish, Helen Dean. *Four and Twenty Blackbirds: A Collection of Old Nursery Rhymes*. Philadelphia: Lippincott, 1937.

Hall, Donald. *Ox-Cart Man*. New York: Viking, 1979.

Holbrook, Stewart. *America's Ethan Allen*. Boston: Houghton, 1949.

Johnson, Crockett. *Harold and the Purple Crayon*. New York: Harper, 1958.

Joslin, Seslye. *What Do You Say, Dear?* Reading, Mass.: Addison-Wesley, 1958.

Krauss, Ruth. *A Hole Is to Dig*. New York: Harper, 1952.

————. *I'll Be You and You Be Me*. New York: Harper, 1954.

————. *A Very Special House*. New York: Harper, 1953.

Langstaff, John. *Frog Went A-Courtin'*. New York: Harcourt, 1955.

Lawson, Robert. *They Were Strong and Good*. New York: Viking, 1940.

Leaf, Munro. *Wee Gillis*. New York: Viking, 1938.

Leaf, Munro, and Robert Lawson. *The Story of Ferdinand*. New York: Viking, 1936.

McCloskey, Robert. *Make Way for Ducklings*. New York: Viking, 1941.

————. *Time of Wonder*. New York: Viking, 1957.

Manheim, Ralph, trans. *E. T. A. Hoffmann's Nutcracker*. New York: Crown, 1984.

Minarik, Else H. *Little Bear's Visit*. New York: Harper, 1961.

Ness, Evaline. *Sam, Bangs and Moonshine*. New York: Holt, 1966.

————. *Tom Tit Tot*. New York: Scribner, 1965.

Nic Leodhas, Sorche. *All in the Morning Early*. New York: Harper, 1963.

Petersham, Maud, and Miska Petersham. *The Rooster Crows*. New York: Macmillan, 1945.

Rojankovsky, Feodor. *The Tall Book of Mother Goose*. New York: Harper, 1942.

Sendak, Maurice. *In the Night Kitchen*. New York: Harper, 1970.

———. *Maurice Sendak's Really Rosie: Starring the Nutshell Kids*. New York: Harper, 1975.

———. *Outside Over There*. New York: Harper, 1981.

———. *Where the Wild Things Are*. New York: Harper, 1963.

Udry, Janice M. *Moon Jumpers*. New York: Harper, 1959.

Van Allsburg, Chris. *Ben's Dream*. Boston: Houghton, 1982.

———. *The Garden of Abdul Gasazi*. Boston: Houghton, 1979.

———. *Jumanji*. Boston: Houghton, 1980.

———. *The Mysteries of Harris Burdick*. Boston: Houghton, 1984.

———. *The Polar Express*. Boston: Houghton, 1985.

———. *The Wreck of the Zephyr*. Boston: Houghton, 1983.

Viguers, Ruth Hill, Marcia Dolphin, and Bertha Mahony Miller, comps. *Illustrators of Children's Books: 1946–1956*. Boston: Horn Book, 1958.

Ward, Lynd. *The Biggest Bear*. Boston: Houghton, 1952.

Zolotow, Charlotte. *Mr. Rabbit and the Lovely Present*. New York: Harper, 1962.

5
Shape: *The Big Snow, White Snow Bright Snow,* and *The Snowy Day*

White Snow Bright Snow won Roger Duvoisin the 1948 Caldecott Award. His expressionistic illustrations accompanied Alvin Tresselt's poetic story about a snowstorm's effects on people in a small community. The next year's Award winner was *The Big Snow* by author-illustrators Berta and Elmer Hader, who realistically portrayed the consequences of a winter storm for animals in the woods. And in 1963 Ezra Jack Keats won the Medal as well as the hearts of children everywhere with his intimate depiction of one boy's small adventures in the first snowfall of winter in *The Snowy Day.*

Living just miles from each other in the greater New York City area, the renowned American illustrators for *The Big Snow, White Snow Bright Snow,* and *The Snowy Day* verifiably endured some of the same northeast snowstorms, however inspired they were to picture such events in singularly personal and strikingly different ways. All died within a single decade, leaving a rich legacy of a combined output of over three hundred illustrated books for children.

Berta and Elmer Hader

The Haders' inspiration for *The Big Snow* was an "astonishing snowfall" in 1947. It became known as the "Big Snow" in the area around their home in Nyack, twenty-five miles north of New York City. Berta and Elmer had built their sandstone house on a tangled and steep woodland hill overlooking the Tappan Zee Bridge that crosses the Hudson River and enjoyed playing host to wild animals that came from the woods in Palisades Park behind their property. The "Big Snow" blocked the animals' access to food: "The feeding stations on the ground were buried too deep to be reached by the most energetic scratching and those hanging in the trees were heavily blanketed with snow that was turning to ice," the Haders recalled in their 1949 Caldecott acceptance speech. Once the snow finally stopped, the two artists began to shovel paths, scatter seeds and corn, put out pans of food, and drag hay from the shed for their "feathered and furry friends," just as they later pictured in *The Big Snow*. "The food problem and the beauty of the snow-covered hillside struck us both as a good subject for a picture book. The models and the background for the pictures were right outside our windows. With the subject agreed on, the story seemed to write itself."

Faithful to the beauty of their live models and hillside, the avowed animal lovers painted and drew woodland scenes with such a reverent attitude that for many children *The Big Snow* provides a first introduction to the diversity of American wildlife—and its vulnerability. Primary-age children enjoy gathering information about the natural world beyond their immediate environment. From such wildlife studies they learn how large or small an animal may be in relation to others, what details characterize male and female in a species, what anatomical distinctions separate one class of creature from another, and most important to conservationists like the Haders, what amount of care and respect from humans is required for such creatures' survival.

Except for the figures of the Haders themselves toward the end of the book, *The Big Snow*'s art resembles much found in nonfiction books intended for children's edification about nature. In subject matter and romanticized artistic style, the book can also be compared with the work of John James Audubon, the nineteenth-century painter and naturalist. Because of their naturalism, *The Big Snow*'s illustrations are accepted as true and real, which in most respects they are. However, Mrs. Cottontail, Mrs. Chipmunk, ground hog, wood rat, and the birds all communicate with each other in English. When this fantasy situation is not continued throughout, young listeners are sometimes disappointed by its absence. At least the animals are not rendered ludicrous by unnatural facial expressions or gesturing mannerisms that would spoil their worth as real-life studies for children. And as in McCloskey's portrayal of the Mallard family, the Haders create a feeling of intimacy by showing the creatures close to the audience or in cozy relationship with others of their kind.

The Haders' home on the Hudson, pictured in *The Big Snow*, was known as "Willow Hill" because of big trees that shelter a pool at the foot of a waterfall tumbling over moss-covered rocks set into the hillside. The construction of this remarkable house by the Haders themselves parallels the development of their collaborative career. Foundations for both were laid in 1919, when Berta Hoerner and Elmer Hader were married and began work together illustrating children's feature sections in magazines and shortly afterwards acquired the hillside overgrown with brush where they would build their home. Berta's childhood had been spent in Mexico, Texas, New York, Seattle, and San Francisco; along the way she dropped ambitions for a career in journalism so as to give all her time to art. A California native, Elmer spent two-and-a-half years in Paris studying art and then served as a military engineer during World War I. Both ambitious newlyweds were determined that the site for their new home be just right to allow them to "pick up where we left off when the war interrupted our lives" and to nurture not only their life together as artists but also their shared love of nature.

There were no architectural blueprints for the house, and so it just grew. Similarly, there were no articulated plans for the Haders' early book-illustrating career. It began with seven titles in 1927–28 for the Happy Hour series by Macmillan. *The Picture Book of Travel* (1928) was the first book they wrote as well as illustrated, and in 1930 *A Picture Book of Mother Goose* established them firmly as rising young talents in children's illustrated literature. During the decade that followed, the artists often wrote and illustrated three books of their own in the same year that they illustrated as many as six by other authors.

Meanwhile their house of wood and stone took shape with giant fireplace nine feet wide, hand-sawed floor board and beams, numerous terraces to take advantage of sun or shade. Willow Hill acquired sleeping room for as many as fourteen guests (Berta counted among many friends Maud Petersham and Rose Wilder Lane, writer daughter of Laura Ingalls Wilder). Their friends the birds were presented with handmade birdhouses that had real hinges on the doors, and other animals rescued from distress were named Phoebe and Squirrely. Likewise in their career, more and more animal books appeared, such as *Friendly Phoebe*, *Little White Foot*, and *Quack-Quack*. Two were named Caldecott Honor Books, *Cock-A-Doodle-Doo* in 1940 and *Mighty Hunter* in 1944. Especially admired was *Little Appaloosa* (1949), inspired by Elmer's memories of his own boyhood pony.

The Haders themselves understood best this interrelationship between home-building and book-building. They wrote about both experiences, first in "Working Together: The Inside Story of the

Hader Books" in 1937 and later in *The Little Stone House* in 1944. In "Working Together," the collaborators explained in simple words how they discussed the subject for a book, decided on the intended audience, and developed the ideas and pictures together (sometimes one started an illustration and the other finished it). They did not try out their ideas on the intended audience because "comments and criticism from the younger generation can be very disconcerting if not altogether discouraging." In *Little Stone House* their explanation of how they started building Willow Hill and modified it over the years provides us with a revealing metaphor as well for their collaborative career in children's books during their remarkably constructive lifetimes.

Roger Duvoisin

Uppermost in Roger Duvoisin's mind as he began his 1948 Caldecott acceptance speech was apparently the same paralyzing snowstorm that the Haders portrayed at Willow Hill in *The Big Snow* and described in their 1949 Award speech. Around Duvoisin's home in Gladstone, New Jersey, the famous twenty-four-inch snowfall of 1947 "stopped trains dead in their tracks." The artist spent two days shoveling "to clear our five-hundred-foot drive of *White Snow Bright Snow*"; there was no water, light, or heat for almost two weeks. The Award-winning title had been published before the snowstorm, and the illustrator felt sure that "no one could have felt any sympathy for the book" if they had realized as "I have known all along, that the book brought the winter upon us." Of course, the very next year's Caldecott winner was the Haders' portrayal of the winter Duvoisin's *White Snow* had brought upon them all.

Duvoisin himself described his pictures as personally inspired by "childhood love for snow, like all childhood memories, strong enough in all of us to make us open our hearts to everything connected with snow . . . the secret urge to go out and feel the snow, to plunge our hands into it, to make snowballs and snowmen . . . [an artist's] recalling the wonderful and charming impressions of his childhood so that he may pass them on to children of new generations; to recreate for them the world which made his own childhood happy." The artist created childlike perceptions of dramatic changes in landscape brought about by a first snowfall, of gaiety and fun for children while grownups fall victim to the weather, and of varying shifts in mood as dark sky whitens before turning into clear blue of morning.

Even children who have not experienced a heavy snowfall enjoy watching for the four main characters as they go about their duties—but some youngsters express the wish that children in the story also had been specifically characterized. *White Snow* is concerned with the snow's effects on a small group of people in a neighborhood, and the concept of groups and interdependence of people is of interest to primary-aged youngsters who are just forming relationships with others.

Perhaps then Duvoisin thought back to boyhood enjoyment of wintertime in his birthplace, Geneva, Switzerland, where later in school he studied music as well as art, and out of school began to paint scenery, murals, posters, and illustrations. Interest in ceramics led him into managership at a young age of a century-old pottery plant in France, and a flair for bright colors and eye-catching designs led to jobs with textile firms in Lyons and Paris. In 1927 an American fabric manufacturer paid his expenses to the United States with the understanding that he work for the company at least four years. Recently married to Swiss-born Louise Fatio, the young designer sailed the next week for New York, where the couple found an apartment in Brooklyn and settled down for the only time in Duvoisin's life that he was "tied to regular hours and a routine job . . . surprisingly tolerable" while he improved his schoolboy English with aid of an English-French dictionary. Both husband and wife became U.S. citizens in 1938; Roger, Junior, later became a neurologist and Jacques an architect, as had been Duvoisin's father in Switzerland.

When son Roger at age four requested help with a drawing, he propelled his father into a career as children's author-illustrator. Duvoisin's job had abruptly ended during the depression, and so the artist, encouraged by successes with free-lance illustrating for magazines and book advertising, turned out two illustrated stories inspired by and written for Roger, *A Little Boy Was Drawing* and *Donkey-Donkey*. Nine other titles with Duvoisin as author and illustrator followed in the 1930s and 1940s before the appearance in 1950 of popular silly goose *Petunia*, who was "glad to help" and starred in five more titles through 1965. Other books of the 1950s included *A For Ark* and *One Thousand Christmas Beards*. In 1961 Duvoisin created another loveable animal character, hippo *Veronica*, who appeared in three more titles in quick succession over the same number of years. Five other books were published in the 1960s, and in the 1970s Duvoisin introduced more new animal characters— *Jasmine* the cow, *Periwinkle* the giraffe, *Crocus* the crocodile, and *Snowy and Woody* the bears, in addition to publishing other titles. The last book with Duvoisin as author and illustrator was a crocodile sequel, *Importance of Crocus*, published posthumously in 1981.

Duvoisin's parallel career as illustrator for other authors of folklore, children's classics, and history as well as nature, fantasy, and holiday stories began in 1936 with three titles, most notably William Rose Benét's collection *Mother Goose*. Another title appeared almost every year—and sometimes as many as six in a single phenomenal year's time—for over forty years. The list encompasses over two dozen publishers and more than sixty authors, including Charlotte Zolotow, Mary Calhoun, Adelaide Holl, and William Lipkind. The 1947 publication of *White Snow Bright Snow* began the auspicious thirty-year collaboration of Alvin Tresselt with Duvoisin. They produced seventeen more titles, including the 1966 Caldecott Honor Book *Hide and Seek Fog*. Duvoisin's banner year was 1950: he published *Petunia*, two books with Tresselt, three more titles illustrated for others, and the first *Happy Lion* book, his first collaboration with his wife, Louise Fatio.

Duvoisin and Fatio's home in New Jersey not far from the Haders' in New York was planned and partly built by them in the 1940s in a rural setting on a wooded hill. The property was a refuge for wildlife as well as a menagerie of domestic pets—like ducks who followed behind Jacques when he was a boy—all buried when the time came in a private animal cemetery reserved for pet and predator alike in the fifteen acres of Duvoisin land.

In the Duvoisin home hung paintings by Henri Matisse and Raoul Dufy, leader and disciple respectively in the early twentieth-century French group know as Fauvists, who celebrated what was felt rather than what was seen through explosions of violently bright and crudely harsh colors in juxtaposition. The Fauvism movement was at its peak in France during the years that Duvoisin as a young man studied there; its attitudes emerge triumphant in the best of Roger Duvoisin's picture books. The delightful personalities and comical adventures of Petunia and the Happy Lion enchant children everywhere. The nature books, especially with Tresselt, stand noteworthy as uniquely personal artistic statements for children about small and large events in the world around us.

Ezra Jack Keats

In New York City forty miles due east of Duvoisin and an even shorter distance downriver from the Haders lived Ezra Jack Keats. In 1947, the year of the "Big Snow," *Collier's* gave the thirty-one-year-old artist his very first illustration assignment. Up to that time Keats had succeeded as a prize-winning high school painter awarded three scholarships upon graduation, a WPA muralist, a comic-book artist, and a camouflage expert during World War II. Except for the three years' duty in the service, a year studying art in Europe, and some later traveling to other countries, this prolific illustrator lived and worked in New York. He spent his childhood in Brooklyn and his adult life in an apartment near Central Park.

After 1947 Keats's magazine and book-jacket illustrating led to many story-illustration assignments. McGraw hired him for five titles of the series that began in 1957 with *The Indians Knew* and *The Pilgrims Knew*, and for four titles of the Danny Dunn series. Through the 1960s the artist continued to illustrate popular books still found on shelves today, with texts by Millicent Selsam, Ann Nolan Clark, Margaret Friskey, Paul Showers, Patricia M. Martin, and others. In 1960, favorable response to his collaboration with Pat Cherr for *My Dog Is Lost!* encouraged him to write as well as illustrate *The Snowy Day*, which appeared in 1962. Keats continued to contribute an original creation to children's literature almost every year through *Clementina's Cactus* in 1982, while illustrating only a few selections by others. These included *In a Spring Garden, The King's Fountain*, and *Two Tickets to Freedom* by Florence B. Freedman, the illustrator's high school English teacher and a friend of the Keats family throughout the years.

Some of Keats's books were illustrated versions of traditional songs and stories, such as *Over in the Meadow, The Little Drummer Boy*, and *John Henry*. There were also fun-loving animal books, such as *Kitten for a Day, Skates!*, and *Psst! Doggie*; titles with girls as main characters, such as *Jennie's Hat* and *Maggie and the Pirate*; and mood pieces like *Apt. 3*. For preschool and primary-age youngsters the collection of a dozen titles often called the Peter Books forms a series around a neighborhood gang with Peter as nucleus and with real-life problems to be solved. Starting with the boy alone in *The Snowy Day*, the series continues through his and his friends' adventures and ends with one friend's establishment in another neighborhood altogether. For years, teachers, librarians, and school media specialists, along with their young audiences, have enjoyed "watching

Peter grow" as each title is read aloud, new friends are introduced, and old ones return.

Keats's mixed-media drawing relies on collage and geometrical abstraction. It met well-deserved success in *The Snowy Day* and subsequent titles. In 1962 the artist related in his acceptance speech that he "had no idea as to how [*The Snowy Day*] would be illustrated, except that I wanted to add a few bits of patterned paper to supplement the painting. . . . before I realized it, each page was being handled in a style I had never worked in before. . . . the mother's dress is made of the kind of oilcloth used for lining cupboards . . . snowflakes [were made from] patterns [cut] out of gum erasers. . . . gray background for the pages where Peter goes to sleep was made by spattering India ink with a toothbrush." The contrasting bold shapes and colors may have been influenced by Paul Klee, Henri Matisse, Paul Delaunay, and such nineteenth-century Japanese paintings as those of Hokusai.

Keats has been heralded as the children's illustrator who in the 1960s breached the intolerance of black children as main characters in American picture books. Keats himself explained in "A Conversation with Ezra Jack Keats," put out by the Children's Book department of Macmillan:

> For about ten years I illustrated other people's books. There were two things that troubled me at that time: one was that in many of the manuscripts I was given there was a peculiar quality of contrivance and rigid structure; the other was that I never got a story about black people, black children. I decided that if I ever did a book of my own it would be more of a happening—certainly not a structured thing, but an experience. My hero would be a black child. I made many sketches and studies of black children, so that Peter would not be a white kid colored brown.

Events of an intensely personal and autobiographical nature influenced the settings, character motivations, and events of Peter Books beginning with *The Snowy Day*. Keats recreated his own childhood remembrances or similar events, contributing to young children's overwhelming intuitive acceptance of the "rightness" of the situations shown. For example, throughout the titles we see an urban environment with increasingly less tolerable conditions. Keats's own childhood was spent in a "run-down tenement in the East New York section of Brooklyn"; he was the youngest of three children of immigrant parents who in their teens fled persecution of Jews in Poland. The bullies depicted in *Goggles!* came from Keats's recollection that he was "intercepted once by some tough older neighborhood boys when I was about eight. I had a painting of mine under my arm. They closed in and pulled it out of my hands. . . . When they learned that I had done the painting, they began to treat me with respect. From then on, when they'd see me, I'd be greeted with 'Hi, Doc!' " He also recalled from age nine becoming the neighborhood "Pied Piper. . . . I began to tell stories to the kids . . . make them up as I'd go along." This experience was recreated in the street performances of Peter and Archie in *Hi, Cat!* and in Susie and Roberto's puppet show in *Louie*. The artist also admitted to being awkwardly shy in junior high school around girls like Harriet Tawarski, who "turned my legs into accordians." This "mixed up" feeling was later attributed to Peter in *A Letter to Amy*.

Keats's mother was approving, helpful, and encouraging, like Peter's mother in the first four books and like Peg in *Louie's Search*, who says about her son, "What? IMPOSSIBLE! He's the best boy in the world!" The artist's mother once showed off to neighbors the kitchen table he'd completely covered with drawings of exotic people and cottages with smoke coming out the chimneys: "Now isn't that nice! You know, it's so wonderful, it's a shame to wash it off." He also said that his mother would "wake him to see the colors of dawn over the city," and these early mornings have been recalled in *The Snowy Day* and *Dreams*. Dramatic skies are found in almost every Keats book, and the artist described his childhood experience creating the first one: "I covered a board with my blue paint. I dipped my brush into the white paint and dabbed it onto the board, shook the brush a little and let it trail off. I stepped back and got the greatest thrill I can remember. I saw a little cloud floating across a blue sky . . . . Even today, when I look up and see a tiny cloud floating across the sky with little wispy ends trailing off, I think of that time." Keats's readers can share that feeling most especially in the mountain-climbing illustration from *Snowy Day* and rainy-day scenes in *A Letter to Amy*.

Keats's father was a Greenwich Village waiter who often saw down-and-out artists, and he was torn between pride in his son's work and dread over his future—he brought the boy tubes of paint but said they were swapped for a bowl of soup by starving artists. When the elder Keats died, the son found in his father's wallet old clippings about his awards that had never been mentioned between the two of them over the years. Figures of fathers in Keats's books are few: the gruff stepfather Barney appears in *Louie's Search* and

Regards to the Man in the Moon, and a nice mustached gentleman is seen in *Whistle for Willie* and *Peter's Chair.*

The last Peter Books have plots concerning Louie and demonstrate such subtle parallels with Keats's own life that one wonders if this poignant character is not the artist himself as a painfully sensitive child. In *Louie* the boy retreated to his room, where he sucked his thumb and daydreamed, while in *The Trip* and *Regards to the Man in the Moon* he escaped from loneliness by flying away to fantasylands. Keats said that as a boy he would "hole up and draw" to flee from unhappiness and humiliating defeats, creating art from anything he could find, once even painting with Mercurochrome. In *Louie's Search,* the boy's unpleasant encounters with a baker and Barney hark back to times during the depression when Keats was sent to buy the family's groceries on credit "to the accompaniment of abuse from the shopkeepers about our unpaid bills. . . . Diminished and humiliated, I returned with the barest necessities, and those painful messages."

The figure of Louie on his long walks is reminiscent of Keats's own walks as a youngster—"anywhere, I thought—so long as it was away from home." He sometimes found himself in another neighborhood that seemed to him to be "another planet . . . lined with quiet lanes of huge gnarled trees, lush lawns . . . well-kept houses . . . trimmed shrubbery . . . new avenues of peace and enchantment." Fantasy trips recur throughout Keats's books as escape from childhood's frustration, pain, or anger, and in one illustration for *The Trip* is found a small photograph of the artist himself, looking with amazed envy as Louie and friends fly by in a plane.

Our introduction to Louie, however, occurs when his speechlessness is shaken by the appearance of Gussie. He utters his first word, "Hello!" Throughout his own life, Keats marked changes in his career as shock waves of recognition for things innately important to him: his first creation of a little cloud floating across a blue sky; his discovery as a teenager of the Arlington Branch of the Brooklyn Public Library, in which he began to read the art books; his marvel at Daumier's painting *Third Class Carriage* on a visit with his father to the Metropolitan Museum of Art; his time spent with a child in Kentucky, who appeared in his first illustrated book, *Jubilant for Sure;* and his "total captivation . . . offering me fresh pleasure at each encounter" with four photographs in the May 13, 1940, issue of *Life.* He kept these photos on his studio wall for over twenty years, and their image of a little black child's "expressive face, body attitudes, the very way he wore his clothes" became the inspiration for Peter himself.

Thus this illustrator's remarkable tenacious memory nurtured his every move in art and allowed him to use the past to create meaningful works for children in the present. When asked what was the greatest source of material for his books, Keats replied, "Well, as an editor of mine once said, I'm an ex-kid." In "Ezra Jack Keats Remembers: Discovering the Library" (*Teacher*, December 1976), he wrote about his yielding to an irresistible yearning to return to the Brooklyn library he had discovered as a boy:

> Halfway up the steps I wondered, "Would [my books] be there?" I hurried to the top and looked for the picture books. I scanned the shelves—there they were. I stood looking at my own books on the shelves and mused at the wonder of it all. What long and winding paths had taken me from that staircase [leading to the art books] to this one?

The path Keats took was indeed a fortunate one for children, past, present, and future, and for the child in us all.

Book Design

White Snow Bright Snow and *The Big Snow* in hardbound editions are both vertical rectangular, and *The Snowy Day* is horizontal rectangular. Although *The Snowy Day* is smaller, its simple and bold illustrations make it suitable for a large audience. All three books make use of double-page as well as single-page fields of action, and the first two include on a few pages some smaller vignettes with accompanying texts. Offset lithography was used to print the acetate color separations in *White Snow*, the watercolor paintings in *The Big Snow*, and the collage technique in *The Snowy Day*. Later editions of *White Snow* and *The Big Snow* show improvements in quality of covers and paper, so that these books stand up to heavy use as does the durable 1962 Viking hardbound edition of *The Snowy Day*.

Much of each book's overall impact is the direct result of choices of colors, audience's viewpoints, and picture composition that takes into account text placement and the invisible line of the gutter. The Haders in *The Big Snow* are most successful with full-color illustrations of animals and woods in naturalistic earthtones; many children wish that the entire book had been illustrated in such sensitive, delicate watercolors. Black-and-white drawings are masterful and quite attractive in themselves, but juxtaposed with the color illustrations these drawings seem less important, even though the very essence of the story is equality in care for all animals in the snowstorm. In *The Big Snow* as in *The Little House*, the small illustration on the last page is anticlimatic. The more appropriate ending would seem to be the page just before, in which all animals "heard the glad tidings and joined the happy throng." The audience's viewpoint is most often at a comfortably normal eye level, but a few worm's-eye level close-ups give youngsters the same satisfaction in implied texture and anatomical details of little creatures that they experienced in *Make Way for Ducklings*.

The Big Snow offers excellent examples of exquisite balance within an artistic field of action. The illustrations are not framed by lines or even the outer perimeters of the page but rather by decorative placement of drawn or painted leaves, grass, snowbanks, or sky, resulting in irregular or free-form shapes for the illustrations themselves. These outlines play as much a part in balancing the figures and colors within the pictures as do the figures and colors themselves. The strictly paragraphed text is arranged formally beneath or above these illustrations, providing a structured area of words as asymmetrical balance for the irregularly shaped areas of art. In a few instances, text is placed more informally.

Macmillan's Collier Books paperbound edition of *The Big Snow* cannot be wholeheartedly recommended for use in art appreciation because it distorts some colors, resulting in muddy browns and garish reds, and because its tighter binding occasionally interferes with the free-form outlines for illustrations. In the sound filmstrip by Weston Woods, some compositions were slightly restructured to fit in single film frames. Regrettably, the production left out not only one lovely color picture of a gray squirrel but also the two pages that illustrate the counting of individual snowflakes. The filmstrip can still be recommended, however, for its sensitive additions of color to black-and-white illustrations. For very young children, the filmstrip may be projected while lengthy text is condensed by an adult reading aloud.

In *White Snow Bright Snow* choices of colors, viewpoints, and compositional arrangements are not as uniformly pleasing to young children as in *The Big Snow*. Roger Duvoisin used an eclectic design style that later became identified with him, most notably through the exotic adventures of such barnyard characters as Petunia and Veronica. A less experimental design might have been more appropriate for *White Snow Bright Snow* since certain page layouts do result in a confusing conglomeration.

The artist's use of the first three double pages points up such problems. A background of gray brushed across the pages implies the overcast sky of approaching winter. However, it cannot be understood as the same background for the different vignettes. Not only would the postman, farmer, policeman, and policeman's wife not appear in the same setting, but the distance and angle for the audience's viewpoint is altered from left to right pages and even within the pages themselves. Poses of postman, farmer, policeman, and wife are separate vignettes, but the gray background with falling snowflakes gives the children the false impression that the setting is the same for all. The second illustration, in which children stand beneath a gray sky on the left, is more readily understood by youngsters as a single-page illustration, even though the same gray is repeated somewhat unattractively as background for text on the opposite page.

Placement of Tresselt's text itself is one of the book's single biggest flaws. It has both very formal text placements opposite illustrations and very informal shapings within illustrations or to the side of vignettes. The result too often is confusion as to sequence and overcrowding of artistic figures within compositions. The erratic placements for text contribute little to compositional balance within vignettes, which are already perplexing due to their gray coloration and mixture of viewpoints. To children, the most successful illustration is a wordless double-page spread of the town under a blanket of snow, even though text describing the automobiles as "big fat raisins" is awkwardly placed on the preceding page.

Added to this frequent lack of artistic balance is interference by the gutter in every double-page spread. Paths lead nowhere, and buildings are abruptly chopped off. In various illustrations, a boy, a dog, a man, a No Parking sign, and most important, the postman who falls into a snowbank have each disappeared within the binding's crease. They can only be restored by viewing the Weston Woods sound filmstrip version of the book. For these restorations and for dramatic improvements in balance, the filmstrip is strongly recommended for art appreciation of *White Snow*.

The Snowy Day has become a classic example of design simplicity for picture books. Throughout the little story, absolute stability prevails through consistent use of single- and double-page fields of action, a viewpoint at normal eye level, and simple text that is uniformly placed toward tops or bottoms of illustrations. Keats was less formal with text arrangement than were the Haders in *The Big Snow* but demonstrated more formality than did Duvoisin in *White Snow*. In *The Snowy Day* the short text is occasionally shaped to fit within an illustration, but these brief lapses into informality are exactly suited to the message of the text itself and thus add to the design.

Keats's illustrations are all structured on an invisible horizontal baseline that extends off the pages themselves, implying that the audience is witness to only a portion of indoor as well as outdoor scenes. Double-page spreads demonstrate the artist's absolute control of simple shapes and bold colors to balance compositions. Single-page illustrations are presented in pairs that move the story forward step by step. The pictures in which Peter dreams and then wakes up are well-balanced within themselves, but their colors are less successful presented side by side than are other colors used in previous illustrations. The double-page illustration of the little boy climbing a snowbank on one page and then sliding down on the other is called a *continuous narrative*, since the repeated figure of Peter in two places within the same setting implies a figure in motion.

The Viking Seafarer paperbound edition can be recommended for use in art appreciation, since it exhibits better reproduction of the vibrant colors in the original *The Snowy Day* than does another paperbound by Scholastic. A short Weston Woods sound filmstrip is also commended for its faithful reproduction of Keats's colors, but lamentably, the quick single-page sequences have been rearranged, and the continuous narrative effect of the snowbank illustration is lost when it is divided into two separate frames.

Art Appreciation of *The Big Snow*

When a picture book is being read aloud, *shape* is the first artistic element a young child looks for. Artists who properly understand dramatic balance for storytelling purposes within compositions arrange their shapes so that the child's eye may travel across many shapes in a single picture but finally rest on the dominant shape. Properties of the shape are then recognized by the viewer: texture, color, line, use of light and dark, and spatial relationship within the composition. If length of text allows time for the child's eye to explore, other shapes and their uses may also be noted.

Many artists can be identified not only by the kinds of shapes and proportions they most often use, but also by the proportion between shapes within a field of action. In the fine arts this sense of proportion is one aspect of an artist's style—it makes paintings by Picasso or pieces of sculpture by Michelangelo recognizable as having been created by them. In children's illustrated literature, lithographed drawings in *Make Way for Ducklings* or bold woodcuts in *Drummer Hoff* can be identified as the work of Robert McCloskey or Ed Emberley. Also important to point out to children is that, just as Picasso used shape differently during various periods of his development, so have some Caldecott artists been awarded the Medal more than once for widely divergent uses of shape.

The Big Snow, White Snow Bright Snow, and *The Snowy Day* have been chosen for study not only because each displays superbly for children a different artistic attitude toward *shape* but also because the three books offer an opportunity to introduce artists who established their reputations through collections of titles that demonstrated a "family" of shapes. Other books from collections by the Haders, by Duvoisin (especially in collaboration with Tresselt), and by Keats (at least through the series about Peter and his friends) can also be studied.

Shape tends to be defined as predominantly naturally *organic* or mathematically *geometric*. The difference is easiest for children to recognize through comparisons. Different systems of proportion may also be taught through juxtaposition. Children may therefore benefit by studying all three Caldecott "snow books" during a single session or at least within a very short period of time. Discussion of implied contour and texture through use of organic shape and idealized proportion will rely primarily on the frontispiece illustration in *The Big Snow,* called here "Animals in the Snow." To discuss geometric shape and natural proportions, study will begin with "The Haders" on the book's copyright page. Hierarchic proportion is seen on two pages called here "Snowflakes" on pages 27–28.[1] Uses of systems of proportion for implied depth will be discussed in *White Snow Bright Snow* and the study will conclude with an introduction to simplification of organic shape as found in *The Snowy Day.*

IDEALIZED PROPORTION OF ORGANIC SHAPE

Two-dimensional organic shape in art resembles three-dimensional, free-form, or biomorphic configurations usually associated with the natural world. Organic shape portrays living organisms, plants and

---

[1] Pagination begins on first page with text.

animals, the growing and changing things of earth. The creatures, trees, bushes, and even the falling snowflakes in "Animals in the Snow" are organic creations with recognizable shapes. A shape can also be recognized by its outline, whether a hard edge line or a softer contrast of line effects. It can further be defined as *closed* when this outline completely separates it from surrounding space or *open* when the outline is loosely structured to allow other space to penetrate. In both paintings and drawings, the Haders use both hard and soft outlines, and most often the shapes that result are closed. Each of the animals is appropriately modeled and implied to be furry or feathery. The blanket softness of snow contrasts nicely with the rough texture of gnarled tree bark. "Animals in the Snow" thus sets the stage for *The Big Snow* as a collection of wildlife art.

Figures with organic shape often have a geometric underlying structure. *Idealized proportion* attempts to portray this structure with strict ratios for parts in relationship to each other. In this first illustration, for instance, the Haders' devoted reliance on idealized proportion results in presentation of two deer with identical, perfectly formed faces that have as their underlying structures neat little triangles from left eye to nose to right eye. The buck and doe are constructed around basic ovals, verticals, triangles, and circles. Three skunks are also pictured exactly the same, as if one ideal way existed for skunks to be pictured: a large round tail on an oval body with a small round head and triangular ears. In *The Big Snow*, the Haders romanticized American wildlife by representing flawless figures, not only in "Animals in the Snow" but throughout the book.

Idealized proportion can also be applied to the spatial relationship among figures within a composition. The goal is a balance of amounts, sizes, and types of figures within the field of action. Figures in "Animals in the Snow" are ideally proportioned within the picture, since just enough small organic shapes are present to balance the artistic weight of larger shapes, and no shapes overlap to destroy this perfect balance, as undoubtedly they might in a truly realistic setting. Thus, in addition to having ideal proportion, the figures are ideally posed, much like stuffed animals in a formal exhibit.

GEOMETRIC SHAPE AND NATURAL PROPORTION

On the book's copyright page a vignette of the Haders offers an immediate comparison between organic and inorganic or geometric shape. The rectangular shovels, Elmer's round glasses, and Berta's coat buttons are examples of geometric shapes: they are mathematically precise and do not reflect irregularity. In the background are other geometric shapes: a triangular roof, rectangular windows, and square windowpanes. Organic shapes in this picture are the Haders themselves, snowdrifts, and icicles.

A comparison of "The Haders" with "Animals in the Snow" also illustrates the difference between idealized and natural proportion. *Natural proportion* does not attempt to portray a perfectly uniform shape but demonstrates instead an artistic interest in a form's individual characteristics, the less attractive as well as the attractive. Natural proportion was used for the Haders, even though the portrayal was intended as caricaturistic self-portraiture rather than photographic realism. The house in the background was also pictured in more detail as a specific home, as compared, for instance, with Burton's simplistically idealized depiction of her home in *The Little House*.

Natural proportion can also be recognized in placement of figures themselves. The Haders' pose is formal, but the overlapping of snowbanks is natural. The imposition of high drifts in front of figures in many other illustrations like this one not only shows the world as it really is but also emphasizes that snow itself is a main character in the story.

HIERARCHIC PROPORTION WITHIN COMPOSITION

Delicate drawings of snowflakes on pages 27–28 of *The Big Snow* are examples of geometric shapes to be found in nature. Like leaves, pine trees, and some flowers, snowflakes are mathematically precise; juxtaposed with a squirrel, they offer an excellent comparison with free-form irregularity found elsewhere in nature. The falling flakes are shown in *hierarchic proportion*, a scale that dictates large sizes for important figures and small sizes for less important. In the beginning, the snowflakes are quite large. They diminish in size through the series of vignettes and are more naturally proportioned beside the squirrel under his branch at the end. Thus hierarchic proportion calls attention to the fragile flakes at the beginning and to the squirrel later.

The *shape* within an artist's field of action is called a "figure" and the empty background space is termed "ground." Appreciation of negative, unfilled space in works of art can be enhanced by an understanding of the interplay between figure and ground in "Snowflakes." Closed shapes of squirrel and snowflakes are of course the figures, and slight lines imply contour, first for an embankment and then for a limb under which the squirrel takes cover. The snowy white on these two pages, however, is primarily all ground and contributes effectively to the delicacy of drawn snowflake figures. The tree branch is one example of an open shape in which the white of the ground penetrates the white of the snow-laden figure itself.

Outlines of white figures on white ground in "Snowflakes" are interesting for children to compare with the hardbound edition's endpaper designs, in which white flakes are presented on a brilliant blue ground and demonstrate the ambiguity that often results from artistic uses for figure and ground. Our visual experience requires that we recognize the white flakes as the figures, but if the endpaper patterns are viewed in reverse as if they were paper cuttings, then the blue itself also represents intriguing shapes.

Art Appreciation of *White Snow Bright Snow:* Systems of Proportion and Implied Depth

The artistic attitude of Duvoisin in *White Snow* is expressive rather than realistic. He chooses only primary red and yellow as dominant hues to depict people, houses, and natural surroundings that would in reality include more color choices. The artist in fact once said, "The fewer the colors, the greater the challenge." The expressive approach is also seen in the policeman's house, for which the illustrator used cutaway views that endow the audience with super-human powers to see through walls into bathroom and kitchen. The case against realism in *White Snow* is clinched by the illustrator's use of different proportion systems for shapes and even for different figures in the same compositions to imply depth.

This case against realism does not imply that Duvoisin created a fantasy world. Recognizable organic and geometric shapes appear in abundance in this book, and all humans, animals, and buildings have idealized proportion. While idealized shape seems realistic in *The Big Snow*, figures in *White Snow* are simplified, with flat, shallow depth to give artistic impressions much like those in *The Little House*. Note for instance that Duvoisin simplifies houses and people as did Burton and on page 29 the sun and its drawn rays are in formal position.[2] Use of ground colorations for effect on the audience is

[2]*White Snow Bright Snow* has its own pagination, which is used here.

also similar to Burton's: dirty gray sets the mood for dark fall and winter scenes, and the cleanest of whites is used for clear winter skies and for the coming of spring.

Many illustrations by Duvoisin employ natural proportion in sizes and amounts of shapes, overlapping, and audience perspectives. Figures lost in the binding's gutter would undoubtedly have added balance between shapes within some double-page spreads. In some cases, though, rabbits appear too large in relation to children nearby or a house seems very small for its owner standing outside. These digressions are good examples for children of hierarchic proportion used by this illustrator. The policeman on page 13, for example, is oversized compared to other shapes on the facing page. This disparity helps us understand that on both pages all figures are vignettes viewed from different distances and not shown in the same setting with the same depth, as they may seem at first glance.

In one illustration Duvoisin uses *distorted proportion*, in which characteristics of a shape are grossly overstated in relation to its other parts or to other figures. The melting snowman on page 29 demonstrates the often grotesque results of this proportional system, used here to exaggerate the moroseness of large eyes, nose, and pipe on a shrinking, bald, and armless snowman that appeared in the winter so healthy and debonair. Distorted proportion can also render a shape as humorous, which is the reaction of most children to Duvoisin's automobile on page 23. Its geometrical shape is absurdly distorted to look like the organic shape of a "big fat raisin" because the snow has fallen on it. The car also takes on an open shape that allows the ground space to penetrate most appropriately to imply the depth of the snow all around. This bit of distorted proportion appears in a scene with otherwise natural proportion implying much depth in the townscape. The contrast enhances children's enjoyment of *White Snow*'s most popular illustration.

Duvoisin often expressed his artistic ideas successfully within a single system of proportion but on occasion rather unsuccessfully with confusing combinations of systems. As an artist moving away from realistic toward simplified shape, he presents for children an important step in art appreciation, bridging the work of the Haders and Ezra Jack Keats.

Art Appreciation of *The Snowy Day:* Simplification of Shape

A most dramatic approach to shape is found in Ezra Jack Keats's simplified representations in *The Snowy Day*, a Caldecott winner that has been one of the collection's most popular titles since its publication over two decades ago. It differs in style from the two other Caldecott snow books and indeed from all other Award winners that went before. Keats not only painted and drew for his personable little story, but he also cut out paper figures and stamped patterns with gum erasers and by so doing played an important part in promoting paper collage as an effective art technique for picture books. His collages are reminiscent of cutouts by Henri Matisse in their stark simplicity, sinuous lines, and organic shapes that are truly *biomorphic*—reflections of real life rather than ideal forms that can be broken down into their precise parts.

Keats's particular style of collage resulted in bold simplifications of both geometric and organic shape, as compared to idealized portrayals in *The Big Snow* and expressive uses for proportion systems as in *White Snow*. The rounded shapes for Peter and his bedclothes in *The Snowy Day*'s first double-page spread on pages 6–7[3] are testimony to Keats's respect for the graceful balance inherent in three-dimensional organic form and also stand as prime examples of the artist's masterful skill in communicating this sense of grace through two-dimensional simplification. Along with the snow piled high outside the window, Peter and his bedsheet are the only organic shapes in this illustration. The sole bits of detail that further define any figure as natural are the boy's hair, one ear, and an eye. Thus Keats simplifies to the extreme with hard-edged line effects for closed shapes and no other drawn lines, line effects, or shading within the figures. Throughout the book he relies on shape alone to show that the illustrations include anything at all from the natural world.

Figures of bedframe, window, and buildings in this first illustration are all geometric shapes. The room's wallpaper pattern reinforces this visual emphasis, as does the design on Peter's pajamas: Although the flowerlike shapes are organic in appearance, they are strictly laid out in a geometric pattern. Peter is the dominant figure in this composition, strategically placed close to the audience and demanding the viewer's primary attention. His size relationship with the window and scene outside seems quite appropriate. Only when children turn to the figure of the bed itself do they notice that something is in fact askew in this illustration. The bed appears awfully big because the headboard and footboard are laid back like covers on an open book, giving the illusion that both ends of the bed are placed against the same wall. The result is an oversized shape for the bed that bleeds out from the middle toward the audience itself.

---

[3]*The Snowy Day* has its own pagination, which will be used here.

This strategic use of hierarchic proportion seems to place us in the bed as well.

Although the shape of the bed is distorted, the result is not in the least ugly or absurd, as is often the case with distorted proportion. On page 15, Keats demonstrated his preference for a gentle use of distorted proportion by rendering as more amusing than grotesque the near-human shape of a tree startled by a blow from Peter on his walk. The blunt, stunted growth of this scrubby tree is exaggerated through distorted proportion to expose an amiable likeness to a gesticulating, loquacious figure with ample derriére and top-heavy coiffure. The tree and snow shaken loose from the branches in this illustration give excellent examples of simplification of organic shape that is the basis for figures represented by the collage technique of the illustrator. Snow is abruptly separated from the tree and thrown into unusual free-form shapes, with much implied motion humorously frozen in time as Peter smacks with his just-right stick.

The concluding double-page illustration is masterful in its demonstration of hierarchic proportion in reverse and in its use of the directional force implied by a geometric shape. Here Peter and his friend are minute between sloped mountains of snow, and in the usual sense of hierarchic proportion the small size of their figures might tend to relegate them to lesser importance. But they remain the center of attention because of Keats's artistic use of the force known to exist in all geometric shapes. In the implied dynamics of geometry, the circle is thought to imply expansion from its center and the rectangle to exhibit left-right or up-down tension. The square is considered nondirectional but still active through stress from diagonals from corner to corner. The triangle implies force from its point at the apex. In Keats's last illustration, Peter and his friend capture our attention because they are positioned at the apex of a triangle of clear blue open sky, and almost mystically this illustration presents the audience with a reverse artistic hierarchy that results in little shapes being more important to the viewer than big ones. For a youngster the visual implication is that smallest is best—an appropriate image that suits the message found in books by one of the most beloved of all children's illustrators, Ezra Jack Keats.

Effects of Shape

Shape is associated with our own feelings and past experience and whether the organic or geometric shape represents a familiar, known image. If a familiar shape is arranged in understandable juxtaposition with other shapes, acceptance is easy. Sometimes in addition one feels delight in an artist's fresh new insight into a familiar experience. When an unfamiliar shape is presented and juxtaposed with others in a way foreign to the audience, fumbling for interpretation may cause uneasiness or even rejection. Shape itself is the subject of much modern art, where it relies for interpretation more on intellect than on emotion. But even modern artists fall back on the old concept that organic shapes more often evoke a warm response and geometric shapes more often a cold one.

Among the very young, response to organic shapes is usually positive because they recognize such shapes as belonging to the natural world that they inhabit as human beings. But children also live in the artificial world of geometric shapes, and in their early years they often feel most comfortable with a combination of geometric and organic, rather than purely organic subjects such as those in *The Big Snow*, no matter how beautifully they may be portrayed. Earlier and more frequent inclusion by the Haders of natural proportion for people and such geometric shapes as houses on the hill would have made a more visually stimulating series of illustrations for the young. Full-color illustrations can inspire awed admiration for woodland creatures not found in a city child's environment, but the unclimactic and largely expository text slows down the pace of the book, and when read aloud it requires that equal time be spent on black-and-white illustrations less captivating to most youngsters. An exception is the series of "snowflakes" vignettes, which have shorter text and combine free-form organic shape in the personable little squirrel and geometric organic shape in the snowflakes.

Duvoisin also is more effective with a young audience in *White Snow Bright Snow* when his illustrations include geometric as well as organic shapes. For example, most children prefer the townscape with automobile as "big fat raisin" to the similar townscape on pages 16–17 in which the organic shape of the man is lost in the gutter and the dominant figures are therefore geometric—houses, church, and bridge. In one scene, children construct shapes from the snow; students can be encouraged to define the snowman, snowball, and snow-house shapes as geometric, organic, or a combination of the two.

In 1962 *The Snowy Day* introduced collage to many adults and children as a different way to see the world. At its foundation was an understanding of the young child's need for combined organic and geometric shape to sustain interest in a work of art; the artist designed his combination brilliantly through simplification of both.

Colors also define the shapes: the red-coated figure of Peter is sought in every scene outdoors. Indoors his shape in flamboyant pajamas is equally sought after. After twenty-odd years, no question remains that the figure of Peter is authentic to children even though he is portrayed in the simplest of terms. All other shapes in the book are secondary to the boy himself, but figures obviously related to Peter are next in popularity with children: his bed, "his" tree, his angels made in the snow, his mother, and his bathtub with his rubber duck.

For Further Study

1. Children enjoy searching through other books in the collections by the Haders, Duvoisin, and Keats for the "families" of shapes around which these artists established their reputations. The Haders' *Snow in the City* makes an excellent companion piece to *The Big Snow*, and Duvoisin's collaboration with Tresselt produced other seasonal titles, such as *Sun Up*, *"Hi, Mister Robin!"*, *Autumn Harvest*, and *Johnny Maple-Leaf*.

Youngsters definitely should study Peter and his neighborhood friends through Keats's other books that use collage of cut paper and stamped designs: *Whistle for Willie* and *Peter's Chair*. In his later books, painting added more detail to collage; these include *A Letter to Amy*; *Dreams*; *Pet Show*; *Hi, Cat!*; *Goggles!*; *Louie*; *The Trip*; *Louie's Search*; and *Regards to the Man in the Moon*. Fun to look for are not only the figures of Peter and his gang as they grow up but also shapes for dog Willie, a cat, Gussie the hand puppet, an ice cream cone, a parrot in a cage, and a paper mouse, each of which appears in more than one book.

2. Drawing or painting *organic shape* using systems of idealized or natural proportions for implied contour and texture can be introduced with less frustration for children if they are encouraged to create images from the right brain or from "drawing with the eye," which means that an object is drawn by coordinating the movement of pencil or brush with eye movement as the subject is observed and looking at the created figure only after the task is finished.

3. Encourage children to design pictures with hierarchic proportion that expresses feelings about figures portrayed, such as an overlarge, menacing cat next to a diminutive, cringing one (see Caldecott winner *Once a Mouse . . .* by Marcia Brown). Part of a figure can also be distorted for effect—for example, one cat's teeth or claws can be disproportionately large. Another proportion that could be

studied employs micro or macro size relationships for images—for example, the earth compared with the universe or a drop of water compared with an ocean. Children tend to enjoy designing miniature drawings of something large or oversized drawings of something small.

4. List with students the basic geometric shapes found in the room, such as doors, light fixtures, and windowpanes. Instruct them to draw a picture of the room using only the shapes listed. Display photographs of architecture and interior designs that rely solely on geometric shape, and discuss the feelings of coldness, sterility, and harshness often attributed to such designs. Show examples of other design models with plants or other organic shapes added and discuss the feelings of warmth attributed to such combinations of shapes. Encourage children to add such shapes to their own previous drawings of the room and to note the effect.

5. Use a flannelboard to arrange various felt geometric shapes into different configurations, such as those found in *Shapes* by Jeanne Bendick. On the stage of an overhead projector place assorted supplies or tools such as scissors, spoon, and hammer, and from the silhouettes projected onto the screen instruct the children to abstract the figures in drawings that reflect basic use of geometric shape. Use Ed Emberley's series of drawing books (see chapter 3) to create animals, people, and objects from circles, triangles, rectangles, and squares for a class mural with a theme such as "Make a World" or "Our Town in Winter." Also to be enjoyed are books such as *Shapes* by Miriam Schlein, *Shapes and Things* by Tana Hoban, and Marcia Brown's books of photography, *Listen to a Shape, Touch Will Tell,* and *Walk with Your Eyes.*

6. Instruct students to cut geometric shapes from colored paper and arrange them into a satisfying balance of sizes and amounts before pasting them onto a large sheet of background paper. Or construct a collage from almost any assortment of organic as well as geometric shapes, such as buttons, shells, feathers, nails, shapes cut from magazines, wallpaper-sample books, cloth, metallic papers, wood scraps, or sponge, all of which can be attached to paper, cardboard, chipboard, or flat pieces of wood. Collage as a technique invented by the early cubists was intended to provide tactile as well as decorative embellishment, so students should be encouraged to seek out materials with real or implied texture for their collages. The implied texture in a magazine picture of cornflakes, for instance, could be creatively used in the student's picture to represent something entirely different, such as a person's hair. Collages may be

constructed as purely abstract compositions with no intended reference to people, places, or things, or they may be thematically developed around an idea of a favorite story, activity, event, or subject.

7. As an exercise in developing an awareness of artistic figure and ground, the creation of a positive and negative design can be helpful. Fold a piece of light-colored paper in half and instruct younger children to cut out a triangle from the fold, which will make a diamond shape when the paper is unfolded. Older children may cut out a continuous outline for half a snowflake, which will be fully formed when unfolded (study snowflake designs in *The Big Snow* and *The Snowy Day*). Paste the cutout shape itself as positive figure onto a negative ground of darker paper; for ambiguity of figure and ground, paste the remaining lighter paper onto dark paper, which now becomes the figure.

8. Young children enjoy watching closely for visual clues about shapes when *The Snowy Day* is read aloud with mistakes included just for fun. Substitute other things for objects mentioned in the text and encourage the children to make corrections, as in the following example: "One winter morning Peter woke up and looked out the [door]. [Rain] had fallen during the night. It covered everything as far as [she] could see. After breakfast he put on his [pajamas] and ran [inside]. The [dirt] was piled up very high along the [floor] to make a path for walking. . . . " Youngsters can also create metaphors around organic shape applied to geometric shape, as in Tresselt's description of the automobile as "big fat raisin."

9. Discussion about snow and winter in general as presented in these three books stimulates children to observe effects of the season on their own lives. Studying animals who migrate, hibernate, or do neither in *The Big Snow* can lead to investigation of how humans adapt in *White Snow* and *The Snowy Day*. A childish fascination with making things from snow can result in a list of snow creations from the books. Among many other books for primary-age children to enjoy are *Snow* by Roy McKie and P. D. Eastman; *Josie and the Snow*, written by Helen E. Buckley and illustrated by 1967 Caldecott winner Evaline Ness; *Katy and the Big Snow* by Virginia Lee Burton; and *It's Snowing!* by Margaret Cosgrove.

Looking Back, Looking Ahead: Line, Color, Light and Dark, Space

An invisible horizontal baseline in *The Big Snow* orients the audience within deep space. Foreground, middle ground, and background are understood to extend off pages to left and right, but decorative framing by leaves, trees, and snowbanks make the pictures self-contained. Use of browns and grays for paintings and no color at all in drawings provide little visual stimulation except for the advancing brightness of cardinal or bluejay, but the naturalistic quiet of woodland scenes bathed in anonymous light is relaxing to the audience. Interest in a source of illumination is only shown in night scenes where the silvery light of a round winter moon creates shadows as the animals frolic or dig their way up from their dens. Points of interest in most pictures are the darker figures of the animals themselves, with exquisite modeling by edge lines, contour lines, and shading contrasted against the white of page or snow and well balanced by weight asymmetrically. An underlying reliance on symmetry, however, is evident in pairs of single-page illustrations. For instance, a red squirrel on one page faces a gray squirrel on the opposite page, and later a wood mouse faces a meadow mouse, skunk family is opposite raccoon family, and two deer with rabbit are opposite another two deer with rabbits.

In *White Snow*, use of red and yellow with dark blue-gray can be seen as an expressionistic attempt at triad harmony of primary colors with much reliance on the advancing qualities of the two warmer and purer primaries. Red is used not only for houses and clothes but also for skin tones except, inexplicably, for two children in the last illustration. An invisible horizontal base is used within compositions except for some vignettes that exhibit different sizes for characters and imbalance the weight of figures on the pages, creating confusion about space implied. Figures as strong vertical lines hold our attention as points of interest on each page; flat colors with few lines and little shading imply hardly any contour, texture, or depth for these shapes. There is no interest in a source of illumination except for red and yellow lights coming from windows and the formal motif of the sun.

The Snowy Day is based on a superb asymmetrical balancing of weights through colors themselves as well as on the shapes that confine those colors. Line effects are created when one bold hue meets another in stark contrast. Primary and secondary hues advance and recede dramatically when combined with tones or other color forms; varying harmonies of triads, adjacents, opposites, and split-complements create dazzling effects as page after page is turned. In different illustrations, tints of lavender, pink, blue, and even green have been washed over the snow to create the only contour shading in the book. Use of bold flat hues in juxtaposition with their tints or tones often creates soft implied texture of velvet; in other instances, juxtaposition with contrasting hues creates an enamellike feel of glass. To be noted are cloth texture used for Peter's bedsheet, the "scratchy" blue line in the snow caused by his stick, the cottony white wisps of clouds in a winter sky, the sandpaper effect of black-splattered pages for Peter's room, and the crystalline sharpness of snowflakes falling everywhere at the end.

A formal orange sun with wavy rays on a bright orange page is the only depiction of a source of illumination, and that is symbolic. An invisible horizontal baseline is implied by snow or floor extending to either side but there is little implied depth except at the beginning and the end and in a wordless page in which Peter and his tracks form a vertical line as he walks away from the audience. Invisible diagonal lines provide structure for adventures with snowball, snowman, and mountain-climbing, and circular structure is found in Peter's scene with his mother. The use of flat space and horizontal orientation in many illustrations urges the audience to turn the pages to see what happens next—incited by such mysterious enticements as two tracks that become three in the snow—but the colorful shape of Peter himself as strong point of interest keeps attention on each page long enough for a reading of the simple but eloquent text.

Looking Around: *Ashanti to Zulu; Animals of the Bible; Prayer for a Child; Fables; Sylvester and the Magic Pebble; Duffy and the Devil; Arrow to the Sun; Nine Days to Christmas; Abraham Lincoln*

The 1977 Caldecott selection, *Ashanti to Zulu: African Traditions*, is a unique Award winner in that a nonfiction text by Margaret Musgrove and series of single-page framed paintings by Leo and Diane Dillon have a documentary, instructional purpose whereas the majority of other winners are picture-book stories. Customs of twenty-six African tribes in alphabetical order are presented in text formally placed across the bottom of each page. In almost every illustration, a man, woman, child, their living quarters, an artifact, and a local animal are pictured in authentic detail based on months of research that led the Dillons to back issues of *National Geographic*, university experts, libraries, museums, galleries, and the United Nations. Idealized proportion is used for modeling the organic shapes of uniformly proud and handsome people, audacious animals, and geometric shapes of exotic objects. Paintings are executed in pastels, water-colors, and acrylics; the Dillons' style is strikingly similar to that of Viennese artist Gustav Klimt in use of rich, mosaiclike colored patterns for figures and landscapes. The pictures in themselves are not visual narration as such but provide clarification for Musgrove's information, description, or anecdotes. Only a slight connecting textual link continues from page to page. The result is a book with abundant verbal and visual images best appreciated by older children.

Only a few other Caldecott titles are recognized as illustrated collections of textual images rather than story-line narrations. They include *Animals of the Bible* (1938), the first Award winner, which has pictures by Dorothy P. Lathrop, and *Prayer for a Child* (1945) illustrated by Elizabeth Orton Jones, whose *Small Rain* had been an Honor Book the year before. Both Medal-winning titles have single-page framed pictures very formally facing texts on opposite pages. *Animals* also exhibits two wordless double spreads in a collection of over two dozen illustrations portraying numerous characters and various scenes described in Biblical verses selected by children's author Helen Dean Fish. *Prayer* portrays encounters in a little girl's daily life as brought to mind by a frequently reprinted prayer written by poet, playwright, and author Rachel Field for her daughter Hannah. Both books demonstrate a use of idealized proportion for shapes, and by representing people and things not as they really are but in preconceived artistic perfection, both offer model images of people, events, and ideas for edification of the very young.

Lathrop's best-loved subjects were the animals she brought to the studio she shared with her sculptor sister Gertrude, and *Animals* itself was illustrated with painstaking detail in black and white, which is most unfortunate: Lathrop's stature as a color illustrator in the 1920s and 1930s was equal to that of her Art Nouveau contemporaries in fantasy, fellow Americans Jessie Willcox Smith and Maxfield Parrish, the popular Dane Kay Nielsen, and British subjects Edmund Dulac and Arthur Rackham. After a thirty-year span of children's-book illustrating, Jones is easily recognized for her family of shapes typified by sentimental portrayals of children's activities. In *Prayer* she had as models not only a little girl who pretended to live in her studio and many well-worn toys contributed by children of friends but also her own personally vivid memories of comfort, security, companionship, and love in childhood.

Yet one other Caldecott winner provides a series of decorative illustrations tied to many tales rather than one narration: the 1981

Medalist *Fables,* written and illustrated by Arnold Lobel (recipient of a 1972 Honor Book award for *Hildilid's Night*). Here again, framed illustrations occupy single pages facing opposing texts, each an original fable complete with moral. Animals are dressed up as humans in a form of caricature or distorted proportion with humorous intent. Lobel had masterfully caricatured human foibles through animal disguises in his earlier Frog and Toad series (including *Frog and Toad Are Friends,* a 1971 Honor Book) and other books in which grasshoppers moved like Fred Astaire and mice established rapport with an audience from the edge of a stage like Judy Garland. He became a modern-day fabulist (like James Thurber in *Many Moons*) in order to work with favorite animals he'd never used before: a lion who fell on his head, a dog who wished on a magic ring, a pig who dreamed of candy.

Likewise inspired by lion, dog, and pig characters and additionally affected by a childhood fascination with Pinocchio was William Steig in his 1970 Award-winning *Sylvester and the Magic Pebble.* This picture book with single narrative plot has visuals that flow from page to page to document a young donkey's misadventure after encountering a lion and wishing on a magic pebble to turn into a rock. Whether caricature distorted organic shape for entertainment or social statement became a controversial issue in the case of *Sylvester*: law-enforcement agencies objected to portrayal of police as pigs, sociologists studying the American drug culture suggested that Sylvester's turning into a rock was an allegory for "getting stoned," and other reviewers pondered Steig's decision to render Sylvester and his parents as a family of jackasses. Steig again amused and perplexed his public with an offbeat sense of humor in 1977 Honor Book *The Amazing Bone.*

Throughout her artistic training, poking fun at life was unavoidable for Margot Zemach, since no matter how serious she tried to be, all her drawings turned into cartoons. She has now illustrated more than thirty picture books, thirteen in collaboration with husband Harve; her caricaturizations of people have been variously regarded by reviewers as frenetic but harmless (as in 1978 Honor Book *It Could Always Be Worse*), as acceptable when renderings are of lovable nincompoops (as in 1970 Honor Book *The Judge*), often as less acceptable when characters are pictured as loutish buffoons because they are fat (as in 1984 Medal winner *Duffy and the Devil*), and generally as highly unacceptable when they are black, happy-go-lucky, and totally undignified (as in the controversial 1982 title *Jake and Honeybunch Go to Heaven*). Exaggeration or distorted proportion of shape and features resulting in caricature can be seen, then, to bring pleasure when artists appear to be laughing with their victims and to bring pain or embarrassment when an audience senses that the artist is instead laughing at them. Both attitudes are powerful visual tools with long traditions in social commentary, as in works by Honoré Daumier, Randolph Caldecott himself, and political cartoonists throughout the history of journalism.

Harve Zemach's retelling of *Duffy*, a tale popular in the nineteenth century as a Christmas play, is a Cornish version of "Rumpelstiltskin" or "Tom Tit Tot" in language rich with dialect that is as fun for a reader reading aloud as it is for the audience listening. Wife Margot's illustrations, which won the Caldecott Award the very year her husband died, are full of chaotic action and detailed complexity reminiscent of genre scenes depicting events from everyday life, such as many of those by sixteenth-century painter Pieter Bruegel the Elder. Galloping, chasing, tangling, spinning, dancing characters all have the same fat bulging shapes and homely faces—except for the gap-toothed and lecherous devil Tarraway—and all are covered in patterned and textured layers of clothes in earthy tones, except for the squire in a nude scene that in the opinion of most youngsters is one of the funniest in children's illustrated literature.

Filmically spectacular scenes have a far different dramatic impact on a young audience in the 1975 Medal winner *Arrow to the Sun*, one of many versions of a Pueblo Indian tale adapted and illustrated (and simultaneously created as an animated film) by Gerald McDermott. Fiery colors and sharply defined geometric representation of organic shapes are rendered by a combination of gouache, transparent dyes, and collage. McDermott expressed an unusually bold approach to book design, and his page layouts reflect his filmmaker's background through use of continuous narration, wordless spreads, and designs that extend off the page to continue onto the next. McDermott's *Anansi the Spider* was a 1973 Honor Book, and the artist demonstrated in several other books and films his personal fascination with the hero quest as universal theme in literature. This fascination culminated in art and story for *Arrow* that are exciting, intense, and surprising in their conceptual developments from page to page. The illustrator did not attempt a literal re-creation of Southwest Indian art but loosely based his pictures on tribal motifs after study of pottery, weaving, and sand-painting designs. He took artistic license, for example, with kachina images that represent humans throughout the book and are seen together as a highly unlikely group dancing at the end. The "Dance of Life" and a game played with straight sticks as pictured by McDermott exist in no pueblo; Arrow Maker is portrayed with a long beard, which is unheard of for an Indian elder; men and boys are shown working and playing in kilts that are reserved for dances.

The 1960 winner, *Nine Days to Christmas*, is the most realistic of all the Caldecotts. Little Ceci's first Christmas posada and piñata are illustrated by Marie Hall Ets, who wrote the text with Mexico City children's librarian Aurora Labastida. Determined to dispel Americans' stereotypical image of their Mexican neighbors as poor village Indians, Ets employed a natural system of proportion sensitively and sympathetically in quick recordings of arrested moments. Real people and events were observed on bustling city streets and in visits to Chapultepec Park, the public market, a kindergarten, a piñata factory, and homes. Almost like candid photography, contrasts in the illustrations revealed the old and new existing side by side in urban Mexico: a Dairy Queen next to a tortilleria, a late-model Detroit car next to a barefoot flower vendor. With a very informal arrangement of text across single- and double-page spreads, Ceci's story is illustrated in pencil on a gray field of action; warm touches of flat reds and yellows call attention to characters, toys, flowers, and, most of all, a star-shaped, treasured piñata. A popular and prolific contributor to children's literature for over three decades, Ets collaborated again with Labastida on the Spanish version of *Gilberto and the Wind* and was awarded Honor Book citations in 1945 for *In the Forest*, 1952 for *Mr. T. W. Anthony Woo*, 1956 for *Play with Me*, 1957 for *Mr. Penny's Race Horse*, and 1966 for *Just Me*.

Only one other illustration from a Caldecott winner is as faithful to photographic reality: the portrait of Lincoln with son Tad by Ingri and Edgar Parin D'Aulaire in their 1940 Medalist *Abraham Lincoln*. The rocking-chair pose of the president is strikingly similar to a Matthew Brady photograph from the Civil War period, whereas the rest of the D'Aulaires' illustrations in various sizes are more primitively expressionistic in a flat paper-doll style much like that of Duvoisin in *White Snow Bright Snow*. An illustrated storybook with long text often shaped inside decorated margins and beside vignettes, *Abraham Lincoln* features pictures drawn on paper and then copied by Edgar himself onto lithographic stone. Red, yellow, blue, and black were laboriously transferred to separate printing plates; this example of early lithography resulted in wide variance of color reproduction quality in different editions. The European-born D'Aulaires chose American themes for their many books, and before *Abraham Lincoln* was illustrated they studied about the sixteenth

U.S. president for a year and toured three states, walking, camping in a tent, and visiting Springfield and New Salem, Illinois, to get a feel of Lincoln country itself.

Works Cited

Alexander, Lloyd. *The King's Fountain*. New York: Dutton, 1971.

Bendick, Jeanne. *Shapes*. New York: Watts, 1968.

Benét, William Rose. *Mother Goose*. Baltimore: Heritage Press, 1936.

Brown, Marica. *Listen to a Shape*. New York: Watts, 1979.

———. *Once a Mouse . . . .* New York: Scribner, 1961.

———. *Touch Will Tell*. New York: Watts, 1979.

———. *Walk with Your Eyes*. New York: Watts, 1979.

Buckley, Helen E. *Josie and the Big Snow*. New York: Lothrop, 1964.

Burton, Virginia Lee. *Katy and the Big Snow*. Boston: Houghton, 1943.

———. *The Little House*. Boston: Houghton, 1942.

Cosgrove, Margaret. *It's Snowing*. New York: Dodd, 1980.

D'Aulaire, Ingri, and Edgar Parin D'Aulaire. *Abraham Lincoln*. New York: Doubleday, 1939.

Duvoisin, Roger. *A for Ark*. New York: Lothrop, 1952.

———. *Crocus*. New York: Knopf, 1977.

———. *Donkey-Donkey*. Chicago: Albert Whitman, 1933.

———. *The Importance of Crocus*. New York: Knopf, 1981.

———. *Jasmine*. New York: Knopf, 1973.

———. *A Little Boy Was Drawing*. New York: Scribner, 1932.

———. *One Thousand Christmas Beards*. New York: Knopf, 1955.

———. *Periwinkle*. New York: Knopf, 1976.

———. *Petunia*. New York: Knopf, 1950.

———. *Snowy and Woody*. New York: Knopf, 1979.

———. *Veronica*. New York: Knopf, 1961.

Emberley, Barbara. *Drummer Hoff*. Englewood Cliffs, N.J.: Prentice-Hall, 1967.

Ets, Marie Hall. *Gilberto and the Wind*. New York: Viking, 1963.

———. *In the Forest*. New York: Viking, 1944.

———. *Just Me*. New York: Viking, 1965.

———. *Mr. Penny's Race Horse*. New York: Viking, 1956.

———. *Mr. T. W. Anthony Woo*. New York: Viking, 1951.

———. *Play with Me*. New York: Viking, 1955.

———, and Aurora Labastida. *Nine Days to Christmas*. New York: Viking, 1959.

Fatio, Louise. *Happy Lion* and other titles. New York: McGraw-Hill, 1954– .

Field, Rachel. *Prayer for a Child*. New York: Macmillan, 1944.

Freedman, Florence B. *Two Tickets to Freedom: The True Story of Ellen and William Craft, Fugitive Slaves*. New York: Simon & Schuster, 1971.

Hader, Berta, and Elmer Hader. *The Big Snow*. New York: Macmillan, 1948.

———. *Cock-a-Doodle-Doo*. New York: Macmillan, 1939.

———. *Friendly Phoebe*. New York: Macmillan, 1953.

———. *Little Appaloosa*. New York: Macmillan, 1949.

———. *The Little Stone House: A Story of Building a House in the Country*. New York: Macmillan, 1944.

———. *Little White Foot*. New York: Macmillan, 1952.

———. *Mighty Hunter*. New York: Macmillan, 1943.

———. *A Picture Book of Mother Goose*. New York: Macmillan, 1930.

———. *The Picture Book of Travel*. New York: Macmillan, 1928.

———. *Quack-Quack*. New York: Macmillan, 1961.

———. *Snow in the City*. New York: Macmillan, 1963.

Hoban, Tana. *Shapes and Things*. New York: Macmillan, 1970.

Jones, Jessie O., ed. *Small Rain*. New York: Viking, 1943.

Keats, Ezra Jack. *Apt. 3*. New York: Macmillan, 1971.

———. *Clementina's Cactus*. New York: Viking, 1982.

———. *Dreams*. New York: Macmillan, 1974.

———. *Goggles!* New York: Macmillan, 1969.

———. *Hi, Cat!* New York: Macmillan, 1970.

———. *Jennie's Hat*. New York: Harper, 1966.

———. *John Henry: An American Legend*. New York: Pantheon, 1965.

———. *Kitten for a Day*. New York: Four Winds Pr., 1974.

———. *A Letter to Amy*. New York: Harper, 1968.

———. *Little Drummer Boy*. New York: Macmillan, 1968.

———. *Louie*. New York: Greenwillow, 1975.

———. *Louie's Search*. New York: Four Winds Pr., 1980.

———. *Maggie and the Pirate*. New York: Four Winds Pr., 1979.

———. *Over in the Meadow*. New York: Four Winds Pr., 1971.

———. *Pet Show!* New York: Macmillan, 1974.

———. *Peter's Chair*. New York: Harper, 1967.

———. *Psst! Doggie*. New York: Watts, 1973.

———. *Regards to the Man in the Moon*. New York: Four Winds Pr., 1981.

———. *Skates!* New York: Four Winds Pr., 1974.

———. *The Snowy Day*. New York: Viking, 1962.

———. *The Trip*. New York: Greenwillow, 1978.

———. *Whistle for Willie*. New York: Viking, 1964.

———, and Pat Cherr. *My Dog Is Lost!* New York: Crowell, 1960.

Lansing, Elisabeth H. *Jubilant for Sure*. New York: Crowell, 1954.

Lathrop, Dorothy P. *Animals of the Bible*. New York: Stokes, 1937.

Lewis, Richard, ed. *In a Spring Garden*. New York: Dial, 1965.

Lipkind, Will, and Nicolas Mordvinoff. *Finders Keepers*. New York: Harcourt, 1951.

Lobel, Arnold. *Fables*. New York: Harper, 1980.

———. *Frog and Toad Are Friends*. New York: Harper, 1970.

McCloskey, Robert. *Make Way for Ducklings*. New York: Viking, 1941.

McDermott, Gerald. *Anansi the Spider*. New York: Holt, 1972.

———. *Arrow to the Sun.* New York: Viking, 1974.

McKie, Roy, and P. D. Eastman. *Snow.* New York: Random, 1962.

Musgrove, Margaret. *Ashanti to Zulu: African Traditions.* New York: Dial, 1976.

Pine, Tillie, and Joseph Levine. *The Indians Knew.* New York: McGraw-Hill, 1957.

———. *The Pilgrims Knew.* New York: McGraw-Hill, 1957.

Ryan, Cheli Duran. *Hildilid's Night.* New York: Macmillan, 1971.

Schlein, Miriam. *Shapes.* Reading, Mass.: Addison-Wesley, 1952.

Steig, William. *The Amazing Bone.* New York: Farrar, 1976.

———. *Sylvester and the Magic Pebble.* New York: Simon & Schuster, 1969.

Thurber, James. *Many Moons.* New York: Harcourt, 1943.

Tresselt, Alvin. *Autumn Harvest.* New York: Lothrop, 1951.

———. *"Hi, Mister Robin!"* New York: Lothrop, 1950.

———. *Hide and Seek Fog.* New York: Lothrop, 1965.

———. *Johnny Maple-Leaf.* New York: Lothrop, 1948.

———. *Sun Up.* New York: Lothrop, 1949.

———. *White Snow Bright Snow.* New York: Lothrop, 1947.

Williams, Jay, and Raymond Abrashkin. *Danny Dunn* and other titles. New York: McGraw-Hill, 1956– .

Zemach, Harve. *Duffy and the Devil.* New York: Farrar, 1973.

———. *The Judge.* New York: Farrar, 1969.

Zemach, Margot. *It Could Always Be Worse: A Yiddish Folktale.* New York: Farrar, 1976.

———. *Jake and Honeybunch Go to Heaven.* New York: Farrar, 1982.

6

Space: *The Fool of the World and the Flying Ship, The Funny Little Woman,* and *Why Mosquitoes Buzz in People's Ears*

Uri Shulevitz was awarded the Caldecott Medal in 1969 for illustrations in *The Fool of the World and the Flying Ship*, a Russian tale retold by Arthur Ransome, about a humble peasant boy who won the hand of a princess from an unscrupulous czar. In 1973 the Award was won by illustrator Blair Lent for *The Funny Little Woman*, a Japanese tale retold by Arlene Mosel, in which a guileless little cook escapes with a magic stirring paddle from wicked *oni* deep under the ground. Then in 1976 the Medal was received by Leo and Diane Dillon for *Why Mosquitoes Buzz in People's Ears*, a West African tale retold by Verna Aardema, in which jungle animals' simple misunderstandings result in a complicated disaster.

Uri Shulevitz

The artistic career and personal triumphs of Uri Shulevitz can be reviewed over ten-year periods beginning with the decade that starts in 1939. In this painfully significant year, not only was the life of this Polish-born artist changed irrevocably, but the course of human history was altered as well. Shulevitz was only four years old when World War II began with the invasion of Poland. He "vividly remembers the streets caving in, the buildings burning, and a bomb falling into a stairwell of our apartment building one day when I was at home" during the blitzkrieg of September, 1939, in his birthplace, Warsaw. His family fled the capital city and "years of wandering" began for the Jewish refugees. This odyssey finally concluded in Paris, where young Shulevitz went to school for two years and "developed a passion for films and comic books" and a fascination for the architecture to be found in cityscapes, many of which later appeared in his picture books. Shulevitz was told that he began scribbling on the walls when he was still a baby in a cradle, and by age twelve he was encouraged by artistically talented parents to "win first prize in a drawing competition held among all the grammar schools in my district"—undoubtedly a celebrated event in 1947 for a young survivor of the recent war's cruel madness.

The year 1949 began a decade spent in Israel, where the family settled in Tel Aviv and Shulevitz went to high school at night and worked during the day at a variety of jobs. One job—issuing dog licenses at city hall—allowed him "time to read, and for my first attempts at writing." Four years of study at the Teachers Institute of Tel Aviv led to a teaching degree, and during this same period Shulevitz took private art lessons from the painter Ezekiel Streichman and attended evening classes at the art institute. After basic training in the Israeli Army during the Sinai War in 1956, the artist joined the Ein Geddi kibbutz by the Dead Sea for more than a year. During this time he graphically designed his first book, a Passover Haggadah containing the narrative of the Exodus read at Seder. After leaving the kibbutz, he served as art director of a magazine for teenagers.

The year 1959 marked a third major change in Shulevitz's life: at twenty-four, he arrived in New York City to study painting at the Brooklyn Museum Art School. Over the next few years he married artist Helene Weiss, became a citizen of the United States, worked as an illustrator for a New York publisher of Hebrew books for children, and published with Harper his own first book, *The Moon in My Room* (1963). *Moon* signaled Shulevitz's development of a "new, free style" for himself as illustrator and author as he described in *Something about the Author:*

> I was talking on the telephone one day when I noticed the lively doodles I was making with my pencil. These doodles bore no resemblance to the work I was doing for the [Hebrew] publisher . . . . *Moon* contains very brief text and suggestive rather than descriptive illustrations that have the purpose of awakening the child's imagination. . . . Writing, I came to realize, has less to do with language than one thinks . . . . Realizing the excess of words in our culture, I followed an Oriental tradition, trying to say more with fewer words.

Over the next few years, two more of Shulevitz's own books, *One Monday Morning* (also re-created as a film) and *Rain Rain Rivers* (winner of a Bronze Medal at the International Book Exhibition in Leipzig) were like *Moon* in that they "depict a child traveling outside his room without ever really leaving it." In addition, the artist illustrated almost a dozen works by other authors, including Charlotte Zolotow and Mary Stolz, before his first full-color pictures were published in 1968 for *The Fool of the World*, an update from British author Arthur Ransome's 1916 collection *Old Peter's Russian Tales*. During this decade, 1959–68, the artist received a citation from the Society of Illustrators and three times was given a children's book award by the American Institute of Graphic Arts, signifying the enthusiasm with which his illustrative style was received by many segments of the art world.

In 1969, not only was *The Fool of the World* awarded the Caldecott Medal in the United States, but its illustrator was also represented at the International Bienalle of Illustration in Bratislava, Czechoslovakia. Here began a decade in which Shulevitz increasingly illustrated old tales and parables of predominantly Eastern European origin by beloved Yiddish storytellers Isaac Bashevis Singer and Sholem Aleichem or translators I. L. Peretz (whose adaptation of *The Magician* was twice represented in book exhibits) and Richard Lourie (whose version of *Soldier and Tsar in the Forest* offers for children yet another tale from Russia). Two books during this period that were not folktales were Shulevitz's own stories *Oh, What a Noise!* and *Dawn* (winner of numerous awards). These titles perhaps best represent the artist's ability to change his style to fit a story as described in *Something about the Author:*

> [Technique] is best when it is an *organic extension of the content.* I am also constantly searching for a new way of illustrating . . . pen and ink and watercolor . . . scratching with a razor blade the pen and ink line and then reworking for a long time to achieve a certain effect as in an etching . . . using a Japanese reed pen or a Chinese brush . . . . As a child I loved Rembrandt. I still do. His etchings are sublime illustrations.

The artist's lighthearted touch and comic attitude in *The Fool of the World* is reminiscent of paintings by Pieter Bruegel the Elder, whose nickname "Peasant Bruegel" described a similar preoccupation with common folk as artistic subjects. Shulevitz has also stated that in his Caldecott winner he used a compositional approach that corresponds with pictures from the Middle Ages and Russian folk art.

From *The Fool of the World* Shulevitz has cited as one of his own favorite illustrations the double spread "with the ship over the panoramic landscape" on pages 12–13,[1] without a doubt also one of the children's favorites as well. Here the artist is at his best with "suggestive rather than descriptive illustrations that have the purpose of awakening the child's imagination," and the picture speaks directly to the innocent yearning of children to fly like the birds, perhaps to break free of the burdens connected with growing up. The previous page has aroused their curiosity about just what a "flying" ship might look like under way. This curiosity is satisfied quite beautifully with no more reliance on the fantasy element than is necessary to portray such an awe-inspiring event—a flight that turns a real world into an unreal one in which impossible things happen before our very eyes.

A "highroad" or main thoroughfare, is said to cross the land below; it is well defined on the left page along a forest's perimeter. But the old compounding of *high* with *road* or *way* to define an easy or certain course takes on for children charmingly new and simple symbolism in this picture, as a boy far above the countryside is seen riding effortlessly along yet another "highroad" to meet his destiny somewhere in the land beyond. This Russian story is, after all, a morality tale "that shows God loves simple folk"; whatever future obstacles may stand in the way of the boy called Fool, because he "never did anyone a harm," in this illustration he has for a glorious moment beaten all the odds. Youngsters do not miss the casual remark that the Fool is also "simple, simpler than some children," and they take great delight in a "child"-like character's winning so magnificent a prize. As Shulevitz himself analyzed in his Caldecott acceptance speech:

> [The Fool] refuses to be bound by the generally accepted opinion of himself and sets out to find a new world. . . . May I propose here that the source of the Fool's wisdom is the breaking down of *false distinctions* . . . . It seems to me that some of the magic of fairy tales also consists in the absence of distinction, the distinction between the living and the inanimate. Everything is alive, just as in a child's world . . . . Are children foolish to ignore accepted distinctions? Conceivably there is much more to reality than we adults are ready to accept. Perhaps it is the children who are more realistic.

[1]Pagination begins on first page with text.

In another very important respect, Shulevitz has reason to admire his own handiwork in the panoramic illustration of the flying ship, for without it the magical events described later in the text would be less likely to win full acceptance by young children. The "flying" ship soaring through the air is after all the only impossible thing actually shown by the artist. Other magical feats, such as the Swift-goer "stepping across the world in a single stride" to fetch the water of life and the Listener "listening to all that is being done in the world" and hearing the Swift-goer's snoring are ambiguously portrayed: they seem to occur within confines of landscape on the pages. If Shulevitz had not early included his panoramic "flying ship" scene to convince children that magic would indeed occur in this story, then when children later needed to rely on their own fantasizing they might not have trusted the impulse. Thus the artist would have failed at "awakening the child's imagination."

The Fool of the World also appeals to primary-age children's fascination with exotic places and peoples different from their own environment. Shulevitz's pictures resemble photographs of fertile farmland and lovely green forests along many of the rivers in the north of Russia, just before the wide expanse of the steppes begins. Research indicates that in the northern provinces of Russia, peasants of old, such as the ones seen in the book, dressed in a variety of costumes native to their districts; they were characterized by wit and humor, a reputation for obstinacy, and a bit of laziness that big-city Muscovites were not felt to possess. Before ruling prince Yury of Moscow gathered all the provinces together in the sixteenth century, Old Russia was divided into many principalities, each with its own czar or sovereign prince who ruled from an imposing palace set within his domain. These provincial palaces, whether large or small, were walled fortresses, strikingly beautiful inside, with flamboyant displays of bright colors; Byzantine designs in wood, tile, or plaster; and ornamental towers with onion-shaped domes. (Churches like famed St. Basil's Cathedral in Moscow also had onion-shaped cupolas with crosses rather than flags on top and were intended to resemble candles lighting up the heavens.) Children are quite intrigued by these examples in Shulevitz's art of freely translated images of history, landscape, and culture of another time, another country, and another people.

In 1979 yet another decade began auspiciously for Shulevitz: a Caldecott Honor Book selection was his book *The Treasure*, a quiet story with illustrations hauntingly lovely in their subtlety. In 1985 the artist published his own splendid book of art appreciation, *Writ-*

ing with Pictures, adding to his triumphs both artistic and personal over the past four decades.

Blair Lent

Blair Lent's collection of illustrated books exemplifies the widespread American fascination with non-Western art and artistic styles after World War II, especially the influence into the 1960s and 1970s of Asian and African art. During the decade 1964–73, no other illustrator in children's literature was more preoccupied with illustrating tales from other cultures or more recognized for such efforts by the Caldecott committee. Lent's illustrated version of a Japanese story, *The Wave,* from Lafcadio Hearn's original, was named a Caldecott Honor Book in 1965; the Nigerian story *Why the Sun and the Moon Live in the Sky* has been translated into many African languages and was the only Honor Book selected in 1969, when Shulevitz won the Medal for *The Fool of the World.* A Tlingit legend, *The Angry Moon,* was named a 1971 Honor Book, and two years later Lent received the Caldecott Medal itself for illustrations in yet another folktale from Japan, the retelling by Arlene Mosel of *The Funny Little Woman* from the original Lafcadio Hearn in *Japanese Fairy Tales.*

During this remarkable period, Lent's versatility was demonstrated in many other illustrations for tales from around the world: in 1965 the Arabian *Oasis of the Stars;* in 1966 the story about the Russian witch *Baba Yaga,* written under the artist's pseudonym Ernest Small; in 1968 both Hans Christian Andersen's *Little Match Girl* and the Chinese *Tikki Tikki Tembo* with retelling again by Mosel; and in 1973 *Favorite Fairy Tales Told in India.* The prolific artist additionally contributed during this same time span illustrated titles with settings in the Western world: in 1964, *Pistachio,* a reminiscence of circus experiences in France and southern Germany; in 1966 both Franklyn Branley's text from the Hayden Planetarium Christmas show for *Christmas Sky* and Lent's personal favorite of all his books, *John Tabor's Ride,* with "the rolling feeling of the sea" off New England's coast. A final area in which Lent has excelled are the timeless and placeless poetic fantasies found in pictures for his compilation of rhymes, *From King Boggen's Hall to Nothing-at-All* (1967), and for Aileen Fisher's *I Stood upon a Mountain* (1979).

After graduation from Boston Museum of Fine Arts School in 1953, Lent received fellowships from the museum to study in Switzerland, Italy, and a few years later the U.S.S.R. Ideas for his books have come from folklore of other lands or "from experiences I have had on my travels. I would like to be able to say things that relate to my own strong feelings about the world around me." Earlier illustrations were created using cardboard cuts shellacked and then brushed with ink; results were similar to woodcuts in all but the pattern of wood grain itself. Many of these titles were included on selected book lists for children. In addition, *The Wave* received a silver medal at Bienal Internacional de Livro e Arte Grafica in Brazil, and *King Boggen's Hall* won a bronze medal at the International Bienalle of Illustration, Bratislava, Czechoslavakia.

In his later picture-book illustrations, Lent returned to painting, the medium he employed early in his career for one-man shows in Boston and New York and to create his two best-known and perhaps best-loved pictures in *Tikki Tikki Tembo* and *The Funny Little Woman*. Of these books he has said, "I sometimes wonder if I should illustrate books about places I haven't seen, but I can never resist the vicarious journey it always involves. And when the book is a fantasy I feel I am allowed to take some liberties anyway." One creative liberty noticeably effective for storytelling purposes in almost all his books is Lent's use of the cutaway view in which is shown the imagined inside rather than the outside of a figure. This technique, sometimes called *X-ray imagery*, appears in the artwork of many primary-age youngsters as well.

Also apparent in Lent's artistic style is heavy reliance on cultural designs and traditional motifs, intriguing to youngsters who are themselves engaged in learning symbolic representations in their own environment. Lent has said that his masks and costumes and architectural styles are "elaborations on originals . . . not meant to be authentic," but they are as symbols quite adequate for arousing children's curiosity about lands and peoples unlike their own. *The Funny Little Woman* is especially effective in this regard, for in the illustrations are found continuing motifs. The same mask of a three-eyed monster is on all the *onis* (devils) and decorates roofs of their houses as well. The figure of a stone lantern (little shrine for the gods) is in the little woman's garden, is found on the banks of the underground river, and reflects the shape of the *onis'* dwellings themselves. Some Jizo statues (guardian gods) carry staffs with jingling rings sounded as they travel so that not even an insect will be trod upon. The chrysanthemum (symbol of Japan's royal family, used to promote harmony) decorates the beginning and end of the story.

In this internationally acclaimed artist, who all his life "wanted to write and illustrate books for children," the talent and energy necessary to illustrate fifteen titles in as many years have been combined with a strong determination "to stick to what [he] really wanted to do." Lent has described his childhood as unhappy; he grew up in a Boston suburb where "money, appearance, and athletic prowess were considered one's most important attributes," and as a youngster he turned to "books my father would bring me from the secondhand bookstore, books I got out of the library, and books I made myself, as presents for my parents and my grandmother." Years later Lent illustrated many stories—such as *The Wave, Tikki Tikki Tembo, The Angry Moon,* and *The Funny Little Woman*—that appeal to young children in large part because of their unlikely heroes. The small, meek, and outwardly powerless are bestowed with certain inner strengths or magical gifts that enable them to fight forces set against them. According to the illustrator, after completion of *The Angry Moon* he had yet another difficult time in his life, but reading the "comical adventures of the Funny Little Woman lifted my spirits and helped to break the spell."

One direct result of being awarded the Caldecott Medal was, predictably, an increase in royalties from sales of *The Funny Little Woman.* This pleasant consequence enabled Lent to leave his crowded studio in a "city environment . . . congested and noisy . . . [where] I was not working well" and buy land in Connecticut, where he built a small workshop beside his own pond and "embarked upon what I feel will be my best work." How enlightening and rewarding it is for children to hear that the same little woman who has delighted picture-book audiences for over two decades also played a meaningful role in the personal and professional life of her artistic creator as well.

Leo and Diane Dillon

The year 1973, when Lent received the Caldecott Medal for *The Funny Little Woman,* was also the year of publication for *Behind the Back of the Mountain,* a collection of ten black folktales from southern Africa, illustrated by Leo and Diane Dillon. *Mountain* was not a picture book, but in several important respects it played a pivotal role in the development of the Dillons' subsequent success as Award-winning picture-book artists. First, *Mountain* marked the beginning of the Dillons' collaboration with storyteller Verna Aardema, a partnership that later resulted in two highly acclaimed picture books, *Why Mosquitoes Buzz in People's Ears* in 1975 and *Who's in Rabbit's House?* in 1977. Second, *Mountain's* cover design displayed an artistic style that inspired illustrations for the two later picture books, a turn of events explained by the Dillons in their 1976 Caldecott acceptance speech:

> Phyllis Fogelman, editor-in-chief of The Dial Press, called us and asked if we would like to illustrate a tale about animals based on a style we had used on the jacket for *Behind the Back of the Mountain*. We were excited by the possibility of working on a kind of book we'd never done before, and Phyllis began looking for a good manuscript for us. A few months later she sent us Verna Aardema's retelling of the West African folk tale, "Why Mosquitoes Buzz in People's Ears." When we first read the manuscript, we were both amazed that in just a few pages there was such a wealth of material . . . we were delighted with the visual possibilities.

Mountain's decorative style, based on African batik and woodcut, portrays human, animal, and spirit figures in flat shapes and dull color tones accomplished by pastels (sticks or crayons of dry color pigment molded by a glue binder) and frisket masks (adhesive-backed paper cutouts applied as stencils; "one area is done and then masked out, or covered, and the next area is done," explained the Dillons). More vibrant, luminescent colors in *Mosquitoes* and *Rabbit's House* were achieved by watercolors applied by an air brush, a spray gun the size of a large pen used for precise creation of fine lines as well as for spraying of larger areas. The artists turned to this technique to "relieve some of the muddy reproduction we were getting from pastel."

Finally, some animal figures on *Mountain's* cover are repeated in modified form in *Mosquitoes*—similar shapes for crow and leopard are easily spotted in both works, and the crocodile on the front of *Mountain* can be seen as a precursor to iguana himself in *Mosquitoes*. In *Mountain's* illustrations are also lion and rabbit figures found in the artists' Caldecott winner two years later. These few simplified figures remain relatively unchanged from *Mountain* to *Mosquitoes*, but for such animals as python and Mother Owl in the latter book, the Dillons' art demonstrates an influence of African batik, with its variety of repeated patterns and traditional motifs. All figures in both books are graphically delineated by white lines or, as is often the case in *Mosquitoes*, outlines of pale blue strikingly set against white or black backgrounds. In addition, many of the human figures in *Mountain* can be seen as artistic predecessors of African tribal peoples in the Dillons' second Medal-winning picture book, *Ashanti to Zulu: African Traditions* by Margaret Musgrove. The most striking example is the Zulu woman on *Mountain's* front cover, whose costume and proud stance itself are echoed in the artists' Zulu illustration for *Ashanti*.

In acceptance speeches for both their 1976 and 1977 Caldecott winners, the Dillons attempted to answer the question How do you work *together?* by describing what they call the "third artist" created by their collaboration in illustrations for books:

> After we read a manuscript we discuss it, tossing back and forth ideas about possible styles and techniques until we agree on what will work best. . . . The drawings are done in pencil, then refined, and finally the finishes are done in color. . . . But as for who does what—sometimes even *we* aren't sure. Each illustration is passed back and forth between us several times before it is completed, and since we both work on every piece of art, the finished painting looks as if one artist has done it. Actually, with this method of working, we create a third artist. Together we are able to create art we would not be able to do individually. . . . Most people who are familiar with our individual work and our work together see a resemblance but agree that the third artist is, indeed, a separate person. . . . We've always known that in some ways the third artist was quite separate from our personal lives, because in times of anger, when husband and wife aren't speaking, the artist continues to communicate and produce. . . . We've never been able to predict totally what the final product of this third artist will be, since neither of us can actually see what the other is seeing, even though we agree on the words. The surprises have kept us interested. We rely on the advantages that a partnership and collaboration can provide, and we trust each other's judgment and taste. In the early days we worried about the loss of our individual identities, but we have found the third identity is as valid and real and as much *us* as the separate ones.

Such trust obviously was not easily acquired by two highly competitive and individualistic artists, as they have candidly explained in interviews and biographical accounts over the years. When young Diane Sorber from California arrived at Parsons School of Design in New York in 1953, one of the first competitors she met in her classes was an intense young man named Leo Dillon, born in Brooklyn of parents originally from Trinidad. Outside the classroom they became friends and collaborated on such free-lance work as typesetting and silk-screen printing, but inside the classroom they continued to compete and to illustrate independently. After graduation from Parsons in 1956, Diane accepted an advertising job in Albany, and Leo continued free-lancing for men's magazines and books of science fiction in New York. But Diane "knew deep down that I wasn't going to stay away forever"; in 1957 they were married and began a collaborative career in which they called themselves "Studio Two" as a defense against pressures to specialize in any one particular artistic style. They wanted their portfolio to be accepted during interviews as work of a pair of professionals rather than a husband-and-wife team, and Leo said further, "If Diane went, I made it a point to show up. . . . Unless they knew I was black we would be getting work under a false pretense." Caedmon hired them to illustrate record jackets and Washington Square Press to do book covers.

The challenge of working together presented severe problems, but they developed a woodcut style in the early sixties that lent itself to collaboration better than other styles of illustrative media. Over the years, the realization that they shared much in common artistically—a love of research, a dedication to revision, an ironic touch of incongruity, and deep caring for the art they produced—enabled them to merge their separate identities into one "third artist." They began to experiment with many kinds of artistic techniques—acrylic paint on acetate, sandpapered illustration board, crewel embroidery, plastic and "liquid steel," basswood carvings, marbleized paper, bleaching, painting on parchment, frisket masks.

They describe a variety of artistic influences on their work: European artists from Hieronymus Bosch to Henri Rousseau, Edvard Munch, Gustav Klimt, Koloman Moser, American illustrator Will Bradley, and artistic movements from the Renaissance and Baroque to African, Art Nouveau, art deco, and op art. They went on to design book covers for the Regency Books series, Time-Life multivolume library, Bantam Shakespeare series, other science fiction and record jackets, modern fiction titles especially by Harlan Ellison, and textbook anthologies. They have won the Hamilton King Award from the Society of Illustrators and the Hugo Award for science fiction and fantasy art; they taught art for almost a decade at the School of Visual Arts in New York; their young son Lee is a talented artist involved in jewelry design, painting, and sculpture.

Before *Mountain* was published in 1973 the Dillons had illustrated several young-adult fiction titles as well as their first picture book, *The Ring in the Prairie: A Shawnee Legend.* A half dozen other titles, including *Whirlwind Is a Ghost Dancing* and *The Hundred Penny Box* were published before *Mosquitoes*. Afterward came their second Caldecott winner, *Ashanti*, winner of numerous other national awards, and *Rabbit's House*, followed by *Honey, I Love: And Other Love Poems*, *Children of the Sun*, and *Two Pairs of Shoes*, along with book covers for new Farrar editions of Madeline L'Engle's Time Trilogy and the Caedmon record jacket for Roald Dahl's *James and the Giant Peach*.

In their art for adults as well as for children, the Dillons have become particularly well known for uses of visual storytelling devices, including *crypthesthesia*—an image hidden artistically within others to produce a double, "hidden" meaning; *reflections* that offer the ambiguity of mirrored images in glass or water; *metamorphosis*, in which stages of transformation for a figure are presented in a single setting; and *montage*, used to compress within a scene a set of interconnected plots or ideas. For good examples of crypthesthesia and reflections, see Marcia Brown's Caldecott winners *Once a Mouse . . .* and *Shadow; Mosquitoes* itself offers examples of metamorphosis and montage, described later as continuous narrative and double narrative in this chapter's section on book design. At the core of all these visual devices is the idea that more than one image can be presented within a single field of action. Such an expression of multiple thoughts is most appropriate in the work of complicated and sophisticated individual talents Leo and Diane Dillon and their "third artist."

Book Design

The Fool of the World in hardbound edition is horizontal rectangular and of sufficient size for a large group of children to enjoy at the same time. Ransome's text is lengthy for most preschool or primary-age audiences, and the book might be justifiably considered an illustrated storybook rather than a picture book if not for the artist's numerous and on occasion wordless double-page spreads. Shulevitz's bold illustrative style with bright colors on expanse of white space makes truly splendid displays on these full double spreads, and he demonstrates absolute control in avoiding the annoying slice of the gutter here as well as in illustrations that cover two-thirds of the total horizontal expanse. Text in these two-thirds spreads is very formally positioned opposite the illustrations, whereas in full double spreads the artist has placed text in less formal, attractively arranged areas of white space, usually very well balanced below the main body of the composition.

The viewpoint in *The Fool of the World* is successfully shifted from normal eye level to a point high above scenes stretching out below toward a limitless sky. These bird's-eye views suit very well a magical story about a flying ship, "—ay, a ship with wings, that should sail this way and that through the blue sky, like a ship sailing on the sea." Most often compositions are structured on strong horizontal frameworks extending beyond the pages to left and right, but the viewer's attention is firmly held in each scene by equally strong vertical figures of colorful characters, elaborate buildings, or the beautiful little ship itself. Shulevitz took liberties with everyday reality in a few compositions by applying an artistic approach that corresponds to conventions found in pictures from the Middle Ages and Russian folk art. For instance, on pages 16–17 a rocky hillside is used as the same setting for two separate episodes introducing different characters in the story. This is an example of what is called here *split narrative* (compared with continuous narrative in *The Snowy Day*, where the same figure of Peter is shown climbing up a snowbank on the left page and sliding down on the right). Shulevitz repeated the split narrative technique for the next double spread in *The Fool of the World*, in which a lake was used as a single setting for entirely different episodes introducing two more peasants who ride in the flying ship.

Another example is an event portrayed quite literally on pages 30–31, in which the Far-shooter fires at a fly buzzing around the head of the Swift-goer (called "Swift Foot" in other versions of this tale) who's gone to sleep on his journey to fetch magical water of life. In all versions of the Russian folktale, Swift-goer or Swift Foot's journey involved great distance—often described as extending to "the other side of the world." In *The Fool of the World* this journey could have been left to the audience's imagination, but Shulevitz instead narrowed the viewpoint to an immediate scene, in the folk-art tradition of restricting a narrative within the confines of a landscape. The sound filmstrip by Weston Woods separated the double-page spread into two frames to create an implication of greater distance between the Far-shooter and his target near a windmill far away, one of many compositional changes that make the audiovisual production quite helpful for storytelling purposes. No paperbound edition of *The Fool of the World* is available at this time, but Random offers the title as cassette read-along.

The Funny Little Woman is also horizontal rectangular; only slightly smaller than *The Fool of the World,* it is easily enjoyed by a large group of children. Viewpoint is chiefly normal eye level, and the two-thirds and double-page spreads show little interference from the gutter. Lent combined a very formal text arrangement opposite single-page pictures with a less formal placement consistently above double-spread illustrations. In several important ways, Lent compared with Shulevitz makes dramatically different use of the artistic field of action offered by the horizontal expanse of double pages. After an initial double spread in the book's front matter, only two other wordless illustrations engage full double pages; they are based compositionally on a horizontal structure but do not bleed off the pages with lines or colors to imply larger scenes, as in *The Fool of the World.* Instead, the full double illustrations as well as single-page and partial double-spread pictures are confined by softened edges for figures or landscapes, shaping illustrations within the white of the pages, or by blunt modeling of dark, amorphous background areas that position underground scenes within white expanse.

Lent's shift in page design from soft-edged figures with white as background into dark areas imposed onto pages has artistic purpose in that the abrupt change aids the artist in the difficult task of picturing scenes underground as well as aboveground. For children to better appreciate the complexity of the illustrator's book design, a brief examination of the initial four illustrations with accompanying text is helpful. The first shows figures aboveground, with acrylic glazes of bright orange and light tones of yellow and brown added to drawings on pure white pages. The cheerful cutaway scene shows the little woman's home with its immediate environment, and beneath the floor a harmless-looking crack leading into the earth. On pages 2–3 and 4–5,[2] color has been removed from the line drawing to left and right of the house, artistically isolating it. It is precariously perched astride the crack, which expands until in the third illustration it swallows up not only a dumpling but the little woman herself. In the fourth and final illustration in this series, only colorless line drawing defines the house on the hillside as the double-page spread is taken over by earthtones of brown, green, and blue. The composition is strictly confined within a dark area on the page, introducing an ominous, cavelike place beneath the ground where the little woman and her runaway dumpling have landed.

[2]Pagination begins on first page with text.

Beginning here and continuing through all but the last two of the remaining pages, Lent visually tells two stories. The major underground scenes have variously shaped dark background areas that command the audience's primary attention, while minor scenes aboveground continue as delicate line drawings when the little woman is absent. Only at the end, when she returns home safely, is artistic emphasis reversed and color returned to the hillside while underground is rendered in black and white.

The artist's choice of page design to picture two scenes at the same time within the same field of action is similar to a technique in fine art called *horizontal banding*. Frequently appearing in early Christian, traditional Egyptian, and Middle Eastern art, horizontal banding places one scene above another. Different settings are implied for each, and shapes are portrayed in either same sizes or hierarchic proportion. Ancient wall paintings from Theban tombs, frescoes by Michelangelo, paintings by William Blake, and illuminated manuscripts such as the fourteenth-century *Book of Hours* all provide precedents for horizontal banding suitably used here by Lent as an underlying structure for an ancient tale from Old Japan. This example provides children with an intriguing introduction to *double narrative*, as compared with split narrative in *The Fool of the World* and continuous narrative in *The Snowy Day*.

The Funny Little Woman is adequately reproduced as an Anytime Books paperbound by Dutton, and the sound filmstrip by Weston Woods is recommended for children's study of artistic detail, even though colors are not as vibrant and some aboveground line drawings of the little woman's house are omitted. One sequence especially missed shows seasonal changes to indicate the passage of time while she is held prisoner by the wicked *oni*.

When *Why Mosquitoes Buzz in People's Ears* first appeared in 1975, the bombastic, larger-than-life illustrative style of artists Leo and Diane Dillon appeared to many to have departed from usual standards for children's book design. In several areas, however, page layouts in the large, square book rely solidly on established elements of picture-book art: a strong horizontal base provides an underlying framework in double-page spreads; precise planning by the artists avoided interruption by the gutter; many interesting, attractive shapes are well defined but intentionally crowded within the field of action; normal eye-level viewpoint for the audience is consistent except in a couple of instances when dramatic emphasis calls for extreme close-ups. Informal arrangement of shaped text within illustrations demonstrates well-balanced artistic beauty as well as contextual significance. The cumulative tale builds up to an understated and humorous one-word ending. The final and only single-page illustration, with its briefest of brief texts, succeeds in delighting young children with artistic impact in much the same way Sendak's little postscript pleases them in *Wild Things.*

The divergence from the norm in *Mosquitoes* is, then, not found in a truly different book layout but in the Dillons' use of the artistic element *space* and in their unique, cinematic uses of continuous narrative, split narrative, and double narrative. The story begins on the title page itself with a continuous narrative in which mosquito is seen first watching the farmer and then in the same setting turning to fly away. The next double spread continues use of this narrative technique: shown first is iguana's disgust with mosquito's nonsense and then his subsequent exit through the reeds with two sticks in his ears. The complicated artistic combination of a split and continuous narrative is introduced on pages 2–3.[3] Python and rabbit are each shown in two positions; additionally, they appear in the same setting for their separate episodes to create a split narration as well. The next illustration repeats this combination of split and continuous narration as both crow and monkey are each pictured in two positions within a single setting.

After one double-spread illustration in which a formal symbol of the sun is shown in a continuous narrative, the double narrative is introduced. Pictured in the background is monkey's imaginary murder of an owlet as described by Mother Owl to animals assembled in the foreground. In the next several illustrations similar use of double narrative is used for exaggerations about events leading up to the animals' dilemma as portrayed by monkey, crow, rabbit, and python. Finally, in the only two straightforward narrative illustrations, iguana appears to face ridicule for the sticks in his ears and tells his story while mosquito eavesdrops.

Throughout the illustrations are two little additional narratives thought of as "stories within a story"—the Dillons' creation of characters for the antelope and the little red bird as described in their acceptance speech:

> The antelope has a very minor part in the story—he is simply sent to bring Mother Owl and later the iguana before the council. We decided he really wanted a more important part—he wanted to be a star. So he began trying to get attention, peering out and

---

[3]Pagination begins on first page with text.

grinning, hamming it up, until finally on one spread he is seen up front in the center, with a great toothy smile. . . . The little red bird never appears in the text at all. We put her in one spread and became rather fond of her. We began to think of her as the observer or reader and added her to the other spreads . . . . For us she is like the storyteller, gathering information, then passing it on to the next generation.

Mother Owl's hooting for the sun as well as mosquito's guilty hiding and whining are both portrayed as continuous narratives in separate illustrations, and the book concludes with a last continuous narrative as mosquito is punished with a slap, "KPAO!" Thus ends a most ambitious, multileveled artistic rendering of a simple tale about one mosquito and all the trouble she caused.

Filmic techniques of continuous, split, and double narratives in *Mosquitoes* lend themselves superbly to Gene Deitch's animated adaptation in the Weston Woods ten-minute motion picture, and the book is also available as a sound filmstrip and an iconographic film. Scholastic offers a recording narrated by Pearl Primus with traditional African rhythms played on drums. The Pied Piper paperbound edition by Dial exhibits excellent color reproduction but is presented in a vertical rectangular shape with addition of white space on tops and bottoms of pages; this arrangement lessens the dramatic impact of scenes with black background.

Art Appreciation of *The Fool of the World and the Flying Ship*

The element of space in two-dimensional art is the very world itself that the artist creates for the viewer. Whether the artist visually invites the audience into the space of a picture involves decisions about overall composition made long before pen or brush is ever put to paper or canvas. For children, the concept of space is best explained as the result of combined uses of other elements discussed thus far: *lines* that are perhaps fat and continuous to define closeness or thin and broken to imply farther distance; warm *colors* that advance toward the audience and cool ones that recede; contrast or gradation of *light and dark* areas that attract the eye or imply depth by contouring; *shapes* of varying sizes or in overlapping positions that suggest different points of interest within the field of action.

An artist's initial decision about the kind of space to be employed in illustrating a story is basic to children's response. Even though implied depth has been extensively discussed in earlier chapters, a separate analysis is vital to recognize the ways in which all elements come together to communicate space. The complexity of artistic composition itself may create the illusion of three-dimensional space within a two-dimensional field of action. Children can learn that the effect depends not only on *what* elements are used, but also *where* and *how* they are employed.

To study how artistic elements are combined to imply deep *space* from aerial and linear perspectives, two double-page spreads from *The Fool of the World* have been chosen: called here "The Highroad" (pages 12–13) and "Singing Like to Burst" (pages 24–25). "The Palace" (pages 42–43) and "The Bathhouse" (pages 36–37) are used to discuss artistic space using different linear perspectives. Creation of shallow space will be studied in *The Funny Little Woman* and flat or planar space will be examined in *Mosquitoes*. It is recommended that all three titles be close at hand for reference to specific points and for clarification through comparisons. Since one of the primary reasons to select a specific spatial system or combination of systems is to imply effects of *deep, shallow,* or *flat space,* this chapter will not as in previous chapters separate the discussion of effect but will instead include its evaluation within the art appreciation sections themselves.

DEEP SPACE THROUGH AERIAL AND LINEAR PERSPECTIVES

The first of Shulevitz's two wordless double spreads in *The Fool of the World* is a scene in which "the Fool steered for the highroad, and sailed along above it" in his little ship. This very popular illustration usually causes a chorus of spontaneous "ooohs" from younger children, who demand a pause in storytelling to savor visual details in the countryside spread out before them. Unfortunately the text describing "The Highroad" is on the next page, necessitating shuffling back and forth. This is only one of several awkward text placements in this long story that might have benefited from a few additional illustrations. Without a doubt, however, this bird's-eye scene as well as another called "Singing Like to Burst," in which the ship approaches the czar's palace, are both highly successful with children. The two make an interesting comparison of the uses of aerial or linear perspective to create the illusion of space on the pages of a picture book.

Aerial perspective is also often called "atmospheric perspective" in art. It is based on the principle that in the natural world the air itself obstructs our view of figures as they recede, causing edge lines to grow less distinct and light and dark contrasts or colors to decrease in intensity as they take on the coloration of the atmosphere through which they are seen. In fine art, this perspective is defined as different from geometrically based *linear perspective*, in which alterations in figure sizes, directions, and placements within composition rather than atmospheric interference are determining factors for creation of an illusion of three-dimensional space. Such nineteenth-centry Impressionists as Camille Pissarro and Claude Monet demonstrated marked interest in the "dissolving" of objects by atmospheric conditions; J. M. W. Turner was indeed so preoccupied with effects of the atmosphere that he created seascapes in which heavy mist like "tinted steam" enshrouded ships and castles in foreground as well as background. Aerial perspective does not require that a scene be presented from a bird's-eye viewpoint, but for young children the implication of space understandably afforded by use of very high position can demonstrate most dramatically a reliance on either aerial or linear perspectives.

In "The Highroad" can be seen the influence of aerial perspective as the landscape, clearly contoured by drawn lines and line effects in foreground and middle ground, becomes washed-out and blurry in the background. Where land meets horizon, it becomes tinted by whitish coloration of sunless sky at the deepest point of space implied in this picture. Hue intensities of the fields have diminished considerably from those in the foreground and middle ground; contrasts of light and dark have decreased so dramatically that the pale pink tints bleed into the white of the page above; and the edge line for the horizon is thin and broken to create an open shape allowing the sky itself to penetrate. Starkly contrasting white ground of the pages as sky (negative space) in all of Shulevitz's outdoor illustrations adds greatly to the dramatic impact of this brilliant and harmonious balance of warmly advancing primary and secondary hues for figures. In only one other illustration, on pages 26–27, has the artist used aerial perspective to allow this white sky to alter the value and intensity of his hues as they meet the horizon.

The most compelling point of interest in "The Highroad," after the viewer has absorbed the highlighted and solitary little dark figure of the ship itself, is the light and spacious river far below. Placed dramatically at the gutter, it crosses over this invisible center line twice to dwindle away finally into a snakelike visible drawn line ending at the horizon. The point at which the river meets the skyline is approximately centered horizontally on the right-hand page, and the visual attention drawn to this river's end balances asymmetrically the artistic weight of the ship, approximately centered horizontally on the opposite page. Thus the eye is attracted to the ship, then down below to the river, where we follow along its diagonal path until it meanders to the horizon, and finally attention goes back again to the ship to conclude visual orientation to the space confined within the field of action. Only then is noted the diagonal slope of the horizon: to dramatically emphasize distances involved in the Fool's long journey Shulevitz gently slopes or curves many of the horizons, making the pictures look larger by imitating the contour of the earth itself as seen from outer space. Next, children love to pore over little organic and geometric shapes for wagon, windmill, haystacks, peasants, and walled cities placed within the colorful panorama below. Indeed, the illustrator's intent has been to pull the viewer most forcefully into the deep space of this scene, and he succeeds masterfully through use of aerial perspective and creative interplay of the other artistic elements color, line, light and dark, and shape.

The invisible framework in "The Highroad" can be compared with McCloskey's initial bird's-eye scene, "Looking for a Place," in *Ducklings* (see chapter 2) to note differences in uses of the gutter's center line, directional lines for horizon, and strategic placements for points of interest to create deep space. The use of color in *The Fool of the World* and the lack of it in *Ducklings* demonstrate subtleties in gradations of light and dark tones to imply contour and texture. Through such comparisons children can be made more aware of unique qualities of the illustrators' accomplishments, using different mediums and different underlying compositional frameworks for creation of similar scenes.

The audience is presented its closest hierarchic view of the little flying ship in the illustration "Singing Like to Burst." Deep space is implied through linear perspective—size change and placements— rather than atmospheric interference along the horizon as in "The Highroad." In this second wordless double spread, the horizon against the white of sky is well defined and constant in coloration and delineation (notice also its gentle undulation interrupted only by staunch vertical lines of the palace with its flags). Distance between ship and landscape is indicated by the large figure of the ship compared with the small palace and even smaller people and trees.

Two-dimensional art does not present what the viewer knows to be literal truth—for example, a palace is in reality larger than a ship—but the artist fashions in space an illusion that near objects are larger than objects of the same or even greater size seen from farther away. In "Singing Like to Burst," the boy's head approximates the size of the palace's onion-shaped dome, an undeniable visual likeness on the page. Yet the audience does not take this likeness literally but assumes it implies closeness of the boy and distance of the dome.

After children have been introduced to such size changes to imply deep space, two other compositional aspects that heighten implication of depth may be pointed out; they are superbly exhibited in "Singing Like to Burst." The first is the sharply tilted angle of the ship, which calls attention to the oblique linear perspective in which no lines run parallel with any sides of the picture. The viewpoint is from a lower bird's-eye level than in "The Highroad" and is more acutely angled. Not only can we see quite well all the passengers crowded into the little ship, but we can also peer down into the entire palace courtyard. Thus deep space is implied not only laterally but also from great height. The ship's path of gesture as well as two passengers' upraised arms lead the viewer's attention to the palace. Thus, precisely at the halfway point of the story, Shulevitz introduces the czar's domain, the setting for the second part of the plot. Indeed the Fool's run of good luck is here about to be interrupted by impossible obstacles waiting below; so most appropriate for this transitional scene is the use of oblique perspective reminiscent of the "warning" scenes discussed in *Jumanji* (see chapter 4).

The last aspect to be considered in this wordless double spread is Shulevitz's reversal of an artistic convention that dictates the positioning of closest figures toward the bottom of a picture and farthest figures at the top to create an illusion of space. This positioning is based on the principle that the human eye generally looks upward into distances and downward into the immediate environment. Several eye-level illustrations immediately preceding "Singing Like to Burst" do employ such placements. But understandably, to imply space in a bird's-eye level scene, the object nearer to the viewer must occupy a position toward the top of the page, higher than faraway objects below. Contrasted expanse of white pages as sky behind colorful flying ship and palace combine with the composition's oblique angle to further arouse the audience's giddy fascination with this illustration's demonstration of deep space thrown precariously off-balance. The result is a fitting note of premonition for the Fool's uncertain fate.

"The Highroad" and "Singing Like to Burst" should be compared with other outdoor scenes in *The Fool of the World* in order for children to study not only the obscuring effect of aerial perspective versus linear perspective, but also the angles, viewpoints, systems of proportion, and other arrangements of artistic elements used to create deep space throughout the book.

DEEP OR SHALLOW SPACE THROUGH
DIFFERENT LINEAR PERSPECTIVES

One of the many obstacles to be overcome by the unsuspecting Fool is to survive in an iron bathhouse made red-hot by servants of the devious czar. This impossible task is accomplished magically in the story and shown with equally magical charm in Shulevitz's illustration "The Bathhouse." Throughout *The Fool of the World*, the artist demonstrates his affinity for the comic sense of Bruegel-like genre paintings of common folk acting out a proverb. Nowhere in the book is this resemblance any better displayed than in this illustration and in its compositional companion piece on pages 4–5, which show the inside of the Fool's home. Both these two interior scenes resemble theatrical "box settings," with ceiling, back wall, and side walls firmly established on the two-thirds double spreads. In his design, Shulevitz invited the viewer into this shallow space by symbolically placing in "The Bathhouse" two servants at an open door and in the earlier illustration a bearded visitor framed at an open window. The audience is drawn in by paths of gesture from upraised arms, which direct the eye toward the center of each setting where the Fool as main character is found in both.

An additional and more complicated invitational technique employed by Shulevitz in "The Bathhouse" involves linear perspective from three separate audience's viewpoints. Such a combination, traditionally considered to be conflicting within a field of action, is here ambitiously employed to assure the viewer's interest, if not from one angle then from another. For children, this example of multiple viewpoints within the same picture is best understood if the illustration is imagined divided vertically into three parts: on the left the open doorway, in the center the Fool and his friend "lying on the stove and singing songs," and on the right a decorated column. The door is seen from bird's-eye viewpoint, since its top plane is visible. In the center, the stove is seen from just below normal eye level, perhaps as viewed by the figures at the door or even from the level of a child. The decorated column is recognized as an object in itself viewed from "simultaneous perspective" (parts of the same figure seen from different views) because not only does the top of the base appear at the bottom end of the bulging orange shaft, but also the lower portion of the capital piece that supports a vaulted ceiling is seen from below. By masking two parts of the illustration to study only a remaining third at a time, and likewise masking upper and then lower halves of the column to clarify its structure, youngsters can gain awareness of differences among the separate viewpoints and later appreciate abstractionists' uses of simultaneity to create unusual interpretations of space.

Use of multiple viewpoints is often attributed to the analytical cubists as typified by Picasso, but the portrayal of different perspective systems within the same field of action can be traced to ancient times. It has been often misunderstood as resulting from unskilled or primitive talent. For instance in "The Bathhouse" simultaneous perspective of the column may at first be considered awkward, but on further inspection the opposing views of the decoration can be recognized as increasing the little room's implied height. The symbols and familiar gestures combined with the artist's intriguing use of multiple viewpoints for exotic settings has the desired effect: we comfortably accept Shulevitz's invitation to linger awhile to savor details in architecture, furnishings, and personalities within the cozy, confined space of "The Bathhouse." Belying the text's insistence that magic straw on the floor has transformed the room from red-hot into ice-cold (evidenced only by a couple of icicles on the funny tub), much of the scene is composed in warm tones of orange that imply contour for walls and stove and bring the rear of the room closer to the audience. The warm colors are balanced by harmony of opposites, as cool blues recede on a speckled ceiling positioned like a formal arch of night sky full of stars. Even in his interior scenes for *The Fool of the World* Shulevitz included framing curves and slopes imitative of the earth's contour, and in this illustration particularly these combine attractively with organic and geometric points of interest. Expressive, free-form, closed, organic shapes of people form an asymmetrical balance with structured, geometric stove, tub, door, stool, rug, wall, and floor tiles. The stove, the heaviest shape in the composition, is highlighted slightly by a dull source of illumination coming from a tiny window nearby and from an open door backlighted in the middle ground, raising the question of what is to be considered foreground in this unusual picture with its multiple viewpoints. The door is opened at a direct angle advancing toward the viewer, implying that the immediate foreground must indeed include the position held by the audience itself. This is one more example of Shulevitz's interest in artistically involving his viewer in space depicted for the scene.

"The Palace" is one of the most elegant of all Uri Shulevitz's book illustrations, presenting to imagined call of trumpets sounding from above a splendid review of the Fool of the World dressed in finest of clothes. His humble peasant friends stand modest and proud, an admiring court bears gifts and congratulations of the day, and a repentant czar leads by the hand the lovely princess who immediately on her wedding day falls in love "to distraction." Just as in the oldest of commemorative art traditions, in which participants appear precisely posed by their portraitist in order of rank and with dutiful respect paid to beauty of a wealthy patron's opulent surroundings, all necessary ingredients are here formally incorporated to document a most eventful day in the history of this provincial ruler's reign. This event is not really the marriage of his daughter, no matter how clever the son-in-law might prove to be, but the much more powerfully significant acquisition of the coveted flying ship everyone appears here to have forgotten all about.

Once again, through use of more than one artistic technique, the audience is invited to enter the space in which the festivities take place. In this illustration, however, Shulevitz's effort to involve the viewer is formally perfunctory, as befitting the occasion. The first indication of welcome is below the main action in the scene, a white expanse serving to lead the eye to the Fool in the middle ground. The Fool here is the central character among the many figures assembled along a horizontal baseline in the enormous room. This block of white is bordered on either side by the palace floor, which continues off the pages in diagonals equidistant from the gutter. This design implies for the audience a fixed center viewpoint almost in the foreground itself, where the floor has been visually eliminated for an ingenious placement of text. (For the reverse of this shaping of composition to allow unique text arrangement, turn to pages 22–23, in which the figure is in the center and text portions are to the sides.)

The diagonal borders for text as well as the vertically diagonal pattern made by the floor tiles themselves are the first clues to this composition's absolute linear parallel perspective: pairs of diagonal lines from left and right pages would appear to converge ultimately at a vanishing point beyond the horizon. These opposing diagonal lines succeed in pulling attention right into the deep space implied in the middle of the pages. Sizes of floor tiles diminish as they extend toward the back wall, an artistic device to imply depth that dates back to the early Renaissance and to fifteenth-century paintings such as those by Uccello.

The other invitation into the deep space is found in the far wall's arches, which open to the outside. As lightest areas in the composition, they attract the eye to the most distant reaches of the palace hall and contrast with flashy primary and secondary hues in costumes and architectural designs. As the eye travels from the white block of text up the floor to seek this spacious light area, the other indications of linear parallel perspective are encountered. They include diminishing sizes and overlapping of figures, decreasing of intervals between horizontal lines for floor tiles, and implied ultimate convergence of parallel vertical-diagonal lines for tiles. Indeed the small plain wooden window arches confining white areas are sought by the eye before the larger and more flamboyantly colorful ceiling arches engage our attention, simply because the eye requires relief from the gaudy array of bright colors. In addition, these plain windows provide a visual reference for orientation within the deep space of the scene.

Each supported by a differently designed column, the elaborate arches for beams and recesses in yet another Shulevitz sky-ceiling are the artist's bombastic architectural conclusion to his book. They also reinforce the illusion of depth by following the diagonal direction of the floor. Once spatially oriented along a sturdy horizontal baseline and diagonals leading deep within the scene, the viewer then more comfortably surveys the outrageous display of colors like fireworks in every imaginable harmonious combination. Busy lines of every description take every direction to define a myriad of interesting contoured organic and decorative geometric shapes and motifs. Interchanges of light and dark tones cause the eye to jump back and forth. In "The Palace" the artist for *The Fool of the World* may have begun with the decorous framework of customary commemorative art, but, just as a court jester might playfully elaborate in telling a dull tale, Shulevitz provides his own extravagant rendition, with wild bursts of color that blow away cobwebs of pomposity smothering a stuffy artistic tradition.

Art Appreciation of *The Funny Little Woman*: Shallow Space

From the first illustration with text, Blair Lent's pictures for *The Funny Little Woman* demonstrate the artist's interest in the ability of shallow space to heighten the audience's close involvement in a scene. Only near figures, placed against stark white pages as contrasting backdrop, are emphasized. The white ground serves to backlight shapes of house, tree, well, and open figure of the hillside, isolating them as colorful silhouettes separated from any surrounding landscape. The last illustrations include more of the little woman's hillside garden with its path leading across a bridge, but in the first pages of the book Lent has deliberately eliminated all extraneous surroundings, while the cutaway view into the house focuses entirely on the woman as she makes dumplings at her table. The white of the open window behind her calls attention to the smallness of her one-room home, while outside, the white backdrop accentuates the unfamiliar shapes of her water well and little stone lantern—both minor artistic details worth watching as the story progresses.

Unlike *The Fool of the World*, Lent's book has no illusions of deep space created through use of high viewpoints, aerial perspective, or lines bleeding off the pages. Instead, through creation of shallow space in initial scenes, Lent strictly confined attention to but one specific place, cozy and near and familiar—inside a wee house on a hillside. Such restrictive spatial orientation might have seriously hampered his ability to convince the audience when the time came to enter an incredibly foreign setting—a cavern deep under the ground. But in these first aboveground illustrations, the cutaway view for house ingeniously includes a cutaway of the hillside too, with its widening crack shown in the earth. Thus viewers get an early and ominous hint of action that indeed might take place below the little house. Finally this underground world itself is shown through a cutaway—obviously the only way an audience could witness what is going on out of normal reach belowground. It should now be obvious that the artist intentionally established acceptance for this cutaway technique through well-planned use of it from the beginning.

Once the artist transfers primary attention to underground scenes, the hillside scene above is viewed from a greater distance than before and on occasion space is deeper than previously seen. This illusion is created through linear perspective by rendering the house in the background quite small and placing it at the top of compositions to make room for garden and path added in middle ground and foreground. Although far from showing the deep space in *The Fool of the World*, these delicate line drawings are indeed more openly spacious than Lent's earlier paintings of the hillside. Their artistic lightness not only implies less significance for the secondary story in this double narrative but also serves as effective balance for the darkly

modeled areas below in which primary action proceeds. Basic reliance on interplay between light and dark is indeed the artistic
foundation for storytelling dynamics in two spaces, one dank and
gloomy, one clear and airy.

In cold and moldy cave scenes, the artist also depends on gradation or contrast of light and dark tones to imply near-claustro-
phobic shallow space beneath the ground. Much as in *Wild Things*,
a low-keyed underlying tone with dull intensity was chosen as the
initial shade upon which to build gradations for areas so dark that
one is uncertain where one figure stops and another begins—for
example, the green dwellings of the wicked *oni* set against the green
of the cavern wall. The darkest of greens, in the crumbling earth
wall, then meshes with brown tones for tree roots snaking down
toward the underground river, intensifying the feeling of oppressively limited, eroded, airless space. By contrast, vividly warm yellow-orange of the little woman's dress, the unearthly cool light blue-
green of the *onis'* figures with little implied contouring or texturing
except in their grass skirts, and the warm yellow-green of the stone
lanterns' lights as solitary sources of illumination—all stand as points
of interest. They balance each other within each composition by
pulling the eye from figure to figure. Similarly, in earlier illustrations,
drawn lines defining benevolent faces on statues of the gods attract
attention when all else appears unfamiliar and threatening.

Contributing also to the sense of shallow space are the numerous, overlapping, dark-toned organic shapes of gods or boulders
and geometric shapes of the *oni* dwellings crowded in natural proportion one on top of another in the underground river's channel.
Both the river and the path along the cave floor offer a horizontal
base upon which illustrations are structured in linear parallel perspective. However, the crowded overlapping of such numerous figures still creates the impression of an irregular, unstable landscape
with nooks and crannies inhospitable and potentially dangerous to
humankind.

But the funny little woman by her own funniness is triumphant
when faced with evil: she laughs "tee-he-he-he-he!" right through
to the end. This idealized figure symbolizes in the best of folktale
tradition the decent commoner small and weak who bravely challenges the wickedness of supernatural powers.

Art Appreciation of *Why Mosquitoes Buzz in People's Ears:* Flat Space

As compared with *The Fool of the World* and *The Funny Little Woman*
Leo and Diane Dillon's illustrations in *Why Mosquitoes Buzz in Peo-*

ple's Ears are superb examples for children of flat or "planar" space. In this technique, unmodeled, two-dimensional figures are placed within a field of action that has little foreground, middle ground, or background to imply space in linear or aerial perspective. Through dramatic arrangement of areas with level planes of harmonious and balanced contrasts of colors, the artists created contourless, flattened shapes inhabiting a seemingly spaceless setting. The design is reminiscent of the near-dimensionless field upon which Emberley's soldiers gathered in *Drummer Hoff*. The Dillons' organic figures broken down into component parts outlined by white or pale blue also resemble Emberley's irregular shapes fitted together to create brilliant abstracted decorations. The space in which these shapes reside exhibits almost no compositional invitations for the audience to enter. Overlapping and size changes are both evident for figures, and a few of the illustrations demonstrate reliance on a horizontal base, but generally the scenes appear baseless and detached, with only sensuous curves or bold verticals of trees and animals to indicate any hold by gravity.

Good examples of flat shapes displayed in planar space are the first few illustrations in which figures are presented from normal eye level against white ground of the pages and appear as if held in suspension, with no audience orientation to horizon behind or floor beneath. Slight overlapping of shapes in these first pictures was used, not to create an illusion of depth between figures, but to strengthen the filmatic techniques of continuous and split narratives. An especially good example for children appears on page 2, in which five different planes lie flat against each other to imply very shallow space: reeds in immediate foreground, then iguana, another set of reeds, the first figure of the python, and finally his second figure in the middle ground as he slithers wasawusu into the rabbit's burrow.

When night grew long, and black replaced white as ground for the book's main sequence of double pages, the illustrators introduced within the same fields of action the concept of two spaces to accommodate double narratives. In one major dark scene, worried animals are gathered to find out why Mother Owl has not called the sun; in a secondary lighter area hierarchic proportion portrays the various animals' exaggerated misunderstandings of what has gone before. Lighter areas contrasted with the black of night attract audience attention much as in *The Funny Little Woman* and thus visually imply deeper space overall for these illustrations than was found in previous scenes with white backdrop. However, each of these later illustrations in *Mosquitoes* is recognized as based compositionally on planar rather than truly deep space, since the double

narratives actually involve representations of two stories, each occupying flat space within itself. Cool tonal variations of primary and
secondary hues in the darkness are so subtle that only the yellow
of eyes and white of teeth or horns pull the audience's attention
from figure to figure, and within the agitated group gathered in the
jungle night are such conflicting paths of look and gesture as to
create little stories within stories in this complicated tale.

For children's fullest appreciation of artistic planar space, the
last four illustrations in *Mosquitoes* offer additional prime examples
of flat decorative figures in positions with little or no depth. On
pages 20–21 the formerly closed figure of the iguana is disintegrated
into an open shape to allow penetration by the same color for tree
shapes assumed to be in the immediate background. The resulting
flat space is emphasized by hierarchical proportion and overlap of
the eavesdropping mosquito, which places her nearer to the audience. The formal motif of the rising sun in the next double-page
spread is a good example of confined planes of colors: the painted
sun rays lie flat on the page, compositionally shedding light on
nothing around them, reaching out only as far as the limits of black
night sky will allow. The continuous narration here as Mother Owl
turns her head to call the sun is also a fine example of flat space
implied by superimposition of two different poses on the same planar
surfaces.

On pages 24–25, flower petals, receptacles, and sepals are portrayed as distinct planes all lying level against each other on the
page. This illustration can help children understand the Dillons'
technique of breaking down three-dimensional shapes into stylized,
flattened parts. Even more important in this double spread is stylization of a proud, contemptuous human face likewise broken down
into planes, which serve to heighten the suspenseful effect of a
suspicious and watchful eye directed toward the whining mosquito.
Finally, suspense concerning mosquito's fate is ended with a "KPAO!"
This illustration is a truly fine culminating demonstration of the
artists' uses of planar space and continuous narration: seen swatting
mosquito are not one but two views of the hand, one on top of the
other in resounding reverberation of the slapping motion. Because
of the absolute flatness of space implied between hand and ear, the
audience understands full well that mosquito does not survive.

Silly mosquito has been punished; a cheer from the children
goes up for her just reward and for the Dillons' artistry, humor, and
honesty in answering an age-old question of why pesky mosquitoes
persist in buzzing around our ears.

For Further Study

1. *The Fool of the World, The Funny Little Woman,* and *Mosquitoes* make an excellent introduction for children to recurring themes or situations found in folk literature from around the world. The Flying Ship story also appears in a Germanic version in which a boy named Hans gives a ride to Sharp Ears, Sharp Eyes, and Swift Foot; another tale similar to *The Fool of the World* is *The Riddle of the Drum* from Tizapan, Mexico, translated and retold by Verna Aardema. *The Funny Little Woman* can be compared with another folktale from Japan, *The Rolling Rice Ball,* in an English version by Alvin Tresselt, and with many other old stories about runaways like *The Pancake, Johnny-Cake,* versions of *The Gingerbread Boy, The Bun,* and *Journey Cake, Ho!* Cumulative tales with a cause-and-effect pattern as in *Mosquitoes* have played a part in children's literature since Mother Goose rhymes, and another version of *Mosquitoes* is *Why the Sun Was Late* by Benjamin Elkin. Other African folklore with animals that behave like people is found in such collections as *Beat the Story-Drum, Pum-Pum,* illustrated by Ashley Bryan.

The Fool of the World as an illustrated Russian tale can be compared to Shulevitz's pictures for another story from that country, *The Soldier and Tsar in the Forest,* and to Nicolas Sidjakov's Caldecott-winning illustrations in *Baboushka and the Three Kings.* Lent's illustrations for *The Funny Little Woman* follow in the footsteps of his earlier pictures for many tales from around the world: another Japanese folktale, *The Wave;* a Chinese tale very popular with children, *Tikki Tikki Tembo;* an Arabian story, *Oasis of the Stars;* the Russian *Baba Yaga;* the Nigerian *Why the Sun and Moon Live in the Sky;* and the Tlingit legend *Angry Moon.* The Dillons' *Mosquitoes* appeared in the middle of their career as illustrators for several other stories from Africa: *Who's in Rabbit's House?, Ashanti to Zulu, Behind the Back of the Mountain,* and *Songs and Stories from Uganda.*

2. For children to better appreciate the complexities involved in various spatial conventions, they should be encouraged to increase their vocabulary of comparative terms starting with easier concepts such as big versus little, near versus far, inside versus outside, and progress into definitions for more difficult concepts such as open versus closed space, figure versus ground, foreground versus background, bright versus dull. Simple antonym word games can be played with very young children, and as artistic concepts are introduced, finding examples in paintings or photographs should become part of the game.

3. Looking out the window to name objects that stand between the students and a house or building across the street can aid in a definition of foreground, middle ground and background, with deep space identified as occupied by the house or building farthest away. In the context of art, *deep* must be defined for young children as an illusion of far distance rather than an extension far into the earth itself, and *shallow* must be seen as representing close-in space with no illusion of far distance.

Landscape photographs or paintings are useful to point out further examples of artistic composition using foreground ("figures placed in front"), background ("figures far away"), and middle ground ("figures in the space between"). Point out also examples of overlapping (a portion of a figure placed partly in front of another and hiding part of the figure behind) and instances in which size relationships have been altered from reality to imply depth.

Simple foreground, middle ground, and background compositions can be planned by children using a large sheet of paper, a narrow strip with both long edges gently curved, and chalk. The chalk is rubbed onto the curved edges of the strip before positioning it in the middle of the large paper; then the students firmly rub the chalk with their fingers away from both top and bottom edges of the strip onto the paper itself. Lift up the strip, and curved line effects imply three grounds in which students can position figures.

Study paintings that use only length and width to create flat or very shallow space. Compare them with paintings that display size changes, overlapping, and modeling to imply depth as well as width and length. Three-dimensional art usually refers to sculpture in which use of space around a figure is as important as the figure itself. Intriguing to young and old alike can be old Keystone stereoscope and Viewmaster viewers that create an optical illusion of three-dimensionality from pairs of slides or photographs taken from slightly different angles and viewed simultaneously through special lenses. The latest developments in laser-generated visual images has resulted in holograms, which not only are three-dimensional but also change in coloration and spatial orientation.

4. For an exercise in creation of planar space, instruct students to arrange paper figures or geometric shapes within a field of action and to note the flat appearance of their work. Sheets of construction paper used by young children in school have traditionally been standard sizes, nine by twelve inches or twelve by eighteen inches, but favored by many art teachers today is sheet size eleven by fourteen inches (available in bulk from Riverside Paper, Appleton, Wis-

consin), which approximates nicely the rather square book shapes of *The Fool of the World, The Funny Little Woman,* and *Mosquitoes.* If children want to practice replication of perspective systems demonstrated by Shulevitz, Lent, and the Dillons, the shape of the field of action could play a part in their success.

For experience with shallow space, construct box dioramas or small-scale stages made inside boxes like the one Louie designed in *The Trip* (see chapter 5). Background can be painted on back and side walls of the box, or a piece of paper can be curved around the inside from one side of the front to the other to eliminate square corners; small three-dimensional objects or cardboard cutouts may be used in foreground and middle ground. To create a scene with deep space, children can construct a tabletop diorama with no background. Only three-dimensional figures are used, and the whole arrangement is designed to be viewed from all sides.

5. To draw or paint using linear or aerial perspective for implied depth is difficult, and children should be encouraged to experiment and exercise patience in order to acquire the basic necessary skills. Four elementary rules of perspective should be discussed, demonstrated, and then practiced frequently: (a) change sizes of figures; (b) change coloration from bright to dull; (c) change details in figures; (d) use a vanishing point for lines.

Objects as they are shown farther away should be drawn progressively smaller. As a beginning practice, have children draw a diagonal line representing a road and position three figures such as houses along it. The house at the bottom of the line should be drawn largest, the house in the middle somewhat smaller, and the house at the top smaller still. In a later exercise the road may be curved or zigzagged, until children feel confident in eliminating the drawn line altogether. At this point, they may situate their different-sized houses on rounded hillsides, as in *The Little House* (see chapter 4).

For changes in detail, figures and foreground near to the audience should be portrayed clearly, with attention to specific parts; when atmospheric perspective is used, less detail should be evident in distant figures and background. Beginners can practice creation of clarity or blurriness through use of fat continuous lines for closed shapes of large individual trees in the foreground and thin broken lines for open shapes of many smaller trees in a forest in the background (see page 21 in *The Fool of the World* for demonstration of this technique). Details in color also should be practiced, with bright, well-defined areas of color in the foreground and dull, vague washes of color in the background.

For practice in constructing lines that converge at one vanishing point, instruct students to draw a line only a few inches long and then use a ruler to make a dozen or more other lines that all meet at one end point of the first. Heavily shade in every other interval between two lines and note the resulting optical illusion of depth. Drawing perpendicular lines across one shaded area adds the suggestion of train tracks; ask whether an imaginary train would be going away from the audience or coming toward it as the rhinos did in *Jumanji* (see chapter 4). On another paper continue this exercise with a pair of drawn lines with one end open and the other end converging in order to demonstrate how a side view of a building in linear perspective can be accomplished. Draw a square at points of the open end and put a door and window inside it. Follow with a pencil the two converging lines to make top and bottom of the building's side, but halfway back draw a line from top to bottom to show the back of the building. Erase the triangle and add windows, doors, and roof using drawn lines parallel to the first few established guidelines.

For practice with vanishing points for lines, draw as above a pair of lines with an open end and an opposite convergent end. Then add a mirror image with open end points of the two pairs touching. The result will be a diamond shape. Connect the top and bottom lines at the middle and again halfway down each side. Erase triangles at left and right, add doors and windows, and a building seen from its corner is created in linear perspective with two vanishing points, one at either side.

Looking Around: *Saint George and the Dragon; The Glorious Flight; Noah's Ark; The Girl Who Loved Wild Horses; A Story A Story; Once a Mouse . . .; The Egg Tree*

In Margaret Hodges's adaptation of *Saint George and the Dragon*, the 1985 Caldecott winner illustrated by Trina Schart Hyman, readers are invited to enter almost every scene by characters looking directly out at them. In the book's front matter, fairies invite us by look and gesture to witness the arrival of Saint George and princess Una in fog and early morning light cast across the first of many sensuously modeled and softened landscapes. Illusion of deep space is created by atmospheric perspective. The front matter offers the book's only full double-page spreads; one wishes this expansive format had been repeated for the ending scene, which is portrayed anticlimactically in the border of the final page. In the romantic *Saint George*, as in Hyman's 1984 Honor Book *Little Red Riding Hood,* the author masterfully adapts subject matter and artistic influence from early illustrators Arthur Rackham and Howard Pyle. In her legendary landscapes, deep space is created by strong invisible structuring through various viewpoints and by her detailed characterizations of idealized shapes through classic representational use of line, light and dark, and subtle coloration. In the style of medieval manuscript illuminators, the artist decorated initials on the title page and embellished single-page borders throughout the book with flowers and other motifs. Certain little vignettes portray a wee ship's voyage across a treacherous sea as visual allegory for this story of the Red Cross Knight adapted from *Faerie Queene* by Edmund Spenser. Very formal placement of text for *Saint George* includes centering within red-outlined border decorations that in a few instances are elaborations on the words or are used as extensions of the major scene itself, as in the first illustration of the dreadful dragon, whose tail continues within the border space on the opposite page. In this book's complicated page design a repetition of the red border outlines framed illustrations, adding ingeniously to their illusion of depth as they seem to be observed through leaded-glass windowpanes.

Similar to *The Fool of the World* in demonstration of deep or shallow space through different systems of linear perspective is *The Glorious Flight: Across the Channel with Louis Blériot.* This 1984 Caldecott selection was written and illustrated by husband-and-wife collaborators Alice and Martin Provensen, whose distinguished art in the 1982 Newbery Award winner *A Visit to William Blake's Inn* resulted in that book's also being chosen as a Caldecott Honor Book. Many commemorative family portraits found in *The Glorious Flight* compare with Shulevitz's formally posed illustration "The Palace" in their compositional invitations to enter deep implied space. Busy street scenes with shallow space offer excellent examples of more than one vanishing point for lines in single fields of action. One unique scene in particular uses *reverse perspective,* in which lines converge *toward* the audience as it looks up with the crowd toward a dirigible.

A primary intent of the illustrators was to artistically recreate for the audience a feeling of exhilaration in the story's climactic pictures as Bleriot flies high over waves and through fog for twenty miles in his tiny single-engine monoplane. The illustrations leading up to this thirty-six-minute historic event are masterfully linked to create an appropriately suspenseful mood, as time and again the amateur aviator-designer's other planes (one experiment pictured as a continuous narrative) never get far off the ground. The Provensens' paintings, in a style of unpolished and roughly finished early American primitivism, suit very well another story about a flying "ship" or "airship," as airplanes are sometimes called. They lend the correct atmosphere of turn-of-the-century documentation to this true account of events leading up to the first flight across the English Channel, by a Frenchman whose place in aviation history is not as well known as that of the Wright brothers and Charles A. Lindbergh.

Implication of deep space for a desolate, rain-soaked expanse of floodwater was created by use of aerial perspective in *Noah's Ark*. The wordless 1978 Medal-winning title was illustrated by Peter Spier in an array of pictures in many sizes and shapes like a filmmaker's storyboard. The crowded and messy ark is pictured in crowded and cluttered illustrations that rely on linear perspective to define a confined atmosphere of shallow space, much like the underground scenes in *The Funny Little Woman*. Flat space is even humorously implied in one little illustration in which everything is plunged into total darkness, leaving yellow beady eyes as witness that only the owls are awake in the stillness of the night.

Many versions of Noah's story are in print (and a flagrant copy of Spier's itself came out the very year he won the Award, complete with identical images of clear glass jars Spier was criticized for having included in his own book). For this version, the Dutch-born artist studied the detailed description from the Bible, translated a seventeenth-century Dutch verse of "The Flood" by Jacobus Revius, and as in his 1962 Honor Book title *The Fox Went Out on a Chilly Night*, he researched the animals and countryside he chose to record. He often succeeded in combining the comedy and poignancy, the enduring beauty and oppressive filth, the uplifting grandeur and claustrophobic despair of Noah's forty days and forty nights before the ark came to rest, as some say, on Turkey's Mount Ararat, shown at the end.

Author-illustrator Paul Goble's *The Girl Who Loved Wild Horses*, the 1979 Award winner, is unique in its artistic vibrancy and in its reverence for nature, humankind, and the fragile mystical kinship between the two. A synthesis of many stories, it provides a stunning exhibition of flat space, shape, and color used for figures of Indian people, wildlife, landscape, and weather itself. Like *Mosquitoes*, Goble's illustrations are a beautifully stylized wedding of old and new art, here inspired by Indian hide paintings and ledger-book art such as that found in *A Cheyenne Sketchbook* by Cohoe. In Cohoe's book, primitive shapes in earthy colors document battles and hunting expeditions; in *Wild Horses*, similarly bold and colorful shapes document a girl's life in the wilderness, the tribal village she left behind, and the rugged, cathedrallike terrain of the plains' high buttes where the Horse Nation ran free.

Goble had been an industrial designer in England before coming to live in America near the Indian people he had admired since childhood, and like Lent in *The Funny Little Woman* he is faithful to cultural motifs. Tepees in *Wild Horses* have schematized animal designs on them that are much like animals in the plot itself, and authentic colors and patterns are used throughout. Goble's white highlighting of compositions is like that of Lent's aboveground illustrations of the little woman's house on the hill. Goble uses the technique to focus attention on such symbolic representations as the vivid red sun, the Great Spirit's finest creation; proud stances for human and horse alike (to prepare the viewer for the story's transformation of one into the other); and a particularly fine waterside scene that is an example of reflection as mentioned in the discussion of *Mosquitoes*.

Flat space in which shapes overlap in bold planes with no implied depth characterizes the 1971 Medalist *A Story A Story*, an African tale retold and illustrated by Gail E. Haley. From the beginning double-spread title page, illustrations are presented as intimate close-ups of figures and scenes contoured by lines rather than tonal gradations and often extending well beyond outer edges of the fields of action. To decorate Ananse's jungle land and the Sky God's heavenly kingdom, flamboyant green, red, yellow, and blue were added to woodcuts to create illustrations resembling batik patterns stamped upon pages as if they were cloth. To tell the story of the Spider Man, artist Haley immersed herself in African folklore, history, art, music, costumes, and even foods before she developed her pictures. For children a highlight of the book is the series of illustrations portraying Ananse's capture of the fairy Mmoatia, which is one of over three hundred versions of the "Tar Baby" story passed down through oral tradition by slaves brought to America.

Another Caldecott selection executed in woodcut was the 1962 *Once a Mouse . . .*, an East Indian fable illustrated in deep earth tones of red, yellow, and green by Marcia Brown. Three times a winner of the Caldecott Medal, Brown has six times been cited also as an Honor Book recipient. More often than not in her jungle scenes for

Once a Mouse ... she creates a deeper sense of space than Haley does. Figures are often smaller and higher on the pages compared with those in *A Story*, which are close up and sometimes larger than life. Loss of detail in figures pictured in deeper space also adds to Brown's use of the visual device crypthesthesia, discussed in connection with *Mosquitoes*: over a dozen animal images in *Mouse* are camouflaged within the backgrounds, their shapes blended with trees and underbrush (and one should not overlook the shadow of the dog as he turns into a tiger). All this is deliberate visual preparation for the book's final illustration, the mouse itself camouflaged as it runs away through the grass. The magic of Brown's hermit in the story contrasts nicely with the cleverness of Haley's Ananse, and the transformation of the ungrateful tiger back into a mouse again is not only an excellent example of metamorphosis, or continuous narration, but is also one of the finest demonstrations in all of the Caldecotts for artistic use of line, color, and value to create a masterful illusion of two shapes while simultaneously transfiguring one space miraculously into another.

Katherine Milhous's decorative paintings in tempera for the 1951 Award-winning *The Egg Tree* suit her story of a tree trimmed with painted Easter eggs, inspired by folk-art designs of her Pennsylvania Dutch heritage and by a real event in Pennsylvania like that described in the book. One illustration employs a spatial system of horizontal banding as more and more people are pictured coming from near and far to see the Egg Tree; another is given a title in a ribbon banner across the bottom of the illustration itself; and another appears within an arched frame that imitates painting on a wood panel as in the ancient icon tradition. *The Egg Tree* is understood today as an illustrated storybook in the folk-art tradition, to a degree historically reminiscent of illuminated manuscripts with their miniature pictures and ornamental borders, and the artist's use of flat shape, color, and space as decoration reminds one of needlework or tapestry or, at its best, perhaps a Henri Matisse still life of flowers or fruit.

Works Cited

Aardema, Verna. *Behind the Back of the Mountain*. New York: Dial, 1973.
———. *Riddle of the Drum*. New York: Four Winds Pr., 1979.
———. *Who's in Rabbit's House?* New York: Dial, 1977.
———. *Why Mosquitoes Buzz in People's Ears*. New York: Dial, 1975.
Andersen, Hans Christian. *Little Match Girl*. Boston: Houghton, 1968.

Belting, Natalia. *Whirlwind Is a Ghost Dancing.* New York: Dutton, 1974.

Bierhorst, John, ed. *The Ring in the Prairie: A Shawnee Legend.* New York: Dial, 1970.

Branley, Franklyn. *Christmas Sky.* New York: Crowell, 1966.

Brown, Marcia. *The Bun.* New York: Harcourt, 1972.

———. *Once a Mouse . . . .* New York: Scribner, 1961.

———. *Shadow.* New York: Scribner, 1982.

Bryan, Ashley. *Beat the Story-Drum, Pum-Pum.* New York: Atheneum, 1980.

Burton, Virginia Lee. *The Little House.* Boston: Houghton, 1942.

Carew, Jan. *Children of the Sun.* Boston: Little, 1980.

Cohoe. *Cheyenne Sketchbook.* Norman: Univ. of Oklahoma Pr., 1964.

Dahl, Roald. *James and the Giant Peach.* New York: Knopf, 1961.

Dayrell, Elphinstone. *Why the Sun and Moon Live in the Sky.* Boston: Houghton, 1968.

Economakis, Olga. *Oasis of the Stars.* New York: Coward, 1965.

Elkin, Benjamin. *Why the Sun Was Late.* New York: Parents Mag. Pr., 1966.

Emberley, Barbara. *Drummer Hoff.* Englewood Cliffs, N.J.: Prentice-Hall, 1967.

Fisher, Aileen. *I Stood upon a Mountain.* New York: Harper, 1979.

Galdone, Paul. *Gingerbread Boy.* New York: Seabury, 1975.

Goble, Paul. *The Girl Who Loved Wild Horses.* Scarsdale, N.Y.: Bradbury Pr., 1978.

Greenfield, Eloise. *Honey, I Love: And Other Love Poems.* New York: Harper, 1978.

Grimm Brothers. *Little Red Riding Hood.* New York: Holiday, 1983.

Haley, Gail E. *A Story A Story.* New York: Atheneum, 1970.

Haviland, Virginia. *Favorite Fairy Tales Told in India.* Boston: Little, 1973.

Hearn, Lafcadio, and others. *Japanese Fairy Tales.* New York: Peter Pauper Pr., 1948.

Hodges, Margaret. *Saint George and the Dragon.* Boston: Little, 1984.

———. *The Wave.* Boston: Houghton, 1964.

Jacobs, Joseph. *Johnny-Cake.* New York: Viking, 1973.

Keats, Ezra Jack. *The Snowy Day.* New York: Viking, 1962.

———. *The Trip.* New York: Greenwillow, 1978.

Lent, Blair. *Baba Yaga.* Boston: Houghton, 1966.

———. *From King Boggen's Hall to Nothing-At-All.* Boston: Little, 1967.

———. *John Tabor's Ride.* Boston: Little, 1966.

———. *Pistachio.* Boston: Little, 1964.

Lobel, Anita. *The Pancake.* New York: Morrow, 1978.

Lourie, Richard, tr. *Soldier and Tsar in the Forest.* New York: Farrar, 1972.

Mathis, Sharon Bell. *The Hundred Penny Box.* New York: Viking, 1975.

McCloskey, Robert. *Make Way for Ducklings.* New York: Viking, 1941.

Milhous, Katherine. *The Egg Tree.* New York: Scribner, 1950.

Mosel, Arlene. *The Funny Little Woman.* New York: Harper, 1972.

———. *Tikki Tikki Tembo.* New York: Harper, 1968.

Musgrove, Margaret. *Ashanti to Zulu: African Traditions.* New York: Dial, 1980.

Provensen, Alice, and Martin Provensen. *The Glorious Flight: Across the Channel with Louis Bleriot July 25, 1909.* New York: Viking, 1983.

Ransome, Arthur. *The Fool of the World and the Flying Ship.* New York: Farrar, 1968.

———. *Old Peter's Russian Tales.* Nashville, Tenn.: Nelson, 1937.

Robbins, Ruth. *Baboushka and the Three Kings.* Boston: Parnassas, 1960.

Sawyer, Ruth. *Journey Cake, Ho!* New York: Viking, 1953.

Sendak, Maurice. *Where the Wild Things Are.* New York: Harper, 1963.

Serwadda, W. Moses, and Hewitt Pantaleoni, eds. *Songs and Stories from Uganda.* New York: Harper, 1974.

Shulevitz, Uri. *Dawn.* New York: Farrar, 1974.

———. *The Magician: An Adaptation from the Yiddish of I. L. Peretz.* New York: Macmillan, 1978.

———. *The Moon in My Room.* New York: Harper, 1963.

———. *Oh, What a Noise!* New York: Macmillan, 1971.

———. *One Monday Morning.* New York: Scribner, 1967.

———. *Rain Rain Rivers.* New York: Farrar, 1969.

———. *The Treasure.* New York: Farrar, 1979.

Sleator, William. *The Angry Moon.* Boston: Little, 1970.

Spier, Peter. *The Fox Went Out on a Chilly Night.* New York: Doubleday, 1961.

———. *Noah's Ark.* New York: Doubleday, 1977.

Travers, P. L. *Two Pairs of Shoes.* New York: Viking, 1980.

Tresselt, Alvin. *Rolling Rice Ball.* New York: Parents Mag. Pr., 1969.

Van Allsburg, Chris. *Jumanji.* Boston: Houghton, 1981.

Willard, Nancy. *A Visit to William Blake's Inn: Poems for Innocent and Experienced Travelers.* New York: Viking, 1983.

Glossary

abstract nonrepresentational; not depicting any recognizable subject matter; manipulation of subject matter into its parts (shapes, colors, etc.) rather than portrayal of naturalistic appearance

afterimage visual phenomenon in which, after long exposure to an intense color, the eye seeks the same image in the opposite color when looking at a neutral background

asymmetric not identical on both sides of a center line

backlighting light source directly behind a figure, offering direct contrast and resulting in a silhouette or an illusion of two-dimensional flat shape

book design total plan for physical arrangement of a book, including format, front matter, typeface, text placement in relation to artwork, medium employed, and artistic style

center point juncture where horizontal center line meets vertical center line, strong in its ability to draw the eye into a picture

closed shape figure having a continuous outline that separates it from surrounding space

color pigments' abilities to absorb, transmit, or reflect light; colors may be classified as *primaries* (red, yellow, blue), used to create *secondaries* (green, orange, violet), and *tertiaries* (red-orange, yellow-orange, yellow-green, blue-green, blue-violet, red-violet)

color forms tones, tints, shades, grays, white, and black

color separation a separate negative made for each color used in printing; preseparation may be done by an artist using separate overlays for each color

color temperature psychological sensation in which yellows, oranges, reds (associated with sun and fire) are considered warm and appear to advance toward the audience, while greens, blues, violets (associated with water, sky, and trees) are considered cool and appear to recede

complementary hues colors directly across from each other on a color wheel

217

composition   organization of artistic elements in relation to each other and to the whole; the process of design; *closed* composition is anchored firmly within its frame, and *open* composition suggests further activity outside the frame

continuous narrative   one character portrayed in two places within the same setting in a field of action

contour   implied advancing or receding planes, accomplished by contour lines, line effects, and/or coloration that shades and models a figure

contrast (of colors)   juxtaposition of different hues or values within a composition

crosshatching   short, broken, parallel lines crossed over by others at a different angle

crypthesthesia   use of images hidden within other images

deep space   contrast of far distance and nearness within a field of action

depth   implied foreground, middle ground, and/or background achieved through interplay of lines, overlapping, and changes in coloration

disintegration   light from the front of a figure that erases the surface, renders shape two-dimensional, and leaves only the intense sensation of light itself

distribution   evenly dispersed light over a scene

double narrative   two scenes with different characters and settings portrayed within a field of action

double spread   horizontal expanse of two facing pages; also called *landscape* or *panorama format*

easy-to-read book   book with controlled, limited vocabulary for beginning readers

edge line   drawn outline or contour line for figure

elements   line, color, light and dark (often called value), shape, space, texture; use of one or more artistic elements can imply contour and/ or depth; interrelationship of artistic elements results in emphasis, balance or imbalance, continuity, unity

field of action   physical space defined by outer boundaries for a work of art; in picture books, the cover, jacket, single pages, and/or double spreads within which artwork will ultimately be reproduced often after enlarging or reducing

figure   object or shape portrayed; also called *positive* or *filled shape*

fine art   one-of-a-kind creation reflecting self-expression and subject to aesthetic judgment regarding beauty and meaningfulness

flat space   field of action in which length and width are the only two dimensions, and images appear without depth upon the surface; also called *planar space*

folk art   utilitarian creation reflecting traditional motifs of a culture and intended as decoration, instruction, or documentation for a specific audience

foreshortening   calculated contraction of a shape in linear perspective, resulting in proportions that appear to diminish or distort as the shape recedes

format book size (large versus "lap" book) and book shape (square, horizontal rectangular, or vertical rectangular)

forward extension protrusion toward the audience and beyond the field of action

front matter endpapers, half title, title, copyright, dedication, and/or table of contents pages

geometric shape mathematically precise configuration; usually associated with humanmade objects but also found in nature

gradation subtle transition from light to dark on a tonal scale, used to model, shape, or highlight figures

graphic art two-dimensional artwork intended for reproduction

grisaille painting in grays

ground empty, unfilled background area around figure; also called *negative space*

gutter vertical inside crease at a book's binding

harmony of adjacents use of hues next to each other on a color wheel; also called *analogous* colors or *chords* when used in threes

harmony of color forms use of tones, tints, shades, grays, black and/or white in combinations

harmony of dominant tint use of a tint to envelop a scene with one pervading visual sensation, resulting in a softening effect

harmony of opposites use of complementary hues

harmony of split-complements use of a key hue combined with two hues found to either side of the key hue's direct opposite on a color wheel

harmony of triads use of three hues found at points of a triangle superimposed on a color wheel

hatching short, broken, parallel lines used to imply contour, depth, or texture

highlighting lightest color of a figure; reflection of a source of illumination

horizontal banding one scene above another, with different settings for each, and shapes either in the same sizes or in hierarchic proportion; an example of *double narrative*

hue exact name of a color

illustrated storybook narrative with a long text that presents significantly more verbal images than are pictured

illustration visual image as extension of text; *decorative* illustrations are loosely related to the text and mainly serve to embellish printed matter; *instructional* illustrations offer visual information that elucidates text; *documentary* illustrations chronicle fictional or factual events, faces, or figures

intaglio use of dampened paper pressed into inked lines, as in etching or engraving

intensity dullness, brightness, or relative strength of a hue; also called *saturation* or *chroma*; intensity scale runs from *light dull* (weak, lightly obscure, low saturation) to *bright* (strong, pure, full saturation) to *dark* *dull* (murky, darkly obscure, low saturation); these are achieved by adding various amounts of a hue's complementary color

key   relative lightness or darkness; light and bright colors are considered *high* key, whereas dark and gloomy colors are considered *low* key

left brain   hemisphere of the brain in which rational analysis, vocabulary building, and labeling are thought to develop

letterpress   a process of rotary gravure printing using a relief surface

light and dark   use of contrast and gradation of lines and/or colors; also called *value*; called *chiaroscuro* or *light and shade* when specific source of illumination, reflected light, and cast shadows are employed

line   visibly drawn line, which may be thick or thin, straight or curved, continuous or broken, and vertical, horizontal, circular, or diagonal; invisible line as compositional skeletal framework, which falls into such directional categories as staunch *vertical* that holds attention within the field of action, *horizontal* base that extends left to right, framed *circular* pattern that leads the eye around, or frenetic underlying *diagonal* that jerks attention from one point to another

line effect   contrast or gradual transition from one shade to another as opposed to distinctly drawn line; color meets color for shading and implied contouring that creates illusion of three dimensions

lithography   use of plane or flat surface for planographic printing

mass-market picture book   generally speaking, less expensive and considered of lesser artistic and literary merit than a high-quality picture book

metamorphosis   transformation by stages of a figure presented in a single setting

modeling   use of light and dark and gradation of tones to create illusion of three-dimensional solidity

montage   interconnected plots, images, or ideas compressed within a single setting

movement   period in the fine arts; certain attitudes and techniques held in common by a group of artists; stylistic sameness among artists in treatment of subject matter

multiple original   skillful reproduction of original print design

narrative illustration   sequence of pictures that portrays one continuous plot having a beginning, a middle, and an end; may be decorative, instructional, documentary, or in combination but additionally fleshes out characters visually, gives events pictorial substance, indicates a cause-and-effect relationship from one picture to another, and develops atmosphere of time and place pictorially in a way that often results in a visual account apart from text

negative shape   empty, unfilled space in a composition

nonrepresentational art   having no reference to anything outside itself

open shape   broken outline for a figure that allows ground space to enter

organic shape   free-form, irregular configuration as often found in nature, naturalistic; also called *biomorphic*

overlapping   placement of one figure in front of another, hiding part of the figure behind

overprinting   printing on white paper of one color of transparent ink over another to produce a third color

path of look or gesture   wordless communication "line" between two figures within a composition or between a figure and the audience

perspective   *aerial* perspective indicates distance through blurring of lines and color, decrease in sizes, diminishment of details; *linear* or *geometric* perspective is based on calculated alterations in figure sizes, directions, and placements within composition, falling into three systems: *parallel* perspective, in which lines are parallel to all sides of the picture's edge and a center vanishing point generally corresponds to the audience's viewpoint; *angular* perspective, in which vertical lines are parallel with the sides but more than one vanishing point is implied for other lines; and *oblique* or tilted perspective, in which lines are not parallel with any sides, and vertical lines may converge either up or down

picture book   a two-dimensional graphic art form in which the whole book is designed around illustrations as extension of text, providing primarily pictorial and aural experience rather than reading experience, and having pictorial images equal to verbal images

picture-book illustrator   a graphic artist who plans and executes a series of pictures as extension of text, serving a decorative, instructional, documentary, or combined function and often providing a unique visual narration through artistic expressiveness

planography   use of chemically sensitized flat surface for printing

point of interest   an area with much eye appeal in a composition

principles of design   rhythm, repetition, motion, spatial relationship created by use of artistic elements within a composition

print   copy of original two-dimensional artwork

proportion   comparison of relationship between parts of a figure or between figures within a composition as regards dimensions, amounts, and intensities, falling into four main systems: *idealized*, in which classically perfect form is portrayed based on standards that include strict ratios for parts in relationship to each other; *natural*, in which individual characteristics are given honest appraisal and structure is truly realistic; *hierarchic*, in which important figures are portrayed in large sizes and less important are in smaller sizes; and *distorted*, in which characteristics are grossly exaggerated in relation to other parts or to other figures

real image   symbol that represents what is understood by research or observation to exist in the world as we know it, regardless of artistic style; opposite of unreal image, created by the artist's imagination

realism   exact appearance with no distortion, idealization, or hierarchical characteristics for expressive purposes

reflection   image mirrored in glass or water; offers ambiguity of interpretation for the audience

relief printing   use of raised surface as in woodcut

representational art   presentation of recognizable, true-to-life subject matter

right brain   hemisphere of the brain in which pictorial or visual literacy and wholistic perception are thought to develop

serigraphy   use of stencils to treat areas separately, as in silk screening

shade   black added to a color

shading   modeling of a figure by manipulation of contrasted or gradated areas of light and dark to create illusion of solid form

shallow space   picture presented close in to the audience, with little or no evidence of depth

shape   two-dimensional outlined area in pictures; three-dimensional mass, also called *form*, in sculpture; *positive shape* in space is a figure, *negative shape* is the ground

shape family   group of shapes exhibiting sameness of style in characterizations or plots; repeated use of a shape prompts ready recognition of an artist's work

silhouette   two-dimensional flat shape with little detail; a result of backlighting

simplification of shape   elimination of detail to present the essence of a figure

simultaneous perspective   parts of the same figure seen at one time from different viewpoints

single spread   full-page scene or tableau framed by marginal space or bleeding off page's edge

source of illumination   natural or artificial lighting in a picture, either shown within the field of action or implied from beyond its boundaries

space   visual illusion that invites the audience "into" a picture; may be *deep, shallow,* or *flat* (also called planar); results from creative interplay of other elements—color, line, shape, light and dark, texture

split narrative   two episodes with different characters portrayed within the same setting in a field of action

spreading   the illusion that one hue takes on the tone of a neighboring hue, resulting in decrease of contrast

style   characteristics or mannerisms of an artist that reflect individual attitudes, a unique approach, and/or a relationship to a historical period or culture, falling into four categories: *linear*, which emphasizes the drawn line, or in painting the use of outlines and contour lines for closed shapes and space; *painterly*, which emphasizes a more sensuous rendering of open shapes and space by areas of color and tone rather than lines; *lines with paint added*, which emphasize color and tone applied within outlines for closed shapes and space; and *mixed-media imagery*, such as collage, which emphasizes use of such materials as cloth, wood, and paper for texture and for closed shapes or space, and within which additional drawing or painting may or may not be included

stylization   alteration or modification of appearance to emphasize pre-conceived universal physical characteristics, resulting in ideal types not as they truly are but as they should be

symmetric   having perfect balance demonstrating equal weight between two halves; identical on both sides of a center line

text placement   arrangement of words on the page of a book in relation to artwork, falling into five categories: *opposite* or on the page adjacent to the illustration, considered most formal; *beneath or above* (often alternating in high or low position within the same book), considered formal; *shaped* by irregular boundaries to fit inside, around, between, or to the side of an illustration, considered informal; *combined* (two or more arrangements), considered very informal; and *absent*, as in a wordless book, considered most informal

texture   related to the sense of touch, tactile, either actual or implied

three-dimensional art   sculpture and architecture, in which space around a figure is as important as the figure itself

tint   a color to which white has been added

tone   a hue to which its complementary color has been added

two-dimensional art   painting, drawing, mixed-media imagery

unreal image   presentation of an otherwordly creation derived purely from the artist's imagination or dreams

value ladder   range of a hue from lightest (also called high value or high key) to darkest (also called low value or low key) with gradual transitions in between

vanishing point   area where parallel lines would finally converge

viewpoint   eye level of the audience, including *normal, bird's-eye,* or *worm's-eye* view; the position may reflect an emotional or intellectual stance the artist wishes the audience to take toward the subject matter

vignette   small or spot illustration, often balanced with text on the same page

visual literacy   the audience's ability to distinguish between reality and unreality, to appreciate use of details that contribute to the whole, to identify unique properties of the artistic medium used, and to understand the main idea intended by the visual; also called *visual discrimination*

weight   comparative worth in a composition of areas with much eye appeal, depending on their size, shape, color, location, and amount

wraparound   book jacket in which the front illustration continues across the spine onto the back

X-ray imagery   cutaway view for the audience that portrays the imagined inside rather than the outside of a figure

Title-Artist Index

Lyn Ellen Lacy is a media specialist for the Minneapolis Public Schools and a member of the American Library Association. Her articles have appeared in *Teacher, Minnesota Media,* and *Top of the News.* Lacy is the scriptwriter of several biographical filmstrips on children's book illustrators such as Wanda Gag, Maud Hart Lovelace, and Randolph Caldecott, and is a three-time winner of the Minnesota Educational Media Organization's Professional Improvement/Development Award.